WRAPPED IN MOURNING

The Series in Trauma and Loss

Consulting Editors
Charles R. Figley and Therese A. Rando

The Series in Trauma and Loss

WRAPPED IN MOURNING

The Gift of Life and Organ Donor Family Trauma

Sue Holtkamp, Ph.D.
*Something More Grief Counseling
& Bereavement Programs
Chattanooga, TN*

USA	Publishing Office:	BRUNNER-ROUTLEDGE *A member of the Taylor & Francis Group* 29 West 35th Street New York, NY 10001 Tel: (212) 216-7800 Fax: (212) 564-7854
	Distribution Center:	BRUNNER-ROUTLEDGE *A member of the Taylor & Francis Group* 7625 Empire Drive Florence, KY 41042 Tel: 1-800-634-7064 Fax: 1-800-248-4724
UK		BRUNNER-ROUTLEDGE *A member of the Taylor & Francis Group* 27 Church Road Hove E Sussex, BN3 2FA Tel: +44 (0) 1273 207411 Fax: +44 (0) 1273 205612

WRAPPED IN MOURNING: The Gift of Life and Organ Donor Family Trauma

1 2 3 4 5 6 7 8 9 0

Printed by Edwards Brothers, Lillington, NC.
Cover design by Ellen Seguin.

A CIP catalog record for this book is available from the British Library.
   The paper in this publication meets the requirements of the ANSI Standard Z39.48-1984 (Permanence of Paper).

Library of Congress Cataloging-in-Publication Data

Holtkamp, Sue.
   Wrapped in mourning : the gift of life and organ donor family trauma / Sue Holtkamp.
      p. cm. — (The series in trauma and loss, ISSN 1090-9575)
   Includes bibliographical references and index.
   ISBN 1-58391-056-5 (alk. paper)
      1. Grief. 2. Bereavement—Psychological aspects. 3. Loss (Psychology). 4. Organ donors—Death—Psychological aspects. 5. Donation of organs, tissues, etc.—Psychological aspects. I. Title. II. Series.

BF575.G7 H655 2001
155.9′3—dc21   2001037751

ISBN 1-58391-056-5
ISSN 1090-9575

This book is lovingly dedicated to
Robert Eugene Lindsey (July 2, 1948–March 16, 2000).
A brilliant and beloved son-in-law
who quietly and humorously meandered
through our lives, encouraging everyone he met.
Our gentle giant—we quite simply adored you.

And to the families of organ donors—
they who know the true cost of transplantation.

CONTENTS

FOREWORD

It is an unfortunate reality of life, but there are myriad states of affairs that confront the human being with disabling admixtures of trauma and loss. These create a variety of conditions, each with differing intensities of distress and degrees of tenability, for those individuals caught within their parameters. The numbers of potential predicaments notwithstanding, one could search long and painstakingly yet still be hard-pressed to find a situation that embodies more combined trauma and loss than that surrounding organ donor families. Be definition, their unique circumstances, and the resultant psychological demands placed upon them, place such persons in a veritable crucible of human experience, with an amalgam of traumatic stress and traumatic loss that is second to none in kind, complexity, severity, and sequelae.

Although the donor experience essentially strikes at the very heart of a person and family, the issues with which these individuals contend are not relegated solely to their own intrapersonal and interpersonal domains. For better or worse, they necessarily extend outward—encompassed within social realms concerned with morality, ethics, religion, politics, economics, and government. In the midst of a profound, typically peerless private tragedy, those in organ donor families harshly and dramatically confront simultaneously both the boundaries and the bounty of medicine in the 21st century; along the way they are exposed to potentially harmful, as well as helpful, occurrences with capacities to profoundly influence subsequent adjustment.

Organ donation is an example *par excellence* of medical technology's creation of new kinds of problems as it offers improved solutions. Transplantation has been made more possible as a result of a new class of patients determined to be dead via neurological, rather than customary cardiopulmonary, criteria. This has created a nontraditional way to die—brain death—that poses unheard-of demands upon the patient's family and other loved ones to understand that a warm, breathing, often natural-looking body, containing a beating heart, is the shell for a legally dead person. Confusion over the boundaries of life and death abounds. The intimates of the patient are thrust immediately into extreme trauma not only by virtue of the suddenness and circumstances of the patient's injuries, and the resulting loss of the person they had known and loved, but by both the inescapable demands of organ procurement/transplantation for a relatively immediate decision that entails substantial traumatic experiences and sequelae, and (usually) their own lack of prior experience upon which to rely in the current absurd situation.

It is into this poignantly distinctive world of the organ donor family that Sue Holtkamp takes us in her compelling work, *Wrapped in Mourning: The Gift of Life and Organ Donor Family Trauma.* Thoroughly comprehending traumatic bereavement from the inside (as a mourner having lost spouse and child in an airplane crash) and from the outside (as a treating professional), Dr. Holtkamp vividly portrays for us the phenomenological experience of the organ donor family. First, these individuals must confront the death of a loved one that has been characterized by one, some, or all of the six factors that can make any particular death a traumatic one—(1) suddenness and lack of anticipation; (2) violence, mutilation, or destruction; (3) preventability or randomness; (4) loss of a child; (5) multiple death; or (6) the mourner's personal encounter with death secondary to either a significant threat to personal survival or a shocking confrontation with the death and mutilation of others (Rando, 2000)—and that automatically places them at high risk for complicated mourning (Rando, 1993). Then, they are thrust into needing to make an incomparably monumental choice affecting life or death for another person, with their mere occupation of such a position adding to their traumatization and additionally complicating their bereavement.

To further muddy the waters, the particular experiences of organ donor families inherently contain elements that are known both to ameliorate, as well as to exacerbate, postdeath anguish. Thus, organ donation intrinsically contains potential for promise as well as pitfalls. Even the decision not to make a choice that theoretically might have augmented the mourner's difficulties is fraught with problems—that choice, despite its relative attractiveness to the person, also may leave him or her with the absence of something that could have been therapeutic. In other words, what is absent, as well as what is present, can profoundly affect the donor family's bereavement. Organ donation essentially constitutes a double-edged sword: It can cut either one of the ways at a given time or both ways simultaneously, in each case leaving its imprint on those involved. In few other instances does the dilemma *damned if you do, damned if you don't* appear quite so applicable.

As noted, the trauma in the traumatic bereavement created by organ donation stems not only from the specific circumstances of the death of the loved one whose organs are donated, nor from the actual losing of that person. As so vividly described by Holtkamp, the peculiar experiences involved in the organ donation process are traumatizing in and of themselves. This means that they necessarily involve stimuli (external and/or internal), suddenly presented, that are too powerful to be dealt with or assimilated in the donor's usual way; overwhelming that individual, causing disruption in functioning, and creating a state of helplessness typically accompanied by signs of autonomic dysregulation (adapted from Moore & Fine, 1990).

Holtkamp delineates for us these traumatizing aspects of the donation process; along the way specifying donor family needs and identifying therapeutic strategies to respond to—if not actually prevent—donor family distress. Among other critically important topics, she analyzes: (1) the choice itself and the time at which it must be made—in the midst of trauma and in the face of the fact that thanatologists usually advise mourners not to make any major decisions for at least a year after a loved one's death; (2) the unique circumstances of brain death and all this means—including conflicting definitions, confusing terms, going against the donor family's typical previous assumption that breathing and heart beating signifies life, and attempting to grasp the reality of the loss in full view of overwhelming visual cues to the contrary and contending with the resulting cognitive dissonance; (3) the fact that the donor family's creation of meaning via the gift of life through organ donation demands an immediate and unbuffered confirmation of the death of the loved one, and means their agreeing to mutilate their loved one's body and cause a complete cessation of his or her physical existence; (4) the potential complications associated with knowledge that parts of the loved one live on in another human being's body, which is an aspect of this bereavement that has no parallel whatsoever and may actually constitute a new risk factor; and (5) problems when the hospital protocol has permitted, or violation of it has caused, the linking of notification of death directly with request for donation (i.e., there is a failure to decouple); when subsequent behaviors from staff cause regret about the decision to donate; or when the time of death on the death certificate is when organs were removed, thus implying that the loved one was not dead at the time the decision was made and that the donor family members either killed their loved one or exposed that person to pain and mutilation.

Using riveting case illustrations to take us step-by-step through the donor family experience, and solidly anchoring it within the clinical literature from the fields of traumatology and thanatology, Holtkamp convincingly demonstrates the integration of trauma and loss that defines this unique ordeal. She then provides therapeutic strategies and specific techniques to intervene most efficaciously. In so doing, she realizes magnificently the goals set by my co-editor, Charles Figley, and me as we initially established *The Series in Trauma and Loss*, of which this work is an important part. Yet, Holtkamp focuses not solely upon the amelioration of distress and the reduction of risks. She makes it explicit that potential benefits reside as well in the organ donation process. She gives caregivers of all types the requisite information to maximize these, to facilitate adaptive coping, and to forestall further traumatization of donor families—thereby enhancing their probability for ultimately accommodating their loss in a healthy fashion.

Without question, this book is destined to be a classic for those involved in all aspects of the organ donation process. Organ donation is only going to increase as the public becomes even more educated about it, and as there continues to be an elevation in the proportion of sudden, traumatic deaths relative to long-term chronic illness ones. If the information in this work is comprehended, and its guidance followed, donor families will be exceptionally well-served. Unnecessary traumatization and complications in their bereavement will be avoided; healthy adjustments will be promoted.

Therese A. Rando, Ph.D., BCETS, BCBT
The Institute for the Study and Treatment of Loss
Warwick, Rhode Island
August 1, 2001

Moore, B., & Fine, B. (Eds.). (1990). *Psychoanalytic terms and concepts.* New Haven, CT: American Psychoanalytic Association and Yale University Press.

Rando, T. A. (1993). *Treatment of complicated mourning.* Champaign, IL: Research Press.

Rando, T. A. (2000). On the experience of traumatic stress in anticipatory and postdeath mourning. In T. A. Rando (Ed.), *Clinical dimensions of anticipatory mourning: Theory and practice in working with the dying, their loved ones, and their caregivers.* Champaign, IL: Research Press.

PREFACE

Almost daily throughout the late 1970s and early 1980s, an inspiring story about someone's life being saved by an organ transplant was featured news on television and in other media. Television journalists could scarcely contain their enthusiasm and amazement when reporting the latest breakthrough in this remarkable modern medical phenomenon. I shared their wonder and awe. Yet, each time I heard these stories, I found myself asking the same question: "What about the donor family?"

In 1986, I received a call from a young woman who identified herself as Nancy Davis. She said that she was a procurement coordinator from Tennessee Donor Services and that she was concerned about a donor family. This family, she said, seemed to be having a particularly difficult time coping with the death of their loved one, and she had heard that I worked with bereaved families. Nancy wondered if I would be willing to see this family.

That was the beginning of a 15-year-long relationship with Tennessee Donor Services that continues to the present time. Eventually, I would develop and implement a comprehensive aftercare program, Something More for Donor Families, for the families served by this and other organizations. During much of this time, I also facilitated support groups and offered grief therapy for individuals and families whose loved one had been a donor.

From time to time, various individuals have suggested that I write a book about donor family grief. At first, the notion seemed absurd. There were no empirical reports to draw from, no systematic studies on the effects of organ donation on long-term grief, and nothing definitive to tell how the knowledge that parts of the loved one live on in another human being impacts the grief of the donor family.

Yet, I had gained valuable insights into this particular population over a period of 15 years. Like Anna in *The King and I* (1956), it had been necessary to get to know the people with whom I worked. "It's a very ancient saying but a true and honest thought, that if you become a teacher, by your pupils you'll be taught." And so it was for me. The donor families who so graciously and honestly shared their experiences actually taught me.

In lieu of formal studies, I would finally write a book based on what I had learned from these families, and augment that knowledge with information about the transplantation/organ donation surround that I wished I had known when I first started my work. I now consider that information vital to providing intelligent and effective care for donor families.

I chose not to include families of tissue donors in this work, not because their donation is not as important, but because the issues relative to organ donor families are very different and, in some ways, quite distant from those of the tissue donor family.

Because of the organ donor's mode of death—sudden, often violent and untimely—and the unique circumstances of brain death and the knowledge that parts of the loved one continue to live on in another human being's body, I considered it appropriate to view the donor family's experience through the lens of trauma-driven grief.

Information about the surround of organ donation, the unique risk factors for trauma within the donor family's grief, complemented with suggestions for treatment will, I believe, enhance the understanding of caregivers as they seek to ameliorate clinical problems as well as provide a source of healing for the donor family.

This volume is an attempt to answer my original question: "What about the donor family?"

ACKNOWLEDGMENTS

It is a marvel that any books on trauma and loss ever get written. I say this because trauma and loss keep happening to the very people who are trying to write the books—and there is no protection from the wrenching pain of trauma and loss just because you think you know so much about such things. You struggle just like everyone else with all the issues that you've known for a very long time. When you finally remember that you're supposed to be writing a book about the very stuff that you're experiencing, there is a great temptation to be shocked and dismayed.

But here I am. And I am here thanks to a number of people who knew my needs even when I didn't. I am supposed to be the grief "expert" in our family, but early this year it was my family who taught me once again about facing loss with grace and dignity. My daughter, Joy, and her children, Bre and Bret, behaved with utter devotion for those five days in March when we kept vigil outside an intensive care unit; waiting first to hear whether Joy's husband, Bob, would live, then waiting for him to die. Joy's sister, Lyn, was the epitome of what a sister should be when a sibling is in crisis. She was and continues to be tireless and faithful in her support. Lyn's husband, John, was magnificent. He simply was there at every visiting hour, every crisis, and all in between. He cared for his sister-in-law as though she were his own sister. He was there for Joy, for her children, and for Lyn and for me. At the funeral, Bre, age 22, and Bret, age 18, delivered a eulogy for their dad that touched everyone and simply amazed their grandmother. I've never been more proud to be related to these people. That's all I will say about that.

Not surprisingly the friends who have been supportive of this book were also the ones who were there during our great time of need. There is one friend in particular who has been steadfast in her support and encouragement. Janet Salyer has simply "been there" at every twist and turn, through every crisis, and every calamity. She is the kind of friend with whom you can laugh and cry and sometimes not know the difference. We are soulmates to the point of being annoying.

Andrea Gambill, editor of *Bereavement Magazine,* has been such a loyal support through so many years that her superbly timed phone calls and messages of encouragement were simply typical of her kind and generous heart. She is much appreciated.

Since the beginning, when I first became involved in trauma and loss, I leaned heavily on the writings of Therese Rando. I still do. Her invitation to contribute a chapter for one of her books, and her subsequent encouragement to write this book, was pivotal in my decision to do so. Her influence, for which I am so grateful, has been incalculable.

In addition to Dr. Rando's influence and help, I benefited enormously from the encouragement and support of Bernadette Capelle, acquisitions editor of Brunner-Routledge, and other members of that organization.

A word of thanks must also go to my daughter, Lyn Simpson, who edits much of my work and maintains an abiding hope that I will learn what to do with commas. She is priceless. The same may be said of Doreen Wirchansky who has worked with me as my assistant since 1992. She is far more than my assistant; she is my colleague and my friend. I especially appreciate her semigracious acceptance of my disorganized work habits.

Considerable appreciation must be directed to my Aussie colleagues. To Alison Barnwell, Aftercare Coordinator for the Red Cross Transplant Program in Sydney, Australia, who proofed much of this work and challenged my medical myopia. She fills both roles of dear friend and trusted colleague. Special thanks to Dr. Rob O'Neill, Medical Sociologist at Western Sydney University, who has been an enormous support by directing me to computer research programs and encouraging me that this volume was meant to be written and that I could write it.

A special word of thanks must go to Dr. Keith Johnson and Tennessee Donor Services for the long and incomparable relationship we have enjoyed since 1986. This organization has enabled me to work closely with some of the most remarkable people in the world: organ and tissue donor families. Long before it became common practice, this organization invested considerable resources to meet the emotional needs of organ and tissue donor families simply because it was the right thing to do. Without them, this book would not have been written.

This book would lose its flavor without the many stories that organ donor family members shared with me. Permission to use those stories breathed life into our body of knowledge. The same may be said of George Borchardt, Inc., who gave permission on behalf of the author, Richard Selzer, to use a portion of *Whither Thou Goest*.

Hayes Johnson's 1992 editorial, "The Dark Side of Organ Donation," provides a perfect counterpoint for other more positive donor family experiences. Many thanks to Lisa Thomas of the editorial department at *The Sun Sentinel* in Ft. Lauderdale, Florida, for permission to use this provocative editorial.

Throughout the United States and a number of other countries, individuals involved in caring for organ donor families have become my friends and colleagues. These professionals care deeply about the donor family, and work tirelessly to offer them support. It would be impossible to name each of these individuals, so I will thank them collectively for their support and encouragement. They know who they are and they are without exception some of the most unusual, loving, intelligent, sensitive, kind, and funny people that I've ever met. I bow to them and to the work they do on behalf of the organ and tissue donor families.

INTRODUCTION

The transplantation of human organs has captured America's collective imagination more than any other modern medical phenomenon. It is a fascinating subject—literally the gift of life for thousands each year. It is also "one of the most sociologically intricate and highly charged events in modern medicine" (Swazey, 1986, p. 10).

Organ transplantation is highly charged and intricate because of the paradox upon which it rests. For it is never just about life, it is also about death. Renee Fox (1988) refers to organ transplantation as being both life saving and death ridden. It is about putting organs in human beings; yet it is also about taking organs from the bodies of other human beings.

☐ Brain Death and Organ Donation

With few exceptions, transplant organs can only be taken from a new class of patients who died via neurological criteria while being maintained on a ventilator. The old standard for declaring death, not breathing, that had been working since the beginning of time is no longer the only way to define death.

Even Shakespeare's King Lear confirmed the death of his beloved daughter, Cordelia, by putting a mirror to her lips to check her breath.

> She's gone for ever—
> I know when one is dead, and when one lives;
> She's dead as earth—Lend me a looking-glass;
> If that her breath will mist or stain the stone,
> Why, then she lives.
> —(Act V, Scene III, Lines 293–298)

With the establishment of a set of neurological criteria that would define death as the cessation of the brain function, no longer is it easy to know when one is dead, and when one is alive. Breath upon a mirror no long serves to verify our perceptions.

Medical advances of recent years have expanded the parameters of socially and ethically acceptable changes in how and when life comes to an end. A specific instance of this tinkering with death came about during the 1970s when the criteria for brain death was medically and legally formalized. The term, brain death, essentially refers to a set of circumstances that create a nontraditional way to die, and were developed by medical and legal authorities to deal with the progressively sophisticated methods of resuscitation and support measures that resulted in only partial success (Fox & Swazey, 1992). Patients were being resuscitated and maintained on a ventilator that sustained heart and lung function but with complete and irreversible cessation of brain function, including that of the brain stem.

This redefinition of death was formalized by the Uniform Determination of Death Act 1981, which was proposed by the President's Commission for the Study of Ethical Problems in Medicine and Biomedical and Behavioral Research. The redefinition of death also paved the way for obtaining organs for transplantation.

Because the brain stem controls pulmonary and heart function, the patient who is declared brain dead is by necessity always being maintained on a ventilator. For those patients who become organ donors, the ventilator must be continued until the organs are surgically removed in order to assure viability of the transplantable organs. With few exceptions, all transplanted organs come from this newly defined class of patients.

☐ The Organ Donor Family

This nontraditional way of dying created another category of people. They were family members or significant others of the uniquely deceased brain dead patient. The transplanted gift of life comes wrapped in the mourning of these families; the true cost of organ transplants cannot be measured by monetary means, but rather by the trauma experienced by those who mourn.

The miracle of transplantation actually begins when these deeply traumatized families reach beyond their pain and give consent for their loved one to become a donor. Until quite recently these individuals—who far outnumber donors, for it is estimated that eight to ten individuals are affected by each death (Rando, 1993)—tended to fade into anonymity once their loved one became a donor. This reality left 40,000–50,000 new traumatized family members each year, plus an untold number of friends, coworkers, and others to struggle on their own with two unique trauma-related issues linked to organ donation. The first unique aspect of donation is the phenomenon of brain death, which was discussed earlier. The second is the reality that the loved one's organs continue to sustain life in the body or bodies of other human beings.

☐ Parts of the Loved One Live On

Thousands of organ donor families live with the knowledge that the organs that once sustained the life of their loved one are now sustaining the life of a stranger. This aspect of donor family grief is a modern phenomenon that has no parallel. While this reality remains peripheral to the grief of many donor families, for others it becomes paramount and colors their grief in ways that can be both comforting and disturbing.

There appears to be a drive to learn about the recipients of a loved one's organs, and while this component of the donation experience is positive and comforting for some, it is less so for others.

> The responses of donors, recipients, and their families to the experience of organ transplantation suggest that, on preconscious and unconscious levels, they feel that something akin to transfer of psychic and social as well as biological qualities of self to the other has taken place. Partly because of the import of the 'gift of life' that has been exchanged, a blurring of boundaries between donors, recipients, and their families often occur. (Fox & Swazey, 1992, p. 256)

The question that pleads an answer is how does this phenomenon affect the grief of the donor family? Might the experience of meeting—or not meeting—recipients further traumatize the family? Fox and Swazey (1992) suggest that this "blending of self and other can be both uplifting and anxiety provoking" (p. 256). Interaction among the donor's family, the recipient, and the recipient's family can surely be one of the most highly charged and intricate aspects of organ donation. And whether for good or ill, there is no question that for some families it plays a significant role in the grief process.

☐ Organ Donation and Donor Family Trauma

Trauma has been defined as a psychologically distressing event that is outside the range of normal human experience. Many organ donor families experience trauma-driven grief. Since death and the grief that inevitably follows is natural and normal, some argue that it does not qualify as traumatic. They forget that death resides in the normal range of experience only in the global sense of the phrase. Consider the following scenarios:

> Jamie, a 23-year-old woman, stated that she had "pretty much gotten used to being beaten by her husband." But neither Jamie, her family, nor the community was prepared for the day that her 3-month-old baby was savagely beaten to death by that same husband.

> Ella, a widow, doted on her only child, a son. He was a medical student at an ivy-league university and planned to work with underprivileged children. He was a bright light to all who knew him until a drunk driver ran him down in broad daylight while he was jogging on campus.

> Mary lived with her mother-in-law, Doris, while her husband was away in the Navy. She described Doris as her best friend, and the mother she had never had. Three days before Mary's husband was to return home, Doris and Mary's 1-year-old daughter died in a car crash. The day that should have been one of joyous reunion was a day of anguish as Mary and her husband stood by the single casket of Doris, cradling her beloved granddaughter.

There is nothing natural or normal about these events. The *Diagnostic and Statistical Manual of Mental Disorders*, 3rd edition (DSM-III; American Psychiatric Association [APA], 1987) contends that "the most common traumata involve either a serious threat to one's life or physical integrity; a serious threat or harm to one's children, spouse, or other close relatives and friends. In some cases the trauma may be learning about a serious threat or harm to a close friends or relative, e.g., that one's child has been . . . killed" (pp. 247–248).

The family members in each of these vignettes experienced trauma and the trauma-driven grief that would follow. Each death also resulted in organ donation.

☐ The Need for Study

Transplantation has always been about reverence for life. To be congruent, this reverence must extend to the families of those who donate organs. One way this reverence can be extended to these families is through increasing awareness of their grief experience. As we shift our attention to the variegated responses within the grief experience as encountered by these individuals, we affirm, validate, and honor those who make organ transplants possible.

Some studies have already attempted to learn more about the donor family experience (Bartucci, 1987; Batten & Prottas, 1987; Holtkamp, 1997; Pellitier, 1992; Savaria, Rovelli, & Schweizer, 1990; Willis & Skelley, 1992). These studies did not focus on trauma or bereavement per se, but rather sought information related to the hospital and donation experience, including the issue of brain death, reasons for donating, and the donor family's needs before, during, and immediately after the decision to donate as well as their responses to donation.

A basic problem with researching this subject is reflected in low response rates. Batten, Levine, and Prottas (1987) considered the 61% response rate to their survey inadequate, leaving "room for doubt about the characteristics and opinions of those who did not respond" (p. 36). In spite of limited returns, such studies have provided rich details about the donor family's experience immediately before, during, and after donation. The practical value of these studies should never be underestimated. Yet much remains to be learned about the grief that follows the unique experience of donor families, especially the long-term impact of donation.

The disturbingly low response rates to some donor family surveys may present a major obstacle to acquiring adequate data about the long-term effects of donation on grief. A vast majority of donor families, as well as those who chose not to donate, have often remained silent. And it is this silent majority that could contribute much to our understanding.

The reasons why these families choose to remain silent are probably multifaceted. However, Senator Orrin Hatch (R–Utah) made a telling observation when he opened the 1983 congressional hearing about organ donation by saying that anyone criticizing organ donation would immediately be given the Scrooge of the Year Award. It may be reasonable to conclude that both researchers and some family members might be reluctant to share negative thoughts and experiences in deference to all the positive aspects of donation.

Other individuals may remain quiet because they are cognizant of a troubling inequity of mind: while one may have reservations about donating the organs of a loved one, that same individual would have no reservations about accepting a donated organ in order to save the life of a family member.

Most Americans, including donor families, are well aware that lives are saved and other families are spared overwhelming anguish because of this remarkable medical procedure. The tangible and noble qualities of organ donation may stifle the emotional as well as the cognitive concerns that people might find difficult to articulate. Whatever their reasons for not responding to surveys, their silence leaves our body of knowledge lean and wanting.

One consistent response from donor families who are not silent indicates that organ donation provided them with "some comfort" or "solace" in that it brought something of value from their tragedy. Both the medical and media communities have recounted this beneficial aspect of organ donation countless times. Without hesitation, families report that there is great comfort in knowing that something uplifting and noble came from the hateful death of a loved one. However, an abundance of anecdotal data indicates that there is more to the story.

☐ Primary Process Thinking

To be authentic and to serve families of organ donors well, we must be willing to risk qualifying for the "Scrooge of the Year Award" by exploring the other side of this story. This exploration won't be easy. Some of the answers will not be found in clear reasoning. Yet, in order to maintain integrity and neutrality, we must recognize the dynamic and often uneasy relationship between the rational, logical processes and "the messier and less-well-articulated world of emotions, superstition and magic" (Youngner, 1996, p. 34).

Working with the illogical or mystical has seldom been appealing to scholars. Yet, we must not be afraid to confront the dark, the irrational, for the darkness may yield many of the answers for which we search to better understand the impact of the gift of life on the families who give.

An example of the illogical aspect of the American response to organ donation is evidenced in the discrepancy between the number of individuals who claim to approve of organ donation, 85–98 % (Batten & Prottas, 1987; Bartucci, 1987; Savaria, Revelli, & Schweizer, 1990), and the number of those who sign donor cards, 28% (Radecki & Jaccard, 1997). One of several reasons for this discrepancy may be lodged in the tendency to revert to primary thinking when under stress. Severe stress or even unpleasantness can sometimes induce the murky, mystical thinking that defies reason and education, even for the most rational human being.

Recognizing the subterranean psychological tensions that often tug at the more rational and tidy view of donation, with its capacity to save lives, will enable us to consider the promises of paradox found within this medical process. Indeed, if we are to learn what we need to know about donor family grief, this combination of the subterranean psychological forces and rational thought must be accepted and understood.

☐ Contents

This work will attempt to better understand the risks and benefits of organ donation as it impacts the trauma-driven grief of the donor family. By examining the history and context of this phenomenon, how organs are procured, the family's experience at the hospital, their trauma-driven grief, as well as concerns about the delicate relationship between the donor family and the recipient of their loved one's organs, we will build a foundation on which to study the attending therapeutic concerns and effective interventions.

☐ Closing Thoughts

In *Trauma, Transformation and Healing,* Wilson (1989) argues that, "[t]he experience of trauma can transform the human spirit in a variety of ways, which range from extreme diminution of the will to an existential transcendence which is spiritual in nature" (p. xiii).

Courage and professional neutrality are necessary in order to explore possible risk factors related to organ donor family grief that might lead to extreme diminution of the will. As professional caregivers, we must attempt to understand the psychological, social, and mystical issues that reside within the donation transaction, and how these issues impact donor family grief. If we summon the courage to explore this topic openly, the helping professions may encourage and empower these families to understand and cope more effectively with organ donation's more troubling aspects without diminishing its noble and uplifting benefits.

In doing so, we may assist donor families in achieving that existential transcendence which is spiritual in nature. To accomplish this, we must be able to tolerate the paradox of this remarkable medical procedure. The eloquence of one donor mother as she describes her feelings reveals one side of the paradox:

> There has been no relief from the devastating pain of my loss, yet there have been surprising sources of comfort. The most surprising source of comfort was that which came from knowing that my daughter's death enabled others to live and saved their families from the agonizing pain of loss. (Anonymous donor mother, personal communication, 1997)

The other side of the paradox, a darker side, is just as legitimate:

> For a long time after my sister's death, I had nightmares about allowing the

mutilation of her body. I even began to have doubts about the doctor's claims that she had been brain dead, and that she could feel no pain while they took away her vital organs. These reactions hit me like aftershocks for years. (H. Johnson, 1992)

Both scenarios are real and honest. Neither is more right than the other. Within these extremes reside the risks and benefits of organ donation. It is here, in the contrast, that we will learn how both effect the grief of the donor families. Here, too, we will discover the promises within this highly-charged and intricately complex medical reality.

Though offering an overview of variegated responses from donor families, this volume does not claim to offer comprehensive research, nor is it an exhaustive work about the distinctive aspects of donor family grief. Rather, it is an initial attempt to frame a foundation for further study of both the potential benefits and problems that might be generated by the life giving, death-ridden phenomenon of organ donation.

Organ Donation and the Donor Family

Transplantation is made possible because of a new class of patients who have been determined to be dead via neurological rather than cardiopulmonary criteria. This nontraditional way to die, which is commonly referred to as brain death, has created another new category of people: They are family members or significant others of the uniquely deceased, brain dead patient.

While clinical technology associated with transplantation has made remarkable strides in recent years, little has been done to understand the trauma-driven grief of family members of the donor. One reason for the dearth of information about the donor family experience is that transplantation is often perceived as merely a medical procedure. The outcome of such a perception is that the social, spiritual, ethical, and personal dimensions of the donor family's experience with trauma-driven grief are often ignored or are undervalued. The stories of these families do not fit the celebratory tone of transplantation and therefore largely go unheard in a society inebriated by hype and posturing.

It is tempting to believe that the donor family's grief experience is bound by their own loved one's trauma. In reality, stressors that impact donor family grief are in place even before the family's involvement and find roots in the history and context of transplantation and organ donation. Troublesome seeds of mistrust and disquietude are sometimes to be found within medical ethics surrounding this modern miracle. To effectively address the needs of organ donor families, caregivers must first have a working knowledge of the historical and contextual surround of this modern phenomenon.

This chapter will explore the early days of transplantation, including the development of brain death criteria and the psychological issues surrounding this phenomenon. In addition to introducing the organ donor's family and their experience, cultural, religious, and ethical concerns will be considered along with current controversial efforts to expand the donor pool.

☐ History and Context of Organ Donation

Clinical transplantation is a relatively new phenomenon in the medical community. It has been described as one of the most miraculous accomplishments of modern medicine. Yet, success did not come easily (Spital, 1997). Initially, that success was particularly limited because the kidneys first used in transplantation were procured from cadaveric donors. These initial limitations were caused by the rapid deterioration of the organs following cardiac arrest and because of the absence of preservation techniques and ineffective immunosuppressive agents (Spital, 1997). Solving the latter problem was pivotal to the success of transplantation because of the body's insistent refusal to accept tissues or organs that are not its own.

The Early Days of Transplantation

In today's world transplantation has become so commonplace that little thought is given to its early days. Yet, to fully understand the donor family experience, it is helpful to review the highlights of how we've come to be where we are.

On December 23, 1954, Dr. Joseph Murray and his colleagues made medical history when they successfully transplanted a kidney between identical twins (Spital, 1997). By using identical twins, the recipient's body was duped into believing that the transplanted kidney was its own, thereby greatly increasing the chance of acceptance. That first transplanted kidney functioned well for eight years (Spital, 1997).

Soon, other kidney transplants were performed on identical twins and eventually, by choosing the most compatible match from a family pool, other close relatives—preferably parents or siblings—were used to achieve successful kidney transplants.

However, these new medical personalities, the living donors, presented some ethical and psychological problems for the medical establishment.

The ethical dilemma of placing a perfectly healthy individual at risk in order to save—or rather, prolong—the life of another individual provided discomfort for medical professionals as well as ethicists. As Dr. Francis Moore (1964) observed: "For the first time in the history of medicine, a procedure is being adopted in which a perfectly healthy person is injured permanently in order to improve the well-being [not of himself but] of another" (p. 388). The risk is actually greater than permanent injury. There are cases of fatalities among living donors as the result of donation. Even one death is considered unacceptable by the medical community and according to noted transplant surgeon, T. E. Starzl, when such a death occurs it "almost stops the clock worldwide" (Morrow, 1991, p. 57).

Although grief that is associated with fatalities among living donors is not the subject of this work, it is worth noting that over 20% of all current kidney transplants involve living donors. Despite the widespread acceptance of this practice, ethical concerns about the use of living donors continues to haunt transplant programs today (Fox & Swazey, 1992).

Psychological Issues Surrounding Transplantation

While early medical and ethical debates about various aspects of transplantation continued, the psychological issues surrounding this medical procedure also received considerable interest and attention within the transplant community. During those early days before transplantation became routine, transplant surgeons discussed the undue emotional pressure that potential and actual live donors might experience. Even though various mechanisms were instituted to protect the donor candidate from undue pressures, Fox claims that no matter what efforts the medical team made "to protect the members of a prospective recipient's family from feeling coerced or self-coerced, the pressure to offer this 'gift of life' [was] powerful" (Fox & Swazey, 1992, p. 33). Transplant professionals also struggled with complications that could arise from the "creditor-debtor aspects of this unrepayable gift of life, and by the animistic feelings and social qualities of the donor being transferred along with the organ into the body and being of the recipient" (Fox, 1996, p. 261).

Questions about how the live donor would respond if the recipient's body should reject the organ or die were other issues of concern for the early transplant professional. Interestingly, Fox and Swazey (1992) pointed out that the families of present-day cadaveric donors experience some of the same psychological reactions as the live donors and their families.

Transplant teams were startled by the animistic experiences that many donors, recipients, and their families seemed to experience in response to this exchange. Medical professionals were unprepared for this kind of "magical" thinking that surrounded the gift of life (Fox & Swazey, 1992). These concerns, however, would have remained in the margins, affecting a minimum number of people, had transplantation remained within the family.

Expansion of the Transplant Program

Three biomedical events, the criteria for brain death, an effective immunological suppressive drug, and improved surgical techniques, enabled the miraculous accomplishment of transplantation to move away from home. That move changed organ transplantation forever. The first major event came approximately a decade after transplanting human organs became a demonstrated reality.

Improvement in resuscitation and support measures made it possible to save the lives of patients whose brains had been permanently damaged. At this point, medical professionals and legal scholars began to clamor for a new standard for determining and pronouncing death for certain brain-injured patients.

Brain Death

The evolution of the definition of death in terms of the irreversible cessation of brain function would become intertwined with the history of organ donation. In 1968 an Ad Hoc Harvard Medical School Committee published a landmark report that defined death in terms of the abolition of brain function rather than just the traditional criteria of cardiopulmonary cessation.

When death occurs in the traditional manner (i.e., the heart stops beating and the patient stops breathing) even the most obtuse layman can recognize it. However, for the first time in history, death suddenly became "an approximation" (Bernat, 1992), a subject of debate. That debate continues to the present time.

The medical criteria for neurological death required backing from the legal community in order to hold up within the legal system. By 1968 the necessary legal parameters were beginning to take shape.

Legal Parameters

The Uniform Anatomical Gift Act of 1968 (UAGA) became the vehicle whereby all organs and tissues are donated for transplantation purposes

(Rodgers, 1989). By 1972 all 50 states had adopted some version of this law.

Basically, the UAGA designated the individuals who may consent to an anatomical gift upon death and other operating guidelines for organ procurement. The concept of the donor card was developed within this code, as well as guidelines related to the limitations and obligations of physicians. Also covered was the designation of approved facilities to receive donations. In this original version of the law, families of donor candidates could override the wishes of their loved one and refuse to allow the donation to take place (Rodgers, 1989).

In 1987, amendments to this act insisted that the wishes of the donor be honored, eliminating the option of revocation of these wishes by family members on the death of the donor. However, in practical reality, families in the United States still have the final say in whether consent is given.

Throughout the 1970s, brain death criteria were progressively developed through court decisions and by the medical community. The Uniform Determination of Death Act proposed by the President's Commission for the Study of Ethical Problems in Medical and Biomedical and Behavioral Research defined death as "either the cessation of cardiopulmonary functions or of the functions of the whole brain, including brain stem, which controls heart and lung function" (Fox & Swazey, 1992, p. 61). By necessity, patients who meet the latter criteria must be on mechanical ventilation.

Regardless of the laudable intent of the new definition of death, some have expressed concerns that the rush to legislation gave the impression that the new definition was adopted simply to allow organs to be "harvested" for transplant (Annas, 1988; Fox & Swazey, 1992; Joralemon, 1995).

Annas (1988) refers to the fact that solid human organs must remain oxygenated until the moment of recovery in order to be viable for transplant. In other words the organs must be fresh. (The freshness of the donor family's grief reflects a poignant parallel.) This means that with the exception of living kidney donors, transplanted organs must come from individuals on ventilators who have suffered "brain death." In fact, the concept of brain death is central to the success and expansion of the transplantation enterprise. "It establishes a necessary prerequisite for selecting potential donors and provides a conceptual basis for discussing the donation option" (Youngner et al., 1989, p. 2205).

The Donor's Family

Discussing the option for donation takes place with the potential donor's family. Ideally, the option is presented after brain death is an established reality. Many of the family members are parents or other family members of relatively young, healthy people who have been killed in an automobile accident, or by suicide or homicide (Fox & Swazey, 1992; Youngner, 1996). Rando (1993) indicates that "deaths caused by accident, disasters, war, suicide, and homicide, as well as the death of a child, readily qualify as traumatic stressors" (pp. 570–571). Most donor deaths fit that profile. There are other stressors present that are unique to the donor family experience.

For instance, the family must confront the unusual presentation of their brain dead loved one. This new class of patient—legally dead but sustaining life—also presents enormous discomfort for others who are not family members, people within the medical profession, and the general public. The physiological status of the patients (they still have a heart beat; they can digest food and excrete waste products, and they may even bear children) is responsible for considerable confusion (Ott, 1998).

It is not unusual for family members to experience cognitive dissonance when they hear that a loved one is dead, yet see visual cues to the contrary. These cues include their loved one looking quite natural: The chest rises and falls as in normal breathing, and the color is good. Reconciling this visual representation of a loved one with the medical and legal definition of death often involves a struggle even for those who are familiar with the concept of neurological death.

In the face of this mind-bending scenario, families of potential donors must: (a) accept the sudden and often violent death of their loved one, (b) grasp the reality of that loss in full view of overwhelming visual cues to the contrary, and (c) consent to or reject the option to donate their loved one's organs for transplant. And all these tasks must be done while the family is in the midst of denial, shock, and disbelief—hallmark reactions to sudden death.

Unless the subject of organ donation had been discussed beforehand, being asked to make a decision when one is in shock, denial, and disbelief is almost incomprehensible. Advanced directives by the potential donor would greatly reduce, and possibly eliminate, that particular stress on family members. However, advanced directives relative to organ donation should only be made when individuals and families clearly understand what they are consenting to.

Informed Consent

The issue of informed consent has been a personal concern for over 10 years. Any strategies currently used or projected for future use to obtain organs for transplant should hinge on informed consent.

Informed consent must be written in a language that can be understood by the patient, and it must be signed and dated by the patient and at least one other witness. This document must include clear statements that describe the procedure or the test; benefits and risks to the patient; expected consequences of not allowing a particular test or procedure, as well as other procedures or diagnostic aids that are available; and a statement that care will not be withheld if the patient does not consent. Informed consent is voluntary. It must always be obtained when the patient is fully competent (*Signet/Mosby Medical Encyclopedia*, 1985).

Informed consent is rarely present in the realm of cadaveric organ donation. The donor card that a person signs to state his or her wish to become an organ donor contains no clear statements that describe brain death or the specific tests used to determine this diagnosis. Neither does there appear to be a plan to provide such information for registrants within other protocols that are being developed to increase the donor pool. The donor-to-be may be considered competent, but hardly informed.

On the other hand, when consent falls to the family of a donor candidate at the time of crisis, explanations of brain death or surgical procedures are scarcely adequate, given the reality that people understand information more effectively when it relates to their existing views. When information requires radical reorientation and is also disagreeable, it is apt to be distorted or dismissed (Parkes & Weiss, 1983).

Understanding brain death on a preneed basis would not even be an issue had it not been for the second biomedical event that helped transform transplantation into a routine procedure: the discovery of a new immunological drug that would effectively address the problem of biological rejection.

Immunosuppressive Drugs

The discovery of the antirejection drug cyclosporine in the late 1970s ushered transplantation into a new era. Hailed as "superior" and "remarkable," this drug averted or postponed rejection of transplanted organs and became the drug that was generally given to all transplant recipients (Fox & Swazey, 1992). Along with this effective antirejection drug came the ability to transplant a wider spectrum of organs and to perform greater numbers of transplants.

Improved Surgical Skills

The increased numbers of transplant surgeries performed led to the third biomedical event: improved surgical skills and techniques that increased the success rates for transplanted organs. The introduction of cyclosporine and the evolution of improved surgical and organ procurement techniques, combined with the medically and legally accepted definition of brain death, brought about an explosion in the types, numbers, and combinations of organs that could be successfully transplanted.

Given that this explosion and the reality that transplantation was moving rapidly from the classification as an experimental procedure to the treatment of choice for many gravely ill people, it was inevitable that those waiting for organs would soon outnumber those wanting to give organs. The demand for transplantable organs rapidly outgrew the supply.

Factors Influencing Organ Donation

The reasons for the shortfall of organs donated are many and varied; however, rejection may be used metaphorically to describe the failure of individuals to queue up to become organ donors. Richardson (1996) claims that while "many people recognize and appreciate the value of organ transplantation," they simply do not "themselves wish to contribute to the supply of human organs . . . " (p. 75). This resistance or cultural rejection is not limited to any class or level of education; even medical personnel harbor such reservations.

Other researchers (Fiedler, 1996; Fox & Swazey, 1992; Joralemon, 1995; Youngner, 1996) define public rejection as a psychological response that will not yield to reason. Psychological boundaries of the self appear no more readily violated than the biological bounds enforced by the body's immune system. Roots for these protective boundaries may be bound within primary-process thinking.

Primary-Process Thinking

Freud describes the dual dimensions of human thought as primary- and secondary-process thinking. Secondary-process thinking is conscious thinking, primarily verbal and logical. Primary-process thinking involves unconscious or preconscious thinking and dreaming. Ruled by emotions and remote from any logic, it is filled with wishful or fearful misconceptions (Fenichel, 1972).

Many professional analysts have observed primary-process thinking as an integral, though subordinate, part of normal adult mental life (Youngner, 1996). Sleep or metabolic disturbances, drugs or severe anxiety may trigger a lapse into the primary-process mode. During such times magical thinking may replace rational thought.

Mystical, magical thinking is not often compatible with scientific training. In fact, the notion that there are valid thought processes other than the rational, cognitive modus operandi tends to rattle the transplant community. Nothing in their medical or scientific training prepares them for "mystical thinking which is lived and felt rather than abstracted and intellectualized" (Verble & Worth, 1996, p. 201). This mystical thinking often emerges when families experience great emotional stress such as when death occurs and they are asked about organ donation.

The inherent nature of transplantation offers both a stimulus and rich material for primary-process thinking. Aversive qualities of this mode of thought may also complicate the trauma-driven grief experienced by organ donor families.

Primary-process thinking also makes it easier to understand society's ambivalence about donation. This ambivalence is demonstrated by the fact that nearly 90% of those surveyed voiced approval of organ donation, while only 28% made the effort to sign a donor card (Radecki & Jaccard, 1997), and the family consent rate is only 60% (Verble & Worth, 1996). If this ambivalence is present during a relatively stress-free period when individuals might sign a donor card or respond to a survey, how much more challenging must it be when families are faced with such a decision in the midst of great personal trauma?

The general consensus in the bereavement field is that individuals should be encouraged not to make irrevocable decisions during their first year of bereavement. However, organ donation demands an immediate decision. Potential donor families who overcome their ambivalence and consent to donation may reexperience that ambivalence during the grief process. Interestingly, families who decline donation because of the inability to make such a momentous decision during distress, also may later regret their decision.

Religious Issues

Religious and mythical attitudes about death as well as superstitions impact attitudes about organ donation within minority communities and the general population. While most Jewish, Protestant, and Catholic religions within the United States are supportive of organ donation, the fundamentalist Christian and Orthodox Jewish communities hold to the more traditional view, which rejects the concept of brain death entirely, arguing that as long as there is vital fluid flow, movement of air and blood through the body, there is life (Youngner, 1996).

Religious as well as cultural differences color Japanese attitudes toward organ transplants. Shinto, the indigenous religion of Japan, teaches that the souls of the deceased are unstable until they are placated through a funeral ceremony and memorial service (Riether & Mahler, 1995). In addition, both Confucianism and Shintoism prohibit tampering with the dead.

Until very recently, Japan had been involved in a 25-year-long argument over the concept of brain death. One position accepted the medicolegal definition of neurological death while the opposing position argued that the social, religious, and cultural aspects of organ donation have not been adequately addressed. According to Lock (1996), Japan appeared less willing to tinker with larger-than-life human forces. Japan's recent decision to accept the medicolegal definition of brain death presumably indicates a change in this culture's willingness to tinker. There appears to be no consideration as to how this radical change will impact the social, religious, and personal dimensions of life in Japan.

Fears and Care for the Dead

Apart from any religious influence, fear forms the basis for much of the cultural resistance to organ donation. The roots of these fears run deep within hard-to-reach places of the mind and in very old attitudes regarding the body and the dead, a fear of bodily mutilation, and fear of inflicting pain upon the dead corpse (Richardson, 1996). Respect for the deceased and concern about proper treatment of the dead body have been powerful and consistent themes throughout the history of civilization.

There is a distinct dichotomy in transplantation in so much as "the idea of giving organs is uplifting" while the idea of "taking them from newly dead bodies of former loved ones, patients, or our imagined dead selves evokes quite a different set of emotions" (Youngner, 1990, p. 1014). Fear is the primary component of this different set of emotions.

It is a mistake to believe that these fears exist only among the less educated. Many well-educated individuals believe that people need their specific body parts to see God or to enter Heaven. Often the most scientifically oriented will experience feelings of tenderness while selecting the burial clothes for a loved one. Such ideas are part of a mystical mode of thought that rest comfortably beside the usual, more cogent mode.

This tandem thought process takes up residence when traumatized family or governments go to extraordinary lengths and expense to recover bodies that have been lost at sea or other remote places. One need not rely on scholars to demonstrate this less-than-rational regard that people evidence toward the dead bodies of a loved one. When the small plane carrying John F. Kennedy, Jr., his wife, and sister-in-law crashed off the coast of Martha's Vineyard in 1999, enormous amounts of money and energy were expended to recover the bodies. This effort was not unusual, although in this case the costs and efforts may have been considerably more excessive. The desire to recover lost bodies is especially telling in the Kennedy case, for once they were located, the bodies were cremated, then reburied at sea.

The extremes undertaken to recover the bodies of lost loved ones are neither rational nor reasonable, but represent a part of our nature that demands that the body be treated with respect and be given a proper burial.

Since medical technology has insisted that we must choose which signs of life constitute the death of the patient, while other signs of life persist (Youngner, 1996) we must be prepared for the effects of this dual level of thinking by the family of the cadaveric donor. These individuals must come to terms with the tragic, often violent and untimely death of their loved one, the cognitive dissonance associated with brain death, the confusion of boundaries, and the mutilation of dead bodies, which are disturbing but inescapable aspects of transplantation and organ procurement (Youngner, 1996). Thus, for the caregiver, an understanding of the magical, mystical mode of thought that provides context for the donation experience is essential.

☐ Expanding the Donor Pool

The aggressive approaches being promoted, developed, or actually instituted in response to the ever-expanding shortage of transplant organs impact the family and plead our attention. Both medical and legal efforts to increase the number of transplantable organs often involve ethical dilemmas.

All the medical and legal gerrymandering to expand the donor pool has led to a new definition of death, to the use of non–heart beating donors, to the proposed use of anencephalic infants, and other aggressive efforts to obtain more organs. These new efforts can negatively impact the fragile trust of the general public as well as that of the donor family.

As noted earlier, prior to the evolution of brain death criteria during the 1960s and 1970s, some transplants were performed using organs from individuals who died via cardiopulmonary standards. There were serious limitations to this method of obtaining transplant organs due to the warm ischemia (where cells and tissue damage begins and progresses rapidly, thus making the organs unusable) as well as the immunocological rejection of the human body to foreign matter. Current transplant centers appear to have found a way around these earlier problems associated with acquiring organs from individuals who die via cardiopulmonary standards.

Non–Heart Beating Donors

New protocols and procedures for obtaining organs from non–heart beating donors have been developed or are already being implemented by major transplant centers. These protocols and procedures overcome the problems associated with the warm ischemia but raise ominous questions for donor families and their caregivers.

There are some definitive differences between the original and the current procedures to retrieve organs from non–heart beating donors. Early attempts to recover kidneys from patients who died because of cardiopulmonary cessation were not particularly efficient or successful primarily because of the crucial and limited time available for recovery and transplant. Today's non–heart beating donors are ventilator dependent and either they or their families consent to donation prior to death, choosing a time for their death and the consequent removal of organs. This protocol is said to give hopelessly ill patients who wish to die the opportunity to donate organs, even though they fail to meet the criteria for brain death (Spital, 1997).

After the decision to donate has been made—which means that life-support measures and resuscitative efforts are declined—the patient is rushed to the operating room, where, to avoid problems associated with warm ischemic time, preparation for organ procurement takes place and a femoral arterial line is inserted in the patient's body while the patient is still alive (Fox, 1996). Only then is the life-support removed from the patient who is given "comfort" medication, but only for demonstrated need. According to Fox (1996) this procedure "means that the patient may be subjected to invasive, potentially distressful and harmful procedures in order to 'save' organs" (p. 264) for transplant.

A particularly worrisome aspect of this protocol is the expectation that something could go wrong, thus necessitating cancellation of the surgery. In the event of such a case, the patient would be returned to the intensive care unit. The harm this might do to a potential donor's family members is incalculable—and unknown.

There is more. Once the life-support equipment is removed, death is pronounced by cardiopulmonary criteria after a mere two minutes. Fox (1996) also notes that physicians in other medical centers under nontransplantation circumstances usually observe six to seven minutes before declaring death. This procedure appears to move the question of death closer and closer to life.

In spite of the fact that the family has been included in these decisions, it should be of interest to those in the bereavement field, that under this protocol the patient dies totally isolated from his or her family, in a cold, sterile operating room in the midst of strangers who helped prepare his or her body for surgery that may have begun when the patient/donor was only equivocally dead (Fox & Swazey, 1992). Spital (1997) acknowledges, "there is . . . a risk of additional emotional trauma for families" because they were "not able to be present when their loved one died" (p. 84).

Families generally consider it critically important to be present when a loved one dies and grieve the possibility that the beloved might die alone or among strangers. Being present gives the family an opportunity to care for the dying individual. When this opportunity is lost, the family later may experience regrets or guilt, even though they had agreed with the decision to donate.

The University of Pittsburgh protocol for using non–heart beating donors has been revised in such a way that family members may stay with the patient in a nonsurgical setting until death is pronounced. This modification came about because of a family that was "strongly committed to having their relative become a non–heart beating donor, but who insisted on remaining with the patient until death occurred, as a precondition." The revision took place, not because the transplanters viewed the old policy as harmful or morally wrong, but because of the "pragmatic realization that they could make these changes and still obtain the organs they sought" (Fox, 1996, p. 265).

There is another alarming but rarely discussed problem within this protocol that pleads attention. According to Youngner and Arnold (1993), the patients who meet the criteria outlined by this protocol could represent a wide range of end-stage degenerative diseases. "At one end of the spectrum are cognitively intact persons with long-term neurological or cardiopulmonary problems that have left them ventilator dependent" (p. 2771). Persons with amyotrophic lateral sclerosis, high spinal injuries, or severe end-stage respiratory or cardiac disease could be included in this category. In such cases, it could be the patient who decided that his or her quality of life is unacceptable, and it could be this patient who asks that all life-support be removed, choosing his or her time of death. Under this protocol, such patients might also choose to become organ donors (Youngner & Arnold, 1993). This protocol appears to compromise a cardinal rule in transplantation, that life-sustaining organs must not be removed from living persons.

Whether or not there are any cases on record of cognitively intact patients moving through this process is irrelevant. Protocols such as the ones applied to the non–heart beating donors that might include cognitively intact patients choosing to die and donate by protocol may undermine the confidence of the general public and add to the suspicions of organ donor families. Other suggestions for expanding the donor pool also skirt ethical bounds.

Anencephalic Donors

The recently observed missionary zeal with which transplant organs are being pursued has also resurrected a perennial and controversial proposal: the use of anencephalic donors.

Anencephalic infants are born with a "congenital absence of a major portion of the brain, skull and scalp. Neonates with this condition are born without a forebrain and without a cerebrum" (Caplan & Coelho, 1998, p. 89). Ninety-five percent of live-born anencephalic infants die within seven days of birth (Fox & Swazey, 1992). During whatever time they live, these infants have no conscious brain activity. However, they are able to maintain at least some of the body's autonomic function, such as the function of the heart, lungs, kidneys, and reflex actions (Caplan & Coelho, 1998).

The use of anencephalic infants as a source of transplant organs violates the cardinal rule of transplantation: People should not be killed for or by organ retrieval. Yet, it is argued that when parents are confronted with the tragic birth of a child who can never experience consciousness and who will die in a matter of days, they may be comforted by donating their infant's organs to save or improve the life of other children. The Council on Ethical and Judicial Affairs declares that good may come from such a donation, but when contemplating that good, it must be remembered that these organs would be coming from infants who "may be able to breathe, suck, engage in spontaneous movements of their eyes, arms and legs, respond to noxious stimuli with crying or avoidance maneuvers, and exhibit facial expressions typical of healthy infants" (Caplan & Coelho, 1998, p. 82). While some parents indicate their desire for their child to be used for donation in order to bring some good from the heart-rending situation, neither they, nor we, can claim to know the long-term psychological impact should this procedure become law.

What is known at the moment is that this practice would (a) violate the prohibition against removal of organs from living persons, (b) increase the chance of creating further exceptions to enable organ removal from other persons with serious disabilities, (c) result in very few additional transplanted organs, and (d) further erode public trust "in the broader social context in which members of the public harbor concerns about physicians removing organs prematurely from dying patients for transplantation" (Caplan & Coelho, 1998, p. 83). This erosion of trust may come after the fact of donation and undermine the donor family's sense of confidence in their decision to donate.

Shewmon and colleagues (1998) argue that the slope is indeed slippery if we measure personhood by IQ. To do so, they contend, would mean that those with "atelencephaly and hydranencephaly and extreme postnatal forebrain destruction resulting in a persistent vegetative state" would have to be included since they "all involve just as much brain absence as anencephaly" (p. 103). However, serious proposals have been developed to redefine patients who are in persistent vegetative states as legally dead, and that the removal of organs from those in such a state is starting to receive serious consideration within medical literature.

Required Request

Thus far we have explored medical attempts to expand the donor pool. However, legal maneuvers are also being promoted as another means of increasing the number of transplantable organs. Some of these attempts may create yet another opportunity to further traumatize donor families by fueling the suspicion that the needs of living patients outweigh care for the donor.

One early legal maneuver to mitigate the chronic and growing shortage of cadaveric organs for transplant generated the required request legislation. This legal tactic dictates that institutions must present the option of organ donation to families whose loved one has been declared brain dead (Rodgers, 1989; Fox & Swazey, 1992). By 1982 required request regulations had been enacted by most state legislatures and mandated in federal legislation for all institutions receiving Medicaid or Medicare (Fox & Swazey, 1992).

Some hospitals merely ask for consent during the admission process when patients enter the hospital. However, such perfunctory efforts hardly account for the limited success in procuring additional organs for transplant. So meager was this law's effectiveness in generating more organs, that some within the medical community joined legal efforts to promote other laws aimed at increasing the number of available transplantable organs.

Presumed Consent

From the beginning, America has used the "opting in" system of organ donation. In other words, a person who wants to be a donor must say so. The policy (or law) of presumed consent would turn the process upside down and presume that everyone wants to donate his or her organs unless that individual provides written objection prior to death. This system is referred to as "opting out" as opposed to the current "opting in" system. Although current laws already allow the option of deciding what to do with your own organs by signing donor cards and talking with your family, the next of kin can usually override that request by refusing donation at the time of their loved one's death.

Presumed consent would eliminate the family's inclusion in the decision-making process. This opting out procedure has been heralded by such popular magazines as *The Saturday Evening Post* (September–October, 1997) in an editorial promoting the passage of presumed consent laws. Presumed consent is being urged by others who are more forthright about their motives: Presumed consent is effective, they allege, because "consent [for] . . . organ donation is almost always sought from the family" and "the need to obtain family consent presents a formidable barrier to organ procurement" (Spital, 1995, p. 504).

Proponents of presumed consent claim that one aspect of this policy is favorable to the donor family. Rather than emphasizing the fact that medical institutions would not need family consent to begin surgical removal of their loved one's vital organs, they point out that this legal policy would remove the onus of decision from the grieving family (Spital, 1995). There is no statistical evidence that families perceive the decision as onus or that they want it taken out of their hands. On the contrary, there is considerable argument for the value of families being involved in the end-stage decisions related to their loved one (Parks & Weiss, 1983). Making the decision for or against donation is one thing these families can do on behalf of their loved one. It is critically important for the emotional welfare of the donor family that they remain involved in the decision-making process.

Mandated Choice

Mandated choice is another major legal policy being suggested as a means to increase the number of donated organs. Under this proposal, also referred to as "required response," all competent adults would be required to decide and record whether or not they wish to become organ donors (Spital, 1997). In other words, every person would be mandated to make a choice. Some versions of mandated choice allow the potential donor's family the option to override the decision to donate only if that person had made a provision granting his or her family veto power. One may get the distinct impression it would be all the better for the transplant program if there were no family.

A major problem with presumed consent and mandated choice is the lack of access. Regardless of how heroic the effort to reach all people, there still would be some who would remain ignorant of the policy. This group could include the poor, the homeless, the disenfranchised, and those "disenchanted young men (many of them poor and/or black) who are the suicides or victims of traffic accidents and urban violence, and who are eminently suitable *membra disjecta* for transplantation" (Fiedler, 1996, p. 58).

In spite of the more appealing aspects of mandated choice, when compared to the routine salvaging of presumed consent, both policies generate similar problems because each would allow organs to be taken without family permission. The future is now in the sense that on approval from the medical examiner, the Texas House Bill #271 in the Anatomical Gift Act of 1968 allows removal of visceral organs and tissue from cadavers if the next of kin cannot be located after reasonable effort within four hours after pronouncement of brain death (Riether & Mahler, 1995). A pragmatic look at this ruling reveals that visceral organs and tissues could be removed from cadavers without consent from the next of kin, if those next of kin cannot be readily located.

The potential for harm to surviving family members as the result of such a law should be obvious. Sudden death is difficult to grasp. It has no history or context in which a family might gain some perspective and balance. Such a death can be disabling for the survivors. Any protocol that allows donation to proceed without family involvement, creates a potential for even greater harm to that family by exacerbating their inability to grasp the reality of the loved one's death.

In one hypothetical scenario, parents could return from a vacation to learn that not only had their 22-year-old son died, he had also been declared brain dead and four hours later became an organ donor. By the time the parents could be informed of his death, various parts of their child's body could have been scattered across the nation, prolonging or enhancing the lives of others.

When such a hypothetical scenario was described to a focus group, the wife of a recipient responded, "They should have been elated that their son helped so many people." Elation would hardly be an expected response from these traumatized parents. Accepting the sudden death of the perfectly healthy son they had left two weeks earlier would be difficult enough, learning that he had arbitrarily been declared an organ donor would only serve to further traumatize these parents. Cavalier attitudes that discount the donor family's experience issue an open invitation for further complications to their mourning.

☐ Ethical Dilemmas and Slippery Slopes

Although the critique of the ethics of organ donation is not the primary purpose of this work, it is essential that the donor family's caregiver be aware of the entire surround—including the ethical debates—of the transplant process. While those who are scientifically minded defend aggressive measures to obtain organs, arguing that thousands of lives will be prolonged or enhanced by radical methods of procurement, donor families may not be so accepting. Portable ethics and "moveable moments of death" aimed at increasing transplant organs often generate additional public suspicion and distrust of this medical enterprise while undermining the family's confidence in their decision to donate.

Once the trust is compromised, the subjective thought process, which is lived and felt rather than processed abstractly or intellectually (Verble & Worth, 1996), will resist educational efforts to restore it. Attempts at such a restoration, however, will most surely involve the donor family caregiver.

Giant steps further down the slippery slope are already being contemplated and urged in mainstream medical literature. The altruism of the past, which motivates individuals and families to consent to donation, is being aggressively challenged and the repercussions could be serious.

Buying and Selling Life

Some believe that the problem of organ shortage in the United States could be immediately solved by offering monetary consideration for viable organs. This measure would demand a definitive answer about who owns the body of the brain dead patient. Even presumed consent and mandated choice stand or fall on the outcome of the legal and ethical debate about who owns the deceased person's body (thereby owning the body parts). Ownership of the body impacts commodification of human organs.

According to the National Organ Transplant Act (NOTA), it is illegal to "acquire, receive, or transfer any human organs for valuable consideration" (Peters, 1998, pp. 200–201). Proponents of some form of payment or bounty for organs represent a small but an increasingly vocal group. Needless to say, they oppose the current state and federal laws that prohibit buying and selling human organs.

Peters (1998), who supports the gifting of $1,000 to families of donors, asserts that while payment for organ donation may be considered an anathema by some families, "the general public may accept such a concept nearly twice as often as would families who have donated a loved one's organs" (p. 202). Presumably this statistical "twice" was determined from a hypothetical question posed to respondents who have not yet encountered the opportunity to act on their responses. Peters forgets that the weak link between what people say and what they do is well documented (Klassen & Klassen, 1996) and that if the public matched their actions with what they say they support, there would not be a scarcity of transplant organs nor a need for financial incentives.

The selling of organs would have a definitive impact on organ donor families as described below by Murray (1996). Understanding that the "newly dead body possesses a greater moral significance than mere commercial property," Murray claims that monetary incentives for organ recovery could be seen as an attempt to alter the relationship a family has to the body of its newly deceased relative (p. 117). Using a familiar metaphor, Murray continues, "The relationship is transmuted from one of intimate social and moral connectedness to something more like the relationship the owners of old cars have with their vehicles, which are now being stripped of still-useful parts in a salvage yard, impersonal, with the hope that a little utility and a little money can be extracted from the now lifeless hulk" (p. 117). This graphic metaphor exemplifies the general feeling of opponents to commodifying human organs.

People generally donate organs for altruistic reasons and to bring something positive from the loss of their loved one (Vernale & Packard, 1990). However, Peters (1998) challenges the idea of altruism with a cautionary vignette about a donor candidate whose brother "responded to the request [for organ donation] by saying, 'I hated that s.o.b! Go ahead and cut him . . . take his organs! Where do I sign?'" (pp. 198–199). Peters' assumption seems to conclude that since this man was not moved by altruism but by his anger, the procurement organizations should appeal to the mercenary side of human nature. Followed to its inevitable conclusion, the transplant programs would then be able to get more organs from people who hate their relatives.

With what might be termed insight, or at least good common sense, Murray (1996) counters with the suggestion that the family members may love the person who has just died, but they may feel other emotions as well: loss or anger at the person for leaving them or for engaging in risky behaviors that resulted in death; remorse for not having done enough or not having loved the person better; guilt for not protecting the person or at least warning the person to avoid whatever caused his or her death. Anger in response to sudden loss is a "given" to caregivers in the field of bereavement and trauma. It is one of many variegated and intense human responses. Such demonstration of intense anger might have led a trauma specialist to question whether or not it was in the best interest of the first brother to consent to donation for a brother he claims to hate. However, the current organ procurement process does not attempt to evaluate the best interests or motivation of the donor's family members, nor does existing transplant literature appear to consider these issues relevant.

The issue of commodification of organs is very serious and more complicated than it may appear. Ethically, morally, and philosophically I am opposed to the commodification of human organs. However, in practical terms, this issue is far more confounding. During the past 15 years I have found it difficult to intervene on behalf of donor families who are left financially devastated by a loved one's death, without funds even for the funeral, and to realize that everyone connected with organ donation and transplantation—including myself—makes money for the work we do while a donor's family may be left destitute. This is not a simple quandary. There appears no aspect of transplantation or organ donation that is absolute or even uncomplicated.

At this time there is strong opposition to the market system. Caplin and Coelho (1998) find "issues of incentive, compensation, and markets for cadaveric donation" (p. 194) particularly distasteful, citing "significant risks to autonomy and fairness posed by calls for commodification that likewise threaten fundamental values for human life, respect, and self-esteem" (p. 194). Perhaps. But respect and self-esteem seem meaningless when children of donors are sick, unfed, and unclothed. It strikes me that reimbursement is not even the real issue but the inevitable misuse and abuse that such a system would invite.

It is worth noting that in 15 years only one donor family member has suggested to me that they would approve of payment for their loved one's organs. This one individual was 65 years old, blind, destitute, and being evicted from her home.

Amidst the current controversy surrounding the ethical dilemma of commodification of human organs, seasoned professionals are leaving the field. Noted medical sociologist and prolific writer on the subject of organ donation, Renee Fox, is leaving after 40 years of teaching and researching transplant issues. One reason she cites for leaving is "the movement toward the commodification of organs that is taking place, and the reduction of the body to only a 'thing-in-the-world' that . . . commodification implies" (Fox, 1992, p. 262). The intense response to this ethical issue is particularly daunting but it is only one of many that the transplant community must contend with.

Brain Death Debates

While the ethical debate about buying and selling organs continues, the debate surrounding the concept of brain death may stir even deeper concerns. Brain death can be singled out as the most unique experience confronting organ donor families. This solitary feature of donation even separates organ donors from tissue donors. (Tissue may be recovered from individuals who die via cardiopulmonary criteria, rather than just from neurological criteria. This reality greatly increases the numbers of tissue donors.) Brain death is central to the success and expansion of the transplantation enterprise.

Yet, 30 years after the Ad Hoc Committee at Harvard outlined the definition of neurological death, the diagnosis is still being debated. Truog (1998) uses Bernat's (1992) descriptive term, "an approximation," when he argues that even supporters of the current status acknowledge that the criterion of "whole brain" (the brain and brain stem) death is not precise and efforts are being made to even circumvent the usual restrictions of brain death altogether (Truog, 1998).

Moveable Moments of Death

One specific way to circumvent the whole brain death rule is to use donors who die via cardiopulmonary criteria. These efforts raise serious ethical dilemmas and may have a deleterious effect on the donor family.

Referring to the University of Pittsburgh's protocol (see the earlier section on "Expanding the Donor Pool") for retrieving organs from non–heart beating donors, Truog (1998) argues that "by manipulating both the process and the definition of death, these protocols give the appearance that the physicians involved are only too willing to draw the boundary between life and death wherever it happens to maximize the chances for organ procurement" (p. 35). This process, he claims, undermines public confidence.

However, rather than urging a return to brain death criteria for organ retrieval, Truog (1998) heads in the other direction and suggests that increasing the number of donated organs could be accomplished by abandoning the requirement for brain death of the donor prior to organ procurement and, instead, focusing upon an alternative for procurement organs, "such as the principles of consent and nonmaleficence" (p. 35)

Truog claims that policies would have to be changed in such a fashion that all organ procurement would come via a donor or an appropriate surrogate and this donation must not cause the donor harm. These individuals, who would be safe from harm, would include those who are "permanently and irreversibly unconscious (patients in a persistent vegetative state or newborns with anencephaly) and those who are imminently and irreversibly dying"(Truog, 1998, p. 35). Those who could not be harmed do not appear to include family members of the donor or society as a whole. It is unclear why Truog believes this policy, as opposed to the University of Pittsburgh policy, would increase confidence and trust in the transplant programs.

As if these suggestions were not enough to ponder, Truog admits that this alternative approach would certainly require substantial changes in the law. "The process of organ procurement would have to be legitimated as a form of justified killing, rather than just as the dissection of a corpse" (Truog, 1998, p. 35). Truog is correct when he contends that this criteria is already the basis for donations in many circumstances. He references Youngner et al.'s (1989) study that indicates that one-third of health care professionals feel comfortable with the process of organ procurement not because they believe the patient is actually dead, but because they believe the patients are permanently unconscious or imminently dying. This, Truog (1998) claims, is an example of basing the decision to donate on nonmaleficence and consent, rather than on the belief in brain death.

Truog (1998) concludes with the observation that the most challenging obstacle for his proposal would be to "gain acceptance of the view that *killing may sometimes be a justifiable necessity for procuring transplantable organs*" (p. 37; emphasis added). This suggestion may seem farfetched. However, it should be noted that the American Medical Association (AMA) also attempted to modify its stand on the use of anencephalic infants as donors in violation of the "dead donor rule." The AMA decided that the use of the anencephalic infant could be a limited exception to the general standard that requires that the donor be legally dead before permitting the harvesting of organs. This decision was based on the fact that the infant has never experienced, and would never experience, consciousness (Caplan & Coelho, 1999). The AMA never suggested that anencephalic infants were dead, but that since they were beyond harm, they could be killed for their organs. Youngner (1996) offered the reassurance that the AMA never used the word *killed*. Apparently, right and wrong may be a matter of public opinion and timing because the decision to exclude anencephalic infants from the dead donor rule proved so controversial that the AMA committee discarded its attempt to rewrite public policy regarding this issue (Caplan & Coelho, 1998).

With the notion of justified killing for organs skulking about in reputable medical literature, it seems that the skids have been waxed and the transplantation enterprise is part way down the slippery slope. For the purpose of this volume, we must contemplate how this slide might harm the families whose loved ones became a donor or will become a donor in the future. There will be an inevitable emotional fallout as families attempt to reconcile the currents debates about neurological death with what they were originally told.

Evolving Definitions

The entire concept of brain death continues to be a subject of international debate. Medical and technological advances, along with neurodiagnostic developments, are continuing to change the dialogue between medical clinicians, anthropologists, philosophers, and ethicists. Brain death is now an evolving definition (Sullivan, Seem, & Chabalewski, 1999). Up to this point in transplant history, every organ donor family has been assured that brain death meant total and irreversible cessation of brain function, including brain stem. Yet, medical literature speaks casually about evolving information about brain death without ever mentioning the impact that this evolution might have on families whose loved one has already become a donor.

The Challenge to Whole Brain Criteria

Proponents of what is called "higher brain concept" as a means of declaring brain death claim that human life is present only when bodily and mental functions are integrated. These advocates believe that the higher-brain oriented definition is more compatible with common medical reality and that this position eliminates the arguments over minor brain responses such as those described below.

Residual Brain Stem Function

Blood pressure in a normal subject is controlled by a regulatory set of nerves referred to as the automomic nervous system. Alterations in blood pressure are normally observed in response to external stimuli to the body (McCullagh, 1993). Several researchers (Hill, Munglani, & Sapsford, 1994; Pennefather, Dark, & Bullock, 1993; Wetzel et al., 1985) reveal that at the time of organ procurement patients who have fulfilled the tests for brain death often respond to surgical incision with a significant rise in both blood pressure and heart rate. In another study of a series of brain dead patients, researchers found that "changes in blood pressure resembling those to be expected in non-brain-dead subjects were evoked by surgical incision in the course of organ removal . . . " (McCullagh, 1993, p. 46).

When seeking an explanation for the occurrence of significant hemodynamic responses to painful stimuli in cadaver organ donors of this report, Wetzel et al. (1985) concluded that "[t]hese responses were probably attributable to some residual brain-stem function" (p. 127). This explanation is not comforting to advocates of the whole brain concept of brain death or to family members who were led to believe in that concept.

These authors, however, emphasized the prognostic aspects of brain death and paid less attention to the implications of these new observations for the original concept, that is, by definition brain death meant there was total and irreversible cessation of brain and brain stem function. Wetzel et al. (1985) even took care to emphasize, "The new observations did not invalidate the criteria for diagnosis of brain death" (p. 128). While no one explained how there can be residual brain function *and* total cessation of brain stem function at the same time, the authors did concede that "[t]hese hemodynamic changes may frequently produce uneasiness in the medical and nursing staff" (Wetzel et al., 1985, p. 128). One might speculate that knowledge of such changes would also create uneasiness for the donor's family or for those who have donated in the past as they wrestle with questions about whether the loved one was actually dead and whether he or she was able to experience pain. Yet, this concern is never considered relevant enough to discuss within the debates occurring within the medical literature.

Whether one is a proponent of whole brain death, which demands irreversible cessation of functioning of brain and brain stem, or among those who support a higher-brain death, which contends that human life is present only when bodily and mental functions are integrated, these sort of arguments have the potential to cause lasting harm to the donor family and create psychological complications that will not yield easily to therapeutic intervention. Without some type of consensus, a common language and valid principles to guide those defining brain death, the debate and the harm it causes the donor family will continue.

The reader may be tempted to believe that these debates will remain closed to the public domain, but that possibility is no longer an option in our culture. On August 14, 1999, the Arts and Entertainment television channel aired an *Investigative Report* program about organ donation. The questions surrounding the commodification of human organs, the distrust of minority groups, and the debates over brain death were all examined to varying degrees. One particularly intriguing segment of the program involved an interview with an organ broker in California who locates organs that may be purchased in other countries for Americans. Given the bizarre "tabloid mentality" of journalism that exists in the United States other investigations are sure to follow.

Debate is generally healthy, and the continued debate about brain death might be challenging and even exciting for scholars. But scholarly speculation seldom comforts, and within the realm of organ donation portable ethics and moveable moments of death may cause great harm to the donor's family. Where do the slippery slopes lead us? Ethicist Gilbert Meilaender (1996) may have the answer as he shares a tale from the Brothers Grimm about a young man who seems incapable of horror. He not only refuses to shrink back from the dead, he even attempts to play with a corpse. In the end he must be sent away to learn how to shudder.

Unless we learn to collectively care about what is in the best interest of the families who consent to donation rather than working feverishly to exclude them, until we stop tinkering with the time of death and other ethical issues that continually allow the medical and legal professions to move life closer and closer to death, and until we recognize that behind the donated organ is a grieving and traumatized family, we may collectively have to be sent away to learn how to shudder.

☐ Closing Thoughts

Accurate criteria for determining death will prove increasingly important as it becomes more difficult for the public to distinguish which patient is alive and which merely looks alive. While it is imperative that family members know that there is a clear line between life and death, the medical community continues to blur that line and to debate the very issue that organ donor families are encouraged to accept.

"Clear, infallible criteria . . . allows us to assure families and society that one living person will not be intentionally or unintentionally killed for the sake of another" (Van Norman, 1991, p. 3). At the present time, the criteria for brain death does not appear to be as clear or infallible as Van Norman demands and families deserve. This issue of brain death may be the most difficult subject that confronts the clinician attempting to work with the traumatized family member. Just as suspicion and distrust of the medical community appear to play a role in the shortage of organs for transplant, this distrust may resurface as brain death debates and the commodification of body parts increase and as cavalier attitudes toward the donor's family continue. Along with suspicion and distrust engendered by these issues may come guilt and self-recrimination on the part of the donor family that can only further complicate the original trauma.

As this chapter is being written, two of my close friends are waiting and praying that their daughters will soon receive transplants. One daughter was diagnosed with diabetes when she was 4 years old; she desperately needs a kidney. The other young woman developed a rare lung disease soon after her last child was born; her life literally depends on receiving a lung transplant. These gravely ill women and those who love them, wait and worry. All the while organs are being buried that might have helped them. I am acutely and painfully aware of this side of transplantation.

And yet Paul Ramsey's 1970 observation that "our culture is already prepared for technocratizing the bodily life into a collection of parts in which consciousness somehow has residence for a time" (p. 193) seems even more relevant today. The view that everyone is a collection of spare parts, eventually available for transplant, offers clear evidence that regular people and the more aggressive members of the transplant world do not enjoy a shared reality.

Richardson (1996) warns, "It is imperative for the health of Western society that the human rights of the sick without a future be balanced against those of the sick with a possible future. Each is equally human, and their lives are equally sacred." She continues with this warning, "We deny or disregard the humanity of the first at the peril of our own" (p. 96).

Considering the rights of the sick without a future is the first step in providing care for the families of these patients. Clinicians as well as the transplant community must examine the unique issues that color donor family grief and determine how complications associated with organ donation might be prevented or ameliorated. We must do this with both eyes open and without getting blurry, double vision. This two-eyed vision of transplantation will allow us to applaud the incomparable "gift of life" while remembering the cost. Transplantation is about reverence for life; to be congruent, that reverence must be extended to the lives of families who make donation possible.

CHAPTER

Organ Procurement and the Donor's Family

The entire transplant enterprise, with its ability to prolong and enhance the lives of gravely ill individuals, is dependent on the process of organ procurement and the "kindness of strangers" who choose to donate. In turn, the grief of these strangers is influenced by the process of procuring organs. An overview of the procurement surround will reveal numerous opportunities for donor families to encounter either hurtful or healing experiences.

☐ Becoming a Donor

Under the system in the United States, one must consent explicitly to become an organ donor. This opting-in system is based on legal framework provided by the UAGA (see chapter 1), which allows the potential donor to determine whether or not to donate, overriding any family objections (Rodgers, 1989). The UAGA provided for the intent of the deceased to be documented, as well as stipulating that if the decedent's wishes were not known at the time of death, the next of kin would have the right to decide about donating. The UAGA further lists the next of kin in a priority order: spouse, adult son or daughter, either parent, adult sibling, or any other person legally responsible for disposition of the body (Rodgers, 1989).

Technically and legally, the UAGA actually makes the decedent's wishes paramount. The decision of the potential donor is legally binding (Rodgers, 1989). Legal protection was also provided for medical personnel who acted in good faith while they assisted with the donation process (Willis & Skelley, 1992). In spite of the existing legal permission to take organs based solely on the known wishes of the donor, U.S. physicians and others generally refuse to do so without the explicit consent from the donor's family (Fox & Swazey, 1992; Youngner, 1996). To avoid potential medical conflict of interest, UAGA prohibited physicians who were attending the patient before death, from participating in the organ recovery process (Willis & Skelley, 1992). Should this safeguard be compromised, families may question whether everything possible was done to save the life of their loved one who became a donor.

While UAGA provided the legal framework for giving and receiving anatomical gifts, it did little to motivate hospitals to promote organ donation. Congress attempted to provide that motivation by amending the Social Security Act through the Omnibus Budget Reconciliation Act of 1986 (OBRA) to press for greater participation by hospitals receiving Medicare. According to Willis and Skelley (1992, p. 65) this legal maneuver required these hospitals to develop and implement the following: (a) procedures for identifying potential donors, (b) mechanisms to assure that each potential donor's family is made aware of the option to donate, and (c) provisions to document that the local organ procurement organization (OPO) is notified of potential donors.

☐ The Process of Organ Procurement

Other than a few romanticized television versions of transplant professionals dashing off into the night to deliver life-saving organs, the process of obtaining organs, the recovery staff, and their organizations have received scant attention. Yet, all are essential to the success of transplantation.

Organ Procurement Organizations (OPOs)

Donation and transplantation each have different, yet vital, roles to play within this medical process. However, from the beginning, the issues surrounding the recipients of organs were acknowledged to be different from the issues surrounding the donor and their families (Elick, 1997). After the expansion of organ transplantation that followed the Anatomical Gift Act in 1971, it became apparent that based on political and ethical realities donor issues should be separated from those of the recipient. To maintain this separation, central procurement agencies were formed to specialize in organ and tissue recovery (Elick, 1997). In addition to their primary task of expediting donor referrals, these organizations developed community education programs to increase donation, develop working relationships with hospitals, and educate health care professionals. Providing organs for transplant hospitals eventually became the responsibility of the nation's system of organ procurement organizations (Willis & Skelley, 1992). This responsibility made these organizations an integral part of the United States transplant community.

Procurement Coordinators

Pivotal to the efforts of this network of organ procurement organizations are health care professionals known as transplant coordinators. These coordinators actually come in two varieties: the procurement coordinator who identifies and facilitates procurement of organs, and the clinical coordinator who is involved in implantation and recipient care. Both are equally important. However, the procurement coordinator's role and interaction with the donor's family has critical and far-reaching consequences for these families as they grieve the loss of the loved one.

> The night Martin died at the hospital, I was desolate, confused, and angry. In the pain and disbelief that followed the pronouncement that Martin was brain dead, the coordinator from the organ donor program was a solitary comforting presence. It's easy to say he was just doing his job but my family and I agree, he was offering far more than the option to donate. He helped us in so many ways. We will never forget him.
>
> —A Donor Wife

Transplantation requires the close collaboration of a multitude of care providers; it is the procurement coordinator who facilitates the cooperation so necessary in making donation happen. As the transplant programs grew, so did the professionalism of the procurement coordinator. In 1975 the North American Transplant Coordinators Organization (NATCO) was established. In 1981 this organization began offering education and practical training for procurement coordinators. By 1985, NATCO had set up a credentialing task force and prepared for a national certification program, which was formally established to oversee professional standards and academic credentials. By 1997, there were over 700 certified procurement coordinators who were drawn from nursing, emergency and medical technology, social work, and other health-related backgrounds.

The Procurement Coordinator's Role

When an OPO is notified by a hospital that a potential donor has been identified, a procurement coordinator is sent to the referring hospital for further assessment of the patient. The organ donor must be below the age of 70 with no unresolved sepsis, no metastatic cancer, and no communicable diseases. Finally, of course, the donor must be declared brain dead.

The shortage of organs has prompted an expansion of the criteria for organ donors to include older donors and more marginal organs. This expansion may result in added stress for the donor's family if it is discovered during surgery that the loved one's organs are unsuitable or if, after transplantation, the organs fail to function.

> Although he was 65 years old, Prudy was told that her husband, Martin, could be an organ donor. Only after surgery to recover the organs was it learned that due to age-related medical problems Martin's organs could not be used. Prudy was disappointed that there would be no tangible good to come from Martin's death. Her children regretted that their father had been put through the extra trauma of surgery and that they had missed being with him when the ventilator had been removed.

Once it is determined that the patient is a potential donor, the family is approached by the procurement coordinator. When the family consents to donation, the coordinator conducts a family interview to determine any preexisting illnesses such as hypertension or diabetes. Serologic studies are performed to assess for the presence of transmissible diseases such AIDS, hepatitis, and syphilis (Willis & Skelley, 1992).

From the standpoint of increasing the likelihood of donation, the approach used by the coordinator is critical. Bartucci (1987) found that the experience of organ donation in the hospital may help sustain positive feelings about the donation process as a whole. The more positive the family feels about the process the less likely they will experience grief-related complications stemming from the donation. Allowing the procurement coordinator, rather than the physician, to broach the issue of donation has proven more effective because it separates the notification of death from the option for donation (von Pohle, 1996).

In addition to the coordinator's many and varied tasks, he or she must assess the family or next of kin to obtain vital information, such as (Elick, 1997):

1. the identity of the legal next of kin and the role of other family members,
2. the family or next of kin's perception of the patient's status,
3. the degree of understanding that the family or next of kin has of the donation process, and
4. the capacity of the legal next of kin of making an informed decision about donation.

The procurement coordinator must address any barriers to understanding the donation process and the family's willingness to donate. All the while the coordinator is available to answer questions posed by the staff, as well as to provide support and information for the family. Explaining and reviewing the consent form for the family is yet another aspect of the procurement coordinator's duties. When the donor's family consents to donation, but chooses not to remain at the hospital for the extended period of time needed to remove the organs, it is usually the procurement coordinator who notifies them that the surgery has been completed.

Within two weeks of the donation, most procurement coordinators will have written a letter to the donor's family, describing the disposition of the organs that were donated by their loved one. Included in the letter are vague descriptions of the recipient of each organ and their current status (e.g., "Heart was placed with 52-year-old from Ohio, a farmer; the father of twin boys who are seniors in high school. This father has been unable to work for a year; because of his improved medical condition he now looks forward to attending his sons' graduation from high school."). Additional updates on the recipient's status are usually supplied only when explicitly requested by the donor's family. If, for any reason, the donated organs could not be transplanted, this information must be revealed in the most sensitive terms possible. When the recipient does not respond well and the organ is rejected or the recipient dies, writing this letter becomes an even more daunting task. Under such circumstances the loss of the meaning from donation or the loss of the recipient may constitute secondary losses for the donor family that must be processed.

Families have consistently indicated the importance of these letters (Holtkamp & Nuckolls, 1993), for they offer tangible affirmation of the worth of the donor's gift. Some individuals copy the letter for other family members or distribute copies at the donor's memorial service. When small children are involved, family members may place the letter in a scrapbook to be read when the children are older. One mother stated that she wanted to remind her children of what kind of man their father was, kind and generous. It would be difficult to overestimate the value of these letters to the donor's family.

☐ Organ Donation, Grief, and the Donor's Family

According to numerous researchers, organ donation is perceived by donor families as offering some solace or comfort in their grief (Bartucci, 1987; Batten & Prottas, 1987; Holtkamp, 1997; Pelletier, 1993; Savaria et al., 1990). Yet Coupe (1990) contends that while "donation may have a part to play in the family's grieving [for others] donation could be purely a peripheral event. The family has been bereaved and it is for this loss that it needs support" (p. 35). Going home from the hospital without a loved one is the family's focus. Appropriately, it is their loss, not donation, that consumes the energy and absorbs the mind.

Quite understandably, it is in the best interest of the donor program and the entire transplant community for the donor's family to be vocal about the benefits of drawing something of value from something hateful and absurd. However, it might be argued that one cannot testify to an outcome while in the midst of a process. It takes time to know how donation impacts the experience of loss. Nonetheless, organ donation does appear to offer significant comfort for some people. Time and again individuals confide that organ donation was the only thing about a loved one's death that made sense or offered comfort.

☐ Families Who Decline Donation

There are two types of families who do not donate: those who were asked and declined, and those who were never asked. According to Pelletier (1993), family members have identified the need to be approached about organ donation and to have their loved one identified as a potential donor. Cerney (1993) found similar sentiments among family members. When such overtures for donation are not offered, the family may subsequently feel that they have been cheated of the opportunity to bring something positive from their loved one's death.

Other family members may decline donation only to reconsider and experience regrets at a later time. However, the far more prevalent problem occurs when there are conflicting views within the family system regarding whether or not to donate. When the extended family pressures the next of kin either to consent or not to consent to donation, the groundwork for disappointment, conflict, and regret is laid and may later complicate the mourning process.

When the family declines consent to donation, this decision is usually accepted graciously by the organ procurement organization and hospital staff. However, Gyulay (1989) claims that families have reported overhearing the following hurtful statements made by hospital staff: "'Their kid's dead, what difference does it make?' 'You'd think they would want to give another child a chance.' 'So the kid blew his brains out, why don't they want to help a kid that's not crazy?' 'Boy, are they selfish. They're only thinking about themselves.'" (p. 99).

This kind of verbiage may deepen and contaminate the pain of those families who choose not to donate. These and other guilt-producing remarks linger in the minds of family members who may have little understanding of their impact. Subsequently, family members may chafe at any reference to organ donation or anything peripheral to transplantation. Other family members may blanch at seemingly unrelated but coerced responsibilities. One mother who declined donation remarked:

> Every time I hear a program or see one of those announcements about the desperate need for organs or when I see the little faces of desperately ill children who are waiting for organs, I feel as though I'm being indicted for the deaths of people I don't even know. I want to stand up and shout, "My choice not to donate my child's organs did not kill another person. Some disease killed them. I made a decision that was best for my family."

Her point is well taken. The current trend to promote organ donation via inculpation of those who choose not to donate rather than presenting it as a viable medical treatment that may be needed by anyone, becomes detrimental to everyone.

Health care providers must realize that nonconsenting families may not have the emotional strength or energy to be concerned about other families. George Engel (1961) contends that the loss of a loved one is as psychologically traumatic as a severe wound or burn is physiologically traumatic. This thesis should be posted within every critical care unit of the hospital and every organ procurement organization.

The problem of nonconsent actually rests with the process, not with the family system. When a family is enraged to learn that their child or other loved one has died, immediately before, during, or after death is not the optimal time to ask them to consider organ donation. In view of how shrink-wrapped individuals become when they suffer extreme physical or psychological trauma, it is remarkable that any family can think beyond themselves.

It is, in my opinion, an important part of the procurement coordinator's responsibility to discourage mean-spirited comments such as the ones described above and to graciously accept the decisions of families who do not consent.

☐ Religious and Cultural Issues Related to Organ Donation

Knowledge increases understanding that is the deepest form of human connection. Without some knowledge of the religious and cultural backgrounds of the families with whom they work, procurement coordinators and post-donation caregivers are at a disadvantage.

Religious Beliefs

It appears that religious beliefs may either help or hinder organ donation. While dissent is vocalized within the fundamental Christian and Orthodox Jewish communities, there is ample verbal support for donation among other major religions as a form of charity (Fox & Swazey, 1992; Youngner, 1996). However, religion has been implicated as a barrier to organ donation (Basu, Hazariwala, & Chipman, 1989; Gallup Organzation [Gallup], 1993; Moores, Clark, Lewis, & Mallick, 1976; Radecki & Jaccard, 1997).

Some obstacles to organ removal that are attributed to religious fears include the belief that the absence of particular organs when a person dies will have negative effects on the afterlife (Radecki & Jaccard, 1997). As Reitz and Callender (1993) observed, "there is great concern among African Americans that in that great getting up morning, if they leave their organs behind, they won't have them for themselves"(p. 355). It would, however, be a mistake to think of these sentiments as limited to the Black community. One Caucasian mother commented: "He's going to be buried with everything he was born with."

Religious faith and superstition are often coupled but are not necessarily related except, perhaps, in the scientific mind. The frequent juxtaposition of these two belief systems is unfortunate. As noted in chapter 1, even highly-educated, rational minds can meander into mystical and illogical thought processes. Long-forgotten superstitions from childhood may filter forward when a person is in extreme stress. On rare occasions superstitions must be challenged to protect the welfare of the individual. Tampering with faith, however, even when it appears primitive or unreasonable, and even in the name of increasing the number of organ donations, would be to tamper with the emotional health and well being of those in question.

Cultural Issues

Organ procurement professionals as well as bereavement caregivers share the responsibility to understand the cultural backgrounds of the donor families who are in their care. Effective care will be preceded by respect for the cultural diversity found among these families.

African Americans

Although it has been thought that African Americans have been consistently resistant to organ donation, the United Network for Organ Sharing (UNOS) Update (June, 1999) reports that 11.3% of cadaveric donors were Black. Considering a population of 12% African Americans, this ratio does not appear unreasonable. Reitz and Callender (1993) concur, stating that part of the problem is the disproportionate number of African Americans waiting for organ transplantation and that the paucity of potential African American organs available for transplantation is relative to the need rather than the representative percentages of donors. For example, while Blacks make up 12% of the total population, they represent 33% of Americans on dialysis; only 26% of whom will receive cadaver kidney transplants (Callender, 1993). Callender argues from a transplant surgeon's point of view that there is strong indication that the current manner of allocation of organs is not race conscious, therefore contributing to the large number of Blacks on transplant waiting lists.

Reitz and Callender (1993) refer to a pilot project that was developed specifically to review the reasons for low organ donation among African Americans (p. 354). This study revealed several factors that influence the African American reluctance to donate organs.

- Lack of awareness about transplantation
- Religious beliefs and misperceptions (superstitions)
- Distrust of the medical community
- Racism
- Poor access to medical care
- Lack of appropriate organ procurement specialists

These causes for resistance are also outlined by Radecki and Jaccard (1997) and supported by other sources (Callender, 1987; Callender, Bayton, Yeager, & Clark, 1982; Callender, Hall, Yeager, Barber, Dunston, & Pinn-Wiggins, 1991; Davidson & Devney, 1991; Lange, 1992). The question of racism is particularly unsettling for families and caregivers. In *Marketing of*

Organ Donation, Prottas (1983) reported that some Black families felt that organ donation only benefited the Whites. He adds:

> How widespread this attitude is impossible to say, but we can't be too sur-
> prised, that in a racially polarized society, altruism is bounded by the limits
> of racially defined communities even in the absence of specific racial hostil-
> ity, black donor families may easily have a greater sense of alienation from
> and fear of the institutions asking them to donate their relatives organs.
> (p. 355)

There is evidence, however, that this population responds more favor-
ably when there is awareness of African American recipients (Creecy &
Wright, 1990) and when the subject is broached by another African American (Reitz & Callender, 1993). There is also some indication that African
Amercians can best offer other Blacks information, education, and assurance about organ donation in an appropriate and sensitive manner. Yet, at
the present time, only 5% of all procurement coordinators are Black (Reitz
& Callender, 1993).

Correcting this inequity among procurement coordinators is easily accomplished and is actually in the best interest of the OPO as well as the
donor's family because the increased number of African American professionals could help reduce their communities' mistrust of the medical system. Understanding is more readily achieved between individuals who
enjoy a shared reality and background. When distrust usurps understanding, there is a greater risk for family members to experience peripheral
anger or regrets following donation.

Asians

Organ donation is rare among Asians because of superstitions in everyday
life, fear of death, the mystery behind leaving the current world, concern
for preserving the sanctity of the deceased and beliefs that organ donation
is inconsistent with the tenets of the Asian faiths (Radecki & Jaccard, 1997,
p.184).

Latino/Hispanics

Hispanics tend to be unfavorably disposed toward organ donation. Studies
appear unable to determine specific reasons for this. However, some general explanations such as language barriers, religious backgrounds, concerns about mutilation, myth, and superstitions serve as obstacles to dona-

tion (Perez et al., 1988; Rene, Yiera, Daniels, & Santos, 1994; Toldeo-Pereyra, 1992). Curiously, Mexican-Americans seem quite willing to donate and have a greater awareness of the donation process (Radecki & Jaccard, 1997).

Accurate information is essential to the well being of the donor's family. Yet, correct and timely information is only one component of effective communication with people of diverse religions, ethnic beliefs, and cultural differences. The question of trust is as vital as spoken words among minority groups. As one minority mother stated when interviewed for a television documentary, "When my son was injured, I told them [the medical staff] up front that he was not a donor. I didn't want them to take less care of him just so he could be a donor" (Arts & Entertainment TV, 1999). These fears are the greatest among minority groups, many of whom have valid historical reasons for mistrusting organized medicine or for doubting that they will be protected by the legal system (Youngner, 1996).

☐ The Language of Organ Procurement

Regardless of race, religion, or culture, words have tremendous power to heal or to harm. With a subject that generates heightened emotions, it should come as no surprise that the language of organ donation can pose a problem for everyone involved.

Willis & Skelley (1992) claim that for the procurement coordinator "meeting the psychological and emotional needs of the donor family is of paramount importance" (p. 67). While attending those needs, the procurement coordinator's job is complicated by several factors, but few as troublesome and unruly as the language of procurement and donation. Language is important because even small changes in wording communicate a very different message that has a significant impact.

Troublesome Terms

Any words that might imply a cavalier attitude toward the donor's death or donation jeopardizes the consent to donation as well as the psychological well being of members of the donor's family. Several troublesome terms appear frequently in the language of organ donation and seem to confuse even the most experienced transplant professionals.

Informed Consent

There are numerous opportunities for miscommunication while conversing with a traumatized family. One of the most troublesome involves informed consent. What is meant by this term, and is informed consent possible within the process of organ donation?

While informed consent is a legal issue, it assumes moral and ethical dimensions when related to the consent of families to donate their loved one's organs. De Chesser (1986) points out that consent for organ donation is usually given when families are undergoing severe stress. As the result of the donor's sudden death, their relatives are in a state of shock, disbelief, and confusion, which is further complicated by observing the victim being maintained on a respirator. De Chesser argues that it is hard to imagine how families could make an informed consent under these circumstances.

Davis (1989) presents the underlying question: Can a grieving family who has just lost a loved one really be informed regarding donation or the donation procedure? Davis answers her own question by stating, "More likely, the person or persons being informed accepts much of the information on trust—trust that the right thing will be done for the benefit of the patient" (p. 833).

One stated duty of the procurement coordinator is to assess the family's or legal next of kin's ability to comprehend pertinent information and provide informed consent (Elick, 1997; Willis & Skelley, 1992). In *The Fiction of Informed Consent*, La Foret (1976) states that the best and probably only guarantee of a patient's or subject's rights is the integrity of the physician (p. 1585). The donor family's best guarantee of being informed is the integrity of the physician and the procurement coordinator.

Brain Death

A number of linguistic problems begin with the term brain death, which is so basic a requirement of donation. To put it bluntly, this term is confusing, baffling, and unpleasant. Laypersons and the media confuse the term with coma and use it interchangeably. For the lay population this confusion is understandable, but it extends to health care professionals who, as Youngner (1996) observes, "persist in describing patients who have lost all brain function as brain dead rather than simply dead" (p. 45). It actually gets more complicated than that. Youngner and researchers might be further chagrined by confusing uses of the term "brain death" found within professional journals. Examples read:

"To the family, the completion of [the organ removal] surgery may signify that the death has occurred and may therefore allow the grieving process to start" (Hart, 1986, p. 211). It would not be helpful for the donor's family to think of the death coming after the completion of the surgery.

Another suggests that operating room nurses "face the outcome of procurement surgery, the death of the already brain-dead donor" and "[i]n a sense, procurement surgery causes the patient's final death." (Wolf, 1991, pp. 80–81).

Or, "Once a decision for or against organ donation is made, the nurse-family interaction process ends when the patient either is transferred to the operating room or *dies* in the unit" (Vernale, 1991). Hopefully, the potential donor was already dead, but that nuance appears difficult to remember.

In another quote, Soukup (1991, p. 8) refers to the *totally brain-dead patient*, which is accurate in that in the United States the "whole brain criteria" is used to declare a patient brain dead. However, the implication is that a patient can be partially dead.

Youngner (1996) understands all this confusion and is merely voicing the concerns of a number of other researchers (Annas, 1988; Jasper, Harris, Jackson, Lee, & Miller, 1991) who lament the fact that, although all 50 states consider all persons with irreversible cessation of whole brain function as dead, they are called brain dead rather than dead.

The problem with this lament is that these dead patients are different from other dead people, and they have to be called something that indicates that difference. True enough, these patients are legally dead; but no one would consider burying them in their present state. They are dead, yet they are filled with life.

Ordinarily, dead people do not remain on a ventilator, but brain dead people do; dead patients do not breathe, but brain dead patients appear to. People who are dead as determined by cardiopulmonary criterion are not aggressively cared for in a critical care unit for hours. The brain dead patient often is. Dead patients are sent to the morgue not the operating room. These patients are not dead in the *same* way that patients are when they die the old-fashioned way.

Youngner (1996) confronts the general confusion about brain death with a poignant and provocative story that graphically highlights this dilemma.

An 18-year-old woman, whom Youngner calls Janet, was 22 weeks pregnant when she suffered a spontaneous ruptured cerebral aneurysm and was admitted to a critical care unit. Within 24 hours Janet was diagnosed brain dead.

The decision was made to maintain this patient in an attempt to save the life of her baby. After the baby was delivered by Cesarean section eight weeks later, the mother became a multiple organ donor. Because the care of this young woman was going to be difficult, volunteers were asked to provide her clinical care. These individuals became very attached to both the mother and her unborn child. Youngner states that "for many of the staff, taking care of the patient was a religious experience. Its mystical nature was enhanced by the fact that Janet had anticipated her death a week before it occurred, when she told her family that 'if anything happens to me, I want them to do everything to save my baby'" (p. 47).

For eight weeks the nurses cared for Janet, keeping her clean, dressing her in lovely robes, washing her hair every week. Her long, beautiful red hair continued to grow.

One nurse stated, "I could sense the presence of her soul in her body." Another sensed a soul hovering over the body "watching us." Even one obstetrician "was clearly convinced that the whole thing [had] a preordained purpose" (p. 47).

According to Youngner, the medical staff used "alive" speech. They referred to "keeping the mother alive until the baby was born." Janet's mother would think her daughter would die each time she left the room, "yet when I return," the mother says, "she is still with us" (p. 47). Youngner asks, but does not answer, "What is the reality for family members who watched the living body of a dead girl nurture, grow, and issue forth a healthy baby? While Janet's hair grew longer and the nurses washed and combed it, was she *really* alive or dead to them?" Rationally, she was dead; "the signs of life told another story" (p. 47).

When the body is alive and the brain is dead, what else could these unfortunate patients be called, other than brain dead? Youngner, Landerfeld, Coulton, Juknialis, and Leary (1989) charge that even experienced transplant surgeons and nurses often refer to patients as brain dead, then later describe them as dying when the ventilator is turned off. He further contends that this problem will not yield to mere education. Perhaps the problem is not with the term itself, but simply with the inconsistency with which the words are used—and maybe that inconsistency reflects some doubt, however small, that brain dead isn't really "dead dead."

More attention, pre- and post-donation, must be paid to settling the question of brain death. A significant number of organ donor families report that they did not understand the diagnosis of brain death at the time of donation (De Jong et al., 1998). These families may encounter greater risk for additional and unnecessary bereavement complications if doubts arise after donation. The following commentary from Helen Barrett, a donor's mother, suggests the persisting ambivalence concerning this term:

> For us, a clear explanation of brain death when we were talking with the medical personnel was helpful. I have to say that I have wondered since whether or not keeping her on the machines and hoping that something amazing might have taken place, and that we might have made the wrong choice. People are fallible. I don't spend a lot of time wondering about it, and I don't have nightmares about it, and I think that by and large I am able to process the probable fact that nothing could ever have been done. However, those darkest days bubbles it up. (H. Barrett, personal communication, April 12, 1994)

This mother, highly intelligent and well educated, yet with gentle doubts and darkest days, must struggle with understanding brain death on cognitive as well as visceral levels. Even so, it is reasonable to surmise that her experience was less traumatic than it might have been because of the clear explanation of brain death given to her by medical personnel. Conversely, lack of a clear explanation or inferences by reputable sources that brain death is merely a matter of opinion rather than an absolute reality can produce intense, long-lasting consequences for the donor family.

Family members should be helped to recognize that their loved one is dead even though the chest is rising and falling, the skin has good color, and they often appear to be sleeping. Family members also must have a clear explanation as to how the body can be dead and yet have the organs within the body be very much alive. This paradoxical reality makes brain death different from cardiopulmonary death.

Life Support

Often health providers refer to turning off the life-support machine following declaration of brain death. In an attempt to avoid using the term life-support, some nurses will refer to the machine as advanced life-support equipment prior to the declaration of brain death, but use the term ventilatory-support equipment afterward (Soukup, 1991). The nine-syllable phrase "ventilatory-support equipment" seems cumbersome for the busy people who must use it and for most traumatized family members. In addition, calling the same machine one thing before the patient dies and another term afterward seems disingenuous.

Obviously, an ordinary dead person would have no use for life support. Yet, caregivers and family members are familiar with the term life support that is still accurate, and might be acceptable, if families grasp the concept that this machine first supports life for the patient, then for the organs. This term, much like the term brain death, requires considerable communication between the coordinator and the family of the donor. No form of communication or explicit explanations will work all the time; the nature of the family's heightened emotional state precludes that kind of absolute predictability. Repeated explanations over a period of time may be necessary.

Retrieval

When speaking of the surgical removal of human organs, some individuals prefer the term "retrieval." But Youngner (1996) argues that this word "implies that the organs belong to someone other than the donor patient and we are merely taking them back" (p. 48).

Procurement

Procurement is an unhappy word (Richardson, 1996). Procurement speaks of commerce and commodities and has "overtones of weapons procurement for the destruction of unknown individuals at a distance. Historically, procuring has been associated with prostitution" (p. 87). A provocative point is raised as Richardson draws attention to the fact that all uses of the word procurement tend to focus on the recipients' wants and needs rather than the providers'.

Harvesting

By far, the unhappiest word in the transplant vocabulary is "harvesting." This word speaks of pastorality, a time of plentitude and thanksgiving. Harvesting refers to reaping crops, vegetables, and such. As one donor mother noted in her objection: "I was not raising my child to be farmed" (Anonymous donor mother, personal communication, July 24, 1994).

Harvesting of field crops was traditionally done "by sickle or scythe, the same implements used by the Grim Reaper, Death, to sever the thread of life. Last, something deeply important at harvest time is entirely missing here: there is no *Thanksgiving*" (Richardson, 1996, p. 86). While Richardson finds this term particularly odious and while there is considerable protest against the word harvesting, a surprising number of family members accept the word with equanimity.

In a strongly leveled conclusion about such terms, Richardson (1996) stated:

Those who employ these terms reveal unspoken attitudes. Seeking to romanticize the endeavor and conceal unpalatable truths, each term serves to cast the enterprise in a more positive light. Each usage in its own way serves also to devalue, even deny, the humanity of the donor—denying in the process the humanity we all possess.

In this discourse, the enormous value of the donor's gifts has been denied, lost sight of. The donor has become a thing, a nothing: a means rather than an end. (pp. 87–88)

The words procurement, retrieval, and harvesting are unpleasant and dehumanizing as well as misleading. They are beyond redemption and should be discarded, while others, such as brain dead and life support may be so useful that health care professionals and the public simply need consistent affirmation of their meanings.

The language of organ donation, as well as the concepts about brain death, must be examined to determine how they impact the donor's family as well as potential donors and their families. If the goal is to do no harm, language is an excellent place to start.

☐ Other Procurement Issues

There are numerous variables within the process of procuring organs for transplant that may impact donor family grief. A brief overview of several of the most common is offered.

Donor Unsuitability

As noted earlier, family members may experience disappointment when tests reveal preexisting medical problems that preclude their loved one from becoming a donor. This disappointment may add to their anguish and leave them feeling robbed of the opportunity to bring something of value from their tragic loss.

When the patient tests positive for HIV or studies confirm the presence of AIDS, family members may be totally unprepared for such a revelation. Test results may not be available prior to the family leaving the hospital, and in some cases for kidney-only-donations, recovery surgery may have been begun or completed. This information may serve to further traumatize the donor family, leaving them to struggle through difficult peripheral issues after they have left the hospital. Such a scenario is problematic for the health care professional as well as for the patient's family. The responsibility of the OPO and the procurement coordinator involves legal, ethical, and moral decision making that must be determined by the applicable laws of each state. Often the donor's attending physician is offered the opportunity to inform the family but usually the task falls to the OPO's medical director.

Stress Related to Time and Timing

When the death of a loved one becomes a time-bound reality, there may be opportunities for the family to visit with and to do things for their loved one; there is time to say goodbye. This is time's gift. However, while this abbreviated period that allows the family time to absorb the reality of impending death of the loved one is helpful, the invasive and painful medical procedures made in an attempt to save the patient during this time may add to the family's distress as they review the trauma and fret over real or perceived suffering that the loved one endured.

Both time and timing have an important impact on the donor family's experience. In a classic study by Batten and Prottas (1987), problems with timing were found to be one of the most difficult factors that contribute to the risk of further traumatizing the family members. The risk of additional trauma increases when there is:

- Inadequate time for reconciliation to the gravity of the donor's condition. It takes time to absorb bad news: yet there is often a need to rush the process in order to maintain viability of the donated organs. This latter need sometimes takes priority over the needs of the donor's family.

- Inadequate time between the declaration of death and the option of donation (Bartucci, 1987; Gyulay, 1989). Since the early 1990s, OPOs have recognized, demonstrated, and documented the value of separating the request from the declaration of brain death. Delaying the request for donation increases consent for donation. More importantly, it gives the potential donor family some time to process the reality of their loved one's death and its meaning for the family.

- Extended time span between suspected brain death and actual declaration. Some families complain of the time span between suspected brain death and the actual declaration (Soukup, 1991). Occasionally, a family will suspect that their loved one's life has ended. Medical staff may verify that observation, but for various reasons the official declaration of brain death is delayed, causing the family additional distress.

- Extended period of time between consent to donation and actual surgery (Batten & Prottas, 1987). Problems securing the operating room or medical personnel and other logistics may account for delays between the decision to donate and the actual surgical removal of the organs. Soukup (1991) noted that some participants in her study indicated that, "their families were not prepared for the length of time between organ donation and the actual surgical removal of organs" (p. 15). This comment would indicate that preparation for such delays might have been helpful for these families.

- Time necessary to complete surgical removal of organs (Batten & Prottas, 1987). With advanced surgical skills, improved immunosuppressive drugs, and other factors, more organs from each donor are being transplanted. Consequently, it takes more time to remove and secure placement for multiple organs. However, the argument that certain logistics of the procurement process are intractable may not soothe the disquietude of the donor family who feel they were misled regarding time frames.

Some families report feelings of confusion because they were told one time-of-death verbally but a different time was noted on the death certificate. Occasionally families may receive a death certificate that indicates the time-of-death as the time that the ventilator was disconnected following organ removal. The consequences of this error can be devastating to the donor family because if the death did not occur until the ventilator was removed it would mean that the donor had been alive during the time the organs were being removed. This error may increase anxiety or guilt for the donor family, or may intensify their preoccupation with the loved one's suffering.

Residual questions about time and timing may present subsequent problems for the donor's family members. When the family feels rushed or when the notification of brain death and the request for donation is made within the same conversation, the family may infer that the diagnosis was made with donation in mind. The temptation to think of these peripheral stressors as minor is unwise because it is precisely these kinds of stressors that have enormous power to drain away limited energy of the mourner. In the excessive rumination that often follows traumatic loss, families may become fixated on the memory that they felt rushed or that health care professionals were insensitive or less than candid during some phase of the consent process. Such thoughts often lead families to reappraise their decision to donate.

The most consequential problem related to time within the procurement process is time that was lost forever—the time that could have been spent with the loved one, but for some reason was denied the family. Whenever family members are denied access to the loved one, they lose valuable time that might have been used to be with and do for the patient. Time lost in this way seems to correlate with future complications in mourning (Parkes & Weiss, 1983)

Billing Errors

The question of who pays for organ donation and what portion of the hospital bill remains the responsibility of the donor's family may prove awkward for both the family and the health care staff. Confusion about hospital costs and funeral arrangement often cause additional stress to the donor family (Batten & Prottas, 1987; Soukup, 1991; Willis & Skelley, 1992).

According to Willis and Skelley (1992), the OPO coordinator should be the person who discusses billing for the donation. Basically all costs associated with the evaluation, management, and recovery of donated organs are covered by the OPO. The family should not incur any financial burden as a result of their beneficence. Yet, billing errors are inevitable in today's world of impersonal computer-generated statements. When classified as an administrative faux pas, billing errors are easily corrected and the procurement coordinator generally takes care of such matters swiftly and effectively.

Sometimes, however, questions about billing are not always so easily remedied. While the OPO picks up the hospital costs from the time brain death was declared, the family retains responsibility for costs up to that time. While this sounds straightforward and reasonable, complications can arise.

The father of a gravely injured young man who was being cared for at a local hospital was told by the attending physician that his son's only chance of surviving would be at a nearby level-one trauma hospital. The father was also told that it was likely that his son would die and he could be an organ donor if he were at the other hospital. Based on those two possibilities, the father agreed to the transfer.

Within an hour after being airlifted to the level-one trauma unit, the son was declared brain dead and later became a multiple organ donor. Subsequently, the father was billed for the helicopter expense. With meager insurance, this father was unable to pay and felt confused as to why the OPO would not bear the cost for this expense since it was so obvious on arrival that his son could not survive. However, the OPO refused to pay, leaving the father confused as to why multiple organs donated by his son, offered in gracious concern for others, had resulted in expenses that his insurance would not, and he could not pay.

A variation of troublesome billing errors was presented by a donor mother. She had received erroneous statements from both the hospital and the anesthesiologist. As she read the charges for various services, she felt distressed by the dispassionate tone, as well as the itemized listing of invasive medical procedures. An innocent billing error triggered this mother's vivid and not altogether accurate imagination of the entire surgical process, leaving her to doubt her decision to donate her child's organs. This mistake paved the way for further complications in this mother's mourning by tapping into her primal fears about the mutilation of her child's body; restless days and sleepless nights followed. Perhaps these occasional billing problems are unavoidable hazards, but they are not without consequences.

Follow-Up Letters from the Procurement Coordinator

The follow-up letter from the procurement coordinator regarding the placement of their loved one's organs usually has a decidedly positive impact on the donor's family. For many individuals, this letter further validates the family's decision to donate, while others report that this letter merely confirmed their loss. The word "bittersweet" is often used to describe their feelings. Regardless of how families respond, this letter often serves as a catalyst to accepting the reality of the death while affirming the benefits of donation.

The limited information about the recipients offered in these letters may also pique the donor family's desire for more contact with the recipients. Contact between a donor's family and the recipient is one of the most controversial topics within the transplant community. It is not a new issue.

Contact Between Donor Family and Recipient

In the early days of transplantation, transplant professionals were distressed by the way recipients, their kin, and donor families personified cadaver organs. There was concern about how some families not only arranged to meet, but also tried to become involved with each other's lives as if they were indebted and related to one another. These factors led most transplant units to establish the practice of confidentiality regarding the identity of the donor and the recipient (Fox & Swazey, 1992).

The current debate about donor-family–recipient contact centers on the perceived rights of both donor family and recipient to make their own choices regarding whether or not they meet or contact each other. While the issue of contact between these two parties may appear to some observers as much ado about nothing, it has far-reaching, high-risk consequences. The impact of donor-family–recipient contact (to be more fully explored in a later chapter) is one of the most entangled and difficult complications to be addressed in this work. This issue is mentioned in this chapter only because it should be initially addressed within the consent process, with further information offered in the letter to the donor's family following donation.

The procurement coordinator must be careful that the donor's family clearly understands what can and cannot be promised in the area of contact with the recipient. The impact of this aspect of organ donation carries an enormous capacity to influence the long-term well being of the donor family.

☐ Implications for the Procurement Coordinator

The procurement coordinator occupies a position of power that may be used to influence both tone and content of the family's trauma-driven grief. If these professionals seize their positional power to intervene and effectively meet the needs of the donor's family and to eliminate obstacles that may delay or distort the family's experience, the bereaved may move more easily beyond the trauma to normal bereavement. Horowitz (1997) claims that, "a relationship, no matter how new or temporary, is the way to restore trust and to reduce fears" (p. 138). Curiously, many coordinators are not aware of their unique opportunity to share with traumatized families something so rare that it cannot be replicated in the future.

It is a godsend that families of donors usually receive exquisite care, in part because what is in the best interest of the potential donor's family is also in the best interest of the organ procurement program. Although most coordinators are moved by the family's situation and usually respond with genuine compassion, this care is sometimes viewed as self-serving.

In her defense of presumed consent, De Chesser (1986) claims that those involved in organ procurement know effective strategies for producing a donation, such as painting an overly optimistic picture of how the organs will benefit others, while down-playing possible negative outcomes. It should be noted that De Chesser is presenting an argument for a method of procurement that would sidestep the family altogether. She does not explain how ignoring the family (as in presumed consent) would be superior to the current method of procuring organs, which is at least mindful of the need for family involvement.

De Chesser's (1986) claim that procurement coordinators are under enormous pressure from their own OPOs as well as transplant hospitals to produce increasing numbers of transplant organs for gravely ill people cannot be denied. Procuring suitable organs is paramount for procurement organizations; that is their purpose. It does not necessarily follow that procurement coordinators are forceful or inappropriate in their attempts to gain consent from family members.

A professional observation based on my 15-year association with organ procurement organizations is appropriate: organ procurement coordinators, those who work directly with potential donor families, are as trustworthy, hard-working, diligent, committed, compassionate, and caring as any professionals in the health care system. Most procurement coordinators stand in awe of the families of donors and regard them with great respect. "This commitment to help donor families gain some positive consolation from their tragedy is often a greater incentive for the coordinator continually to work long, stressful hours than the waiting recipients' need" (Willis & Skelley, 1992, p. 67). For many of these health care professionals, theirs is not just a job. It is a commitment that goes well beyond the call of duty.

It would be difficult to overemphasize the importance of the procurement coordinator's influence on the donor's family. In spite of the intense shock and disbelief normally experienced during this time of crisis, families usually remember the coordinator by name and express appreciation for him or her.

Procurement coordinators may have only a brief period of time in which to develop a relationship with the donor candidate's family. Even so, a curious bond may develop between them. Rando (1993) speaks of the trauma survivor developing "a sensitivity to individuals unfamiliar with the particular meaning of the trauma who might serve to stimulate unwanted traumatic memories without a constructive context for healing" (p. 591). This sensitivity leads to the development of what Lindy (1985) calls a "trauma membrane" that guards the inner healing process of the individual by forming a protective outer surface. Procurement coordinators are often accepted within the trauma membrane. While others may stir up memories without sharing the family's experience, the procurement coordinator has a shared reality with the donor's family. That shared experience with the family members allows the coordinator to relate as one who "knows." Indeed, to varying degrees these professionals, who "truly know the absurd reality of the traumatic event or have shared its experience—have a special place of closeness" (Rando, 1993, p. 591).

☐ Closing Thoughts

A provocative novel by Paul De Vries (1961) describes the journey of one man, Dan Wanderhope, whose 10-year-old daughter dies some years after her mother. One line from the novel reads, "There may be griefs beyond the reach of solace" (p. 246). This observation augments Coupe's (1990) contention that while organ donation brings life and hope to recipients and may be seen as comforting to many donor families, for others, it remains peripheral. The donor family's loss, like many other losses, may carry a grief that seems beyond solace. As one donor mother noted: "My only child is dead; this is not about organ donation."

Every person involved in organ procurement—from physicians to policymakers to administrators to procurement coordinators to trauma and grief specialists—must remember those two observations.

The Chinese characters that express the word "crisis" mean both danger and opportunity (Aguilera, 1990). The crisis experienced by the donor family certainly offers both. The danger is obvious. It threatens to overwhelm the family and often the caregiver.

The opportunity of this crisis for the family is the option to donate a loved one's organs and bring something of value from the absurdity of the loss. For the procurement coordinator, there is the opportunity to intervene on behalf of the family in ways that no others can claim. When life is no longer an option for a brain-injured loved one, the procurement coordinator, along with well-trained hospital staff, initiates care for the organ donor family that will help set the tone and content of that family's journey through trauma-driven grief.

The Hospital Experience and the Organ Donor Family

Organ donation is a remarkable act of altruism that prolongs or enhances the life of another human being. Only individuals who have been declared dead via neurologically defined, legally and medically sanctioned criteria can become organ donors. Most of these deaths are sudden, unexpected, and sometimes violent. However, organ donor deaths are never instantaneous and usually require some level of emergency care. When life is no longer an option for these patients and when there is no longer brain and brain stem function, the body remains on the ventilator to keep the organs viable for transplant.

The entire transplant enterprise depends on this time frame between the original trauma and the declaration of brain death, for it is this period of forewarning that allows for the option of organ donation (Youngner et al., 1989). This period of forewarning also offers both challenges and opportunities to intervene on behalf of the donor family.

The traumatic drama of donation unfolds within hospital settings—more specifically, in emergency rooms, intensive care rooms, and operating rooms—but the drama really begins in the waiting room, with the donor's family. These family members or significant others of the uniquely deceased, brain dead patient experience more than the usual dimensions of sudden traumatic loss.

There are many types of losses represented among donor families, such as the loss of a life-partner, a sibling, a parent, or other relative. Everyone's experience is important. Since approximately 70% of donors involve the parental loss of a child and because the nature and course of their grief will be complicated not only by the suddenness or the violence associated with their loss, but by the object of that loss, the family of a young person serves as an example throughout this chapter.

> Her name was Eva Leah, and at 19 years of age, she was the "belle of the ball." Everywhere she went she was surrounded by people—peers, teachers, parents—who loved and respected her. Her brother, Jeff, two years younger, quite simply adored her. Her mother, Emma, cherished the fact that they were soulmates. And John, her father—well, there aren't words to describe how he felt about his only daughter.

> Six hours after she waved goodbye to her family as she left for college, Eva Leah died. Within 12 hours her heart, lungs, liver, and kidneys were sustaining life for compatible strangers across the country. Carelessness on the part of another stranger destroyed her car and took her life. The world, as Eva Leah's family knew it, was over. Nothing, absolutely nothing, would ever be the same. They even had a new identity: They were now a donor family.

Transplantation is filled with paradox. While one lives, another dies. While one rejoices, another grieves. The trajectory of the donor's death itself is paradoxical. For while it is sudden, it is also anticipated—for at least hours or days; there is a period of forewarning. During that time of waiting, the donor's family attempts to grasp what has happened to their world.

☐ The Donor's Family

Before discussing the donor family's needs during this time of forewarning, the term "donor family" must be clarified. Referring to the donor's family as one cohesive unit may be misleading; there may be several sets of family members, there may be one single person, or a huge extended family. And they may or may not be cohesive. However, the dynamics of the family as a whole will influence how the individuals will cope with the loss of one of its members, and the response of each individual will color the response of the family as a whole (Rando, 1993).

A family has an unparalleled capacity to provide comfort or to cause havoc. They may offer support for one another or create further aggravation of the primary trauma. When facing the loss of one of its members, the dysfunctional family's usual high anxiety may escalate to the extent that it produces conflict and tension. Triangulation among family members, divorced parents, warring factions, and blended families might create complications that require additional support, understanding, and patience on behalf of caregivers.

There is great diversity among the families of organ donors. These families may be rich or poor, educated or illiterate, religious or irreverent, young or not so young, highly prejudiced or amazingly accepting. Yet, their needs are remarkably similar.

Tasks for the Donor Family

The impact of sudden loss may not be more devastating than other forms of loss; however, it is often perceived as more disabling (Parkes & Weiss, 1983). When sudden death is the result of violent accidents, negligent or purposeful homicide, or suicide, the potential for traumatic stress response escalates. Rando (1993) warns that family members may be overwhelmed when faced with the shock of sudden death and may be consumed with trying to master strong feelings of helplessness and the rush of affect (e.g., shock, fear, anxiety, terror, and vulnerability). Parkes and Weiss (1983) suggest that the "impact of unexpected and untimely bereavement can overwhelm a person's existing ability to cope with stress and trigger reactions that will lead to lasting problems" (p. 239).

The family's ability to cope may be enhanced by assisting them as they attempt to accomplish specific tasks associated with anticipatory grief. The donor's family may not complete these tasks during the period of brief forewarning, but efforts to do so should begin during the hospitalization. The tasks listed below are adapted from Lebow (1976).

1. Accepting the reality of their loss or impending loss
2. Remaining involved with the loved one
3. Remaining separate from the loved one
4. Adapting to role changes and compromised assumptions
5. Bearing the affects of grief
7. Saying goodbye

Accepting the Reality of Their Loss or Impending Loss

Accepting a loved one's death occurs on many levels. During the loved one's hospitalization, this task can be accomplished only on a most primary level. The inability to fully grasp the reality of what has happened, which is the hallmark of sudden loss, is fueled by the fact that much of the donor family's anxiety is focused on what the future will bring. The trauma has occurred, yet the patient is still breathing. Thus, the tension of disbelief is further complicated by the intense hope for the patient's recovery. Unlike immediate sudden death, this situation creates some brief history leading up to the donor's death. Events are taking place within the period of forewarning, including valiant efforts to save the patient's life, decisions concerning care, and usually, time for family and friends to arrive at the hospital.

> Eva Leah's parents arrived at the hospital first. Jeff burst into the waiting room 30 minutes later. Friends and family members began to come and go. "Every time I saw someone I knew walking toward me," noted Eva Leah's mother, "I realized that this was not a bad dream. As I looked into the grief-stricken faces, I knew that I could not deny the seriousness of my daughter's condition."

Each time someone visits and offers support to the family, the reality of the situation breaks through; denial is breached as family members perceive the gravity of their loved one's injury. Some individuals within the family may be too numb or shocked to respond, while others may react with intense expressive emotion. Since this expression of grief serves to help facilitate acceptance, it should not be suppressed but rather encouraged.

Accepting the reality of loss or impending loss is something that every involved donor family member must do. Sooner or later, the family must realize that their loved one is in a life-threatening crisis. Eventually, they must realize that their loved one is dead (i.e., brain dead). The neurological death of this family member is one of the unique factors that will influence donor family grief.

Remaining Involved with the Loved One

Most family members want to do something for their loved one. Yet, the nature of the injury and the presence of medical equipment used to sustain life or to maintain the viability of organs may deprive family members of doing for and being with their loved one. Efforts must be made to circumvent the obstacles that prevent family involvement in the care of their loved one.

Doing for the loved one, however, may take many forms. For instance, even sharing information with the medical staff offers the family something to do while enabling the staff to assess the family's coping patterns, needs, and resources (Holtkamp, 2000). Often when individuals experience trauma, their sense of trust and security is violated. Treatment received in the hospital setting may either increase that sense of violation, or the trust generated by this dialogue (between the family and health care providers) may enhance planning and decision making. In turn, this participation with the medical staff reduces the family's sense of helplessness (Holtkamp, 2000). These moments of being helpful or engaged also offer a brief respite from anxiety or expressive grief. Families of donors may experience subsequent problems directly related to the lack of opportunity to do for and be with their loved one.

> Eva Leah's mother spoke to the importance of the family's participation in care. "When I first saw Eva Leah, she looked as though she were sleeping. I smoothed her hair and stroked her arm, while her father held her free hand. Then I tried to comb her hair, which couldn't be combed. Her father decided he needed to rearrange the sheets, which didn't need to be rearranged. We desperately needed to do something, but could think of only the simplest acts of love."

These forms of care, stroking her arm, smoothing the sheets, holding her hand, may be the simplest acts of love, yet these acts are exquisitely meaningful for the family. Creative ways to provide these opportunities for the donor's families must be found.

Remaining Separate from the Loved One

Health care staff should be ready to balance the family member's need to remain involved with the patient with his or her need to remain separate. To recognize that they are separate from the patient, family members must begin to realize that they will live, whereas the patient will die. This realization is difficult but necessary. The family must be helped to understand that remaining separate does not preclude remaining involved with the patient. These two tasks are pursued in tandem as family members come to understand that their needs are different from the patient's and that taking care of their own needs serves the patient best (Holtkamp, 2000).

Caregivers reinforce this reality by simply encouraging each member of the family to take care of themselves, get enough sleep, or eat to keep up their strength. Reminding people of their specific needs demonstrates how separate and different their needs are from those of the patient. Family members may be encouraged to understand that taking care of themselves is in the service of caring for their loved one.

Adapting to Role Changes and Compromised Assumptions

Although the time between trauma and the patient's death is abbreviated, there may be fragile attempts by the family to explore life's assumptions and personal identities (Rando, 1984). Eva Leah's brother acknowledged such an attempt.

> I always took it for granted that Eva Leah and I would grow up together; marry and come home with the grandchildren. Now we'll never get to do that. Even though she was my big sister, I took care of her. I was her brother. Now I'm nobody's brother.

In this brief vignette, there is evidence of compromised assumptions: "Eva Leah and I would grow up together . . . we would come home with the grandchildren." Also present is the question: "Who am I now? I'm nobody's brother, I have no one to protect." While intervention at this time is limited, future efforts might need to address compromised assumptions as well as altered identities.

Bearing the Affect of Grief

Much of the affective response from families may not occur until the notification of the patient's death. At that point the vigil is over; the worst has happened, and denial is no longer sufficient to ward off the pain.

When families are confronted with the death of their loved one, there are a number of considerations (adapted from Rando, 1984) that caregivers might find helpful.

1. Family members should be reminded that intense feelings are appropriate and acceptable.

2. Some members of the family may need assurances that releasing the emotions a little at a time actually prevents loss of control.

3. Families need a place for the expression of feelings that is comfortable and private. A room that is well stocked with tissue, water, and a telephone would be helpful.

4. Caregivers should remain calm and reassuring. The caregiver need not be stoic. Tears may be a form of advocacy. However, intense emotions will hinder attempts to help the family.

5. When practical matters must be addressed, caregivers may help by

gently facilitating closure for family members who are overcome with strong emotions.

When anger is compounded by the need to blame—so common in traumatic deaths—there may be instances when the reaction of a family member is so strong and demonstrative that caring for the family becomes a security issue rather than a therapeutic concern. While extreme anger is not considered outside the range of appropriate responses, in a public environment it must be dealt with quickly and appropriately to assure the safety of all concerned.

Family members who are quiet and unresponsive may create the opposite situation. These individuals may be so overwhelmed that they often warrant even more emotional support than do members of the family who are able to express their emotions. Occasionally, a family member may cover anxiety with a chatty cheerfulness that appears quite inappropriate. The risk that such an individual might, at any moment, exhibit expressive grief equal to his or her initial denial calls for certain watchfulness.

Under no circumstances should attempts be made to diminish the family's grief. Anything said or done that discounts the enormity of the pain or robs individuals of their experience can be harmful. This is not the time to offer trite simplistic platitudes or to encourage traumatized people that it will get better with time. Even the idea that the mourner will recover may be perceived as a form of discounting if not exquisitely timed.

Saying Goodbye

Goodbyes are seldom easy; final goodbyes bring wrenching heartache. The perception that the patient is being abandoned exacerbates that pain. Offering the assurance that they are merely leaving the hospital experience rather than the loved one may provide some comfort. Reminding the family members of the loved one's ongoing presence in their memories is another effective gesture of reassurance.

Meeting the Donor Family's Immediate Needs

Ninety-five percent of donors are cared for in critical care units (Youngner et al., 1989). The needs of family members whose loved one was cared for in these units have been identified by several studies (Hickey, 1985; Leske, 1986; McIvor & Thompson, 1988; McPhee, 1987; Norris & Grove, 1986) and match the needs of donor families as outlined by Willis and Skelley (1992); Corr, Coolican, Nile, and Noedel (1994); and Holtkamp (1997). An adaptation selected from these two sources outline the needs of a donor's family:

1. Positive identification of the patient
2. Immediate support
3. Assurance that the patient's needs are respected
4. Accurate and ongoing information
5. Opportunity to address unfinished business
6. Access to the patient
7. Clear understanding of brain death
8. Opportunity to come to terms with impending death
9. Sensitive notification of death
10. Accurate and consistent time of death
11. Privacy and permission to grieve
12. The option to donate
13. Times for reconciliation
14. Time to say goodbye
15. Ongoing emotional support

Similarity between the family's needs and the previously outlined tasks are readily apparent. Meeting the family's needs is a way that procurement coordinators and other health care professionals may support the family as they accomplish those necessary tasks.

Positive Identification

The most obvious, essential, and primary need of the donor family is to positively identify the patient. While incorrect identification is rare, a reminder of its importance is warranted. Personal items such as purses or wallets may be lost or scattered at the accident scene. If there is any question about the patient's identity or if there were multiple deaths involved in the trauma, identities must be clarified as early as possible. Only when this identification is certain can the family's other needs be met.

Immediate Support

Support, considered by some experts to be the most important variable in grief recovery (Kirste, Muthny, & Wilms, 1988; Rando, 1993; Raphael, 1986), may reduce the impact of sudden loss. Natural support systems that include family, friends, ministers, chaplains, and others provide valuable support for the donor's family. However, at the hospital the health care professionals' efforts are essential because of their ability to meet specific family needs. This support should be in place prior to the family's arrival at the hospital. The combination of personal and professional efforts on behalf of the donor family may weave a safety net of emotional support which could continue when the family returns to their home.

Health care professionals who imbue their clinical skills with empathy offer highly-traumatized families something of value that is difficult to define, yet easy to recognize. Empathy suggests an understanding that forms the deepest connection between humans. It denotes comprehension, rapport, affinity, and fellow feelings. These characteristics explain why a caregiver is capable of treating a donor family in ways that he or she would wish to be treated. Caring for traumatized individuals, which can be difficult and challenging, demands compassion from organ procurement coordinators as well as hospital personnel. Both are uniquely positioned to help these families begin the exhausting work of mourning.

Assurance that the Patient's Needs Are Respected

As the donor's family members absorb information about their loved one's status, they also welcome assurance that her needs are being met and that she is being, and will continue to be, treated with respect. This assurance of respect must cover all treatments or circumstances, including the surgery to recover donated organs.

Calling the patient by name is a simple gesture that may lessen the impression that the patient lost her identity once she entered the hospital. Whether or not there is viable hope of recovery, the patient is never just a patient or a potential organ donor; *she* is the daughter of distraught parents, sister to a young man who never before encountered death up close; she is a granddaughter, friend, babysitter. She is a person; she has a name. If there is some question about which name to use, the family should be consulted.

Accurate and Ongoing Information

Providing information regarding the patient's trauma, current status, and prognosis on a continuous basis and in a consistent manner is one of the most effective ways health care providers can support the family (Holtkamp, 1997).

Information is empowering. When information about the patient is presented in easily understood language, as free as possible of medical terms, and repeated as often as necessary, family members benefit. Individuals within the family may hear or interpret only parts of the information offered by medical personnel. Efforts to clarify these differences between what was said and what the family heard may reduce tensions and misunderstandings within the family system. Even if a spokesperson serves as liaison between the family and medical personnel, periodic efforts to determine whether there are conflicting perceptions among family members may be helpful for the health care provider as well as for the family.

Staying close to the family, gently providing updates of the patient's condition, and confirming that the forewarnings are understood, allows the caring professional time to assess the family's capacity to cope with the reality of the situation. Wright (1978) stresses the value of this approach.

> Families can be much less reactionary and uncooperative when they are kept informed, in terminology understandable to them, of their significant other's progress. Even when a client's recovery seems uncertain . . . taking a few moments to talk with the family and listen to their perceptions of what is happening can have a tremendous impact on the family's acceptance of the patient's status, [including] the inevitability of death. Though it is simplistic, it is most essential that families and patients know that they are truly cared about as people. (p. 978)

Opportunity to Address Unfinished Business

One beneficial aspect of the window of time between initial trauma and the death of the donor is the opportunity for the donor's family members to address unfinished business. The possibility that this task might be accomplished is heightened each time the family is allowed access to their loved one. The health care staff or the organ procurement coordinator may help the family use this time to express regrets, affection, and appreciation. Even though the patient is unable to respond, his or her presence facilitates this communication. Consistently, loved ones "speak with gratitude of the opportunity to say their good-byes and to express their regrets, joys and affection" (Holtkamp, 2000, p. 518).

Eva Leah's mother expressed the value of this communication:

> We had often said "I love you" to one another. Yet, I needed to tell her once again how much joy she had brought to our lives. I needed to tell her how proud I was of her, how wonderful she was. I wanted her to know that we were there. There are no words to express how grateful I am for those moments.

To offer ample time to address unfinished business, families of potential donors must be granted access to their loved one as often as medically possible. Hospital protocols that do not consider the importance of family involvement suggest professional or administrative myopia.

Access to the Patient

Without question, the opportunity to frequently visit the patient is one of the most supportive gestures that hospital staff can offer a potential donor's family (Back, 1991; Coolican, 1990; Coupe, 1990; Gyulay, 1989; C. Johnson, 1992; Willis & Skelley, 1992). Yet, trauma families often express concerns about a lack of access to the patient.

When death is violent, sudden, and random, the survivor's sense of trust and security is violated. Limiting access of immediate family members to the patient may further strain that sense of security or may "engender mistrust and bitterness toward the hospital and the staff" (Willis & Skelley, 1992, p. 76).

Frequent opportunities to visually assess the lethality of the patient's injuries will at least prepare the family for the reality that the patient's condition is different from when he or she was last seen before hospitalization.

"The last image I had of Eva Leah," said her father, "was when she left for college. With car keys jingling, and filled with laughter, she was the picture of youth and health. Only when I saw her in the hospital hooked up to all that equipment could I realize how critical the situation was."

Clear Understanding of Brain Death

Comprehending brain death is even more perplexing because there is often an absence of external injuries, and because the patient is being supported by a ventilator, there are signs of viability and normal body functions. The body is warm to the touch, the color is good, and there is urine output (Pelletier, 1992). The situation seems surreal and cognitive dissonance may be experienced by involved family members.

"When we were finally allowed to see Eva Leah," her father noted, "it was so hard to believe she was gone. She looked good. There was not a mark on her. Her color was good, her chest moved up and down. It was easy to believe that she was just asleep and would soon wake up and say 'Hi Dad, why aren't you at work?'"

Prior understanding of the concept of brain death does not appear to completely eliminate the gap between intellectual knowledge and emotional acceptance. The family may know that the patient is dead, yet feel as though he or she is alive. Even so, an understanding of brain death prior to need should help those individuals who generally "absorb information most effectively when it fits their existing view. Information that requires reorientation and is, in addition, highly unpleasant, is apt to be distorted, suppressed, or exaggerated" (Parkes & Weiss, 1983, p. 232). Radical reorientation may be required when the visual presentation of death contradicts the family's lifelong views of death.

Throughout this period, the family must continue to struggle with realities that may seem straightforward and obvious to medical personnel. However, "even though bereavement is an established reality, the bereaved still need time and the chance to talk through the implications of their loss and to react emotionally. [Donor families literally] have to prepare themselves for an event that has already taken place" (Parkes & Weiss, 1983, p. 239). Time for this preparation can seldom be accelerated.

Come to Terms with the Impending Death

In the pristine sense of the phrase, only rarely would a family fully come to terms with the donor's impending death at the hospital. Yet, access to the patient and incremental forewarnings may facilitate a certain acceptance of the inevitable outcome, which may be interpreted as coming to terms with the donor's death.

Sensitive Notification of Death

How and where people are informed of the death of a loved one is critically important. This is especially true when death is determined by neurological criteria rather than the traditional method of cardiopulmonary cessation. "It takes time to break bad news and the setting in which communication takes place will influence how it is received" (Parkes & Weiss, 1983, p. 231). Private, comfortable surroundings should be provided for the family when they are notified of their loved one's death. Access to the patient should be immediate.

When death is inevitable, false hope never serves the family well. Parkes and Weiss (1983) suggest that because the peculiarly traumatic impact of sudden, untimely bereavement often overwhelms integrative capacities, the possibility of a terminal outcome must be made known as soon as it is medically recognized. However, family members also need time to absorb the reality of a loved one's condition. Parkes and Weiss concur that "this information [regarding impending death] should, if possible, be communicated gradually so that it will not in itself constitute an overwhelmingly traumatic confrontation with impending loss" (pp. 229–230).

Although families are often in shock and numbed by the prospect of the impending loss, there is often a degree of hypersensitivity (Rando, 1993). Families have the uncanny ability to recall peripheral experiences—often negative or hurtful—that occurred during this stressful time; the notification of death is ripe for such hurtful experiences.

> At 7:30 p.m. on the third day of their vigil, Eva Leah's parents and her brother stood just outside the intensive care unit. Her doctor came out of the unit and approached them. Eva Leah's father tells what happened next.
>
> "I knew from the look on the doctor's face that Eva Leah was gone. But I was still shocked that he told us as we stood in the hallway that Eva Leah was brain dead and without pausing asked if we had ever considered organ donation. I was too stunned to speak but with anger-driven courage my wife spoke: 'We were not raising our daughter to become an organ donor.' We almost decided against donation at that point."

Negative experiences, such as the one described by Eva Leah's father, are obvious and avoidable. Advising a family in the hallway of their loved one's death is inappropriate and insensitive. Regardless of how such information is relayed, the family may have difficulty grasping the reality that the death has occurred. However, that is not an excuse for the doctor's unthinking behavior. Also inexcusable is the linking of notification of brain death and request for organ donation. "Obscene," retorted one donor's mother.

Linking notification of death directly with the request for donation compromises the trauma family's confidence that everything possible was done to save the loved one's life. When notifying the family of the death, information needs to be brief and to the point. "Families . . . have been angered by a long, comprehensive description about what was done, what failed, or what was hoped for before announcement of the death" (Gyulay, 1989, p. 76). Families may later request such information, but not as a preface to the pronouncement of their loved one's death.

Following declaration of brain death, the family must be given a time of death and that time must be given verbally and recorded consistently (Holtkamp, 1997; Youngner, 1992). Youngner (1992) warns that the time when irreversible loss of all brain function was determined is rarely noted as the time of death on death certificates. Instead, time of death is recorded as the time when the ventilator is disconnected in the operating room. The implications of this practice should be obvious. The slightest inference that the loved one was not dead at the time of organ removal could create enormous guilt and anxiety. The fear that organ donation caused the donor's death may fuel primitive fears about mutilation of the loved one's body or intrusive thoughts and images of the love one's suffering. This one seemingly simple error could have devastating and long-lasting impact on the donor's family.

> Emma and John sat quietly in my office. They hated to bother me, they said, but there was a problem that was causing them sleepless nights; and when sleep did come it brought nightmares about their daughter's death.
>
> Emma spoke. "We consented to donation at 7:30 in the evening on August 30th. We received her death certificate in the mail and we gave it to the stonemason who was preparing Eva Leah's monument. We didn't even read it because it was so painful. So final."
>
> "But when the stone was finished we realized the date of death was August 31st. The person at the monument place had copied that date from the death certificate. All we think of now is that Eva Leah wasn't dead when we left her at the hospital; she wasn't dead when they took her organs."

Such preventable errors are extraordinarily hard to ameliorate and often constitute a secondary trauma for the family. Whatever doubts may have been rumbling about in the minds of these parents appeared confirmed. It is never easy, and may not be possible, for this family to erase the question mark that haunts them. At question here was not whether the time of death was exact or absolute, but that the death occurred prior to surgery.

Privacy and Permission to Grieve

As noted earlier, the inability to grasp the reality of the death is a hallmark of sudden loss. As long as there is some hope, families generally react with anxiety; when that hope is gone, when reality breaks through the cushion of denial and disbelief, intense and expressive grief frequently upstages that anxiety. There may be feelings of sadness, fear, or hysteria. People who are overwhelmed with intense emotions may lash out with anger or hostility. Individuals may become excessively demanding to cover their fear and vulnerability (Rando, 1984). Men in particular may use anger as protection against other emotions that they deem unacceptable. Attempts to help may be rebuffed because such gestures only serve to remind some men of their own vulnerability; others may welcome support.

Curiously, while intense expressive grief is not unusual, neither is an absence of strong emotions. Shock, numbness, and disbelief may be so pervasive that family members are simply unable to respond. Caregivers must not assume that a quiet, unexpressive family member needs less support.

Option to Donate Organs

As family members struggle to cope with the neurological death of their loved one, they are confronted with a number of critical decisions. For medical reasons, organ donation is one of those decisions that must be addressed when families are still shocked, confused, disoriented, and vulnerable. If the patient has discussed the issue of donation with the family or if the patient has indicated his or her desire on their driver's license, the decision appears easier for the family. The decision to donate is and must remain an individual matter. Neither the great need for organs nor the value of donation as perceived by other donor's families should obscure the reality that donation is not the best option for some families (Holtkamp, 2000).

While most donor families do not perceive the process of request for donation as additionally stressful or burdensome (Bartucci, 1987; Savaria et al., 1990), some do. "Families are often angered that they have to face these decisions quickly, although the inevitability of the death has been apparent for some time" (Gyulay, 1989, p. 97).

The option of donation may breach family denial, and force them to confront the reality of their loved one's death before they are ready to do so. While this factor alone might be interpreted as stressful, it is also in the service of healthy grieving. Gyulay (1989) indicates that although angered by the hurried atmosphere "most families are grateful that at least something positive comes from such a tragic situation" (p. 97). The conclusion that families may experience difficulties related to the donation process and still believe that donation is a worthy, even noble, cause is pertinent to the study of donor-family trauma. By identifying and working through any negative aspects of the donation process, family members are often able to refocus on the outcome of their loved one's gift.

Signing the consent form may be a traumatic moment for the family because it offers tangible evidence that the loved one is truly dead. However, families often indicate that donation was the only thing that made sense of their tragedy.

Eva Leah's father describes his thoughts on this issue: "The manner in which the doctor raised the question of donation was inappropriate. However, when

we returned to the trauma unit, I began to reconsider the option of donation. The trauma unit was chaos: I was chaotic, crazy. When I was asked
again if I was willing for Eva Leah to be a donor, it was the only thing that
night that had made any sense at all. The act of donation brought something
of worth from absolute madness; however, it also meant that Eva Leah was
truly dead."

As noted earlier, the stress of deciding whether to donate and of signing
the consent form is lessened when the request for donation is distinctly
separate from the notification of the loved one's death.

Decoupling. During the early 1990s a flurry of articles and presentations within the transplant community dealt with the idea of decoupling.
This word, as used within the process of organ procurement, simply means
that the option of organ donation is separated (decoupled) from the pronouncement of death. von Pohle (1996) reports that when an organ procurement representative, rather than the physician, presents the option of
donation, thereby decoupling the possibility of donation from the discussion of neurological death of their loved one, the rate of donation increased
significantly.

Within the disciplines of thanatology and traumatology, decoupling
would have been a given. Out of minimum respect for the grieving family,
it would seem that this separation would have been the natural route
even before decoupling was clinically validated as a means of increasing
donation (von Pohle, 1996). However, this means of increasing consent
actually accomplished more than originally intended. Caring and dedicated organ procurement representatives often greatly enhance the total
quality of care provided for the potential donor's family.

Fantasies and Consent to Donation. Donor families in general, and parents in particular, often report fantasizing about who might
receive the organs; these fantasies usually involve another child close to
the same age as their own child. Discovering that the recipient is much
different than imagined may represent a secondary loss for some families.
If false promises were made during the consent process, the family may
feel deceived. Eva Leah's mother speaks of such reactions.

One of the "selling points" for donation was when I was told that my child's
heart would continue living for years to come. I was led to believe that
because of size and other factors, Eva Leah's heart would go to another
young person. Although my husband and I felt we had donated with no

strings attached, we had consoled ourselves during those first two weeks that Eva Leah had saved the life of another young person. When we were told that a 58-year-old man received her heart . . . well, quite honestly, we were disappointed. How much longer will it live, and why did they not choose a young person?

Because of the traumatized family's limited ability to grasp all that is being communicated, it may be necessary for the procurement coordinator to state clearly that except in rare cases, organs cannot be designated for a specific person or age group. By addressing the topic prior to consent, the organ procurement coordinator may abort fantasies that could lead to disappointment.

Times of Reconciliation

Those who work closely with donor families agree about the importance of a time of reconciliation (Holtkamp, 1997; Willis & Skelley, 1992). There are, however, three distinct occasions when the donor family must be allowed to get used to the idea of death. The first phase of reconciliation occurs when the family realizes the gravity of the situation. The second takes place after the declaration of brain death. Families need time to comprehend this diagnosis, to ask questions, and to discuss what this means to the patient and to the family. Family members may react with shock or with intense expressive emotions during either of these times.

The third opportunity for reconciliation should come after the option for organ donation has been presented. Family members must be allowed time in private, free of coercion, to make the decision that is appropriate for them. Time constraints to maintain viability of the donated organs is a critical issue; however, families must have as much time as possible to consider this option and be provided enough information to make this decision with discernment (Stocks, Culter, Kress, & Lewino, 1992).

Failure to bring up the option for donation could potentially harm family members who might later regret the missed opportunity. The request for donation should never, under any circumstances, be made prior to or in tandem with the pronouncement of brain death. The donor's family must always be offered the opportunity to view their loved one following surgery. When they choose not to remain at the hospital for the extended period of time required for surgical removal of the organs, they may experience a particularly difficult aspect of leave taking. Because the potential donor is still being maintained artificially, some may perceive that they are abandoning the patient, rather than their loved one leaving them. Viewing the body postoperatively may reduce that perception.

Those families who choose to remain at the hospital until the surgery is completed must have continuing support. During this time, the family will continue processing all that has happened; they will benefit by having someone nearby to provide ongoing support. Some families need only a caring attitude on the part of hospital and procurement staff, others may need extensive practical help as well as emotional support.

Saying Goodbye

Part of the family's reconciliation involves an opportunity to say goodbye to their loved one. The act of saying goodbye acknowledges that leave taking is occurring. It is at once an act of love and an act of relinquishment, a reluctant farewell to the fortress that housed the essence of the beloved. Whether this act is verbal or nonverbal, concrete or symbolic, it will always be meaningful to the family members who participate (Holtkamp, 2000, p. 530).

Prior to seeing their loved one, the family members should always be prepared for any visible changes in the patient's appearance and for the presence of medical equipment. Families often imagine something much worse than the reality, yet preparation for visual changes is always wise.

Ongoing Emotional Support

Following consent to donate, it is imperative that support continues for the donor family. Occasionally, a family speaks of feeling discarded once the consent form is signed.

> From the moment we signed the paper, we felt everything change. It was as if they had gotten what they wanted and we were merely in the way. . . . There were no words of consolation, no acknowledgement of the horrible thing [we] were going through, no word of thanks for the gracious gift. There was no offer of a bowl of soup or cup of coffee. (Helmberger, 1992)

Contrast the palpable sense of disenfranchisement described by Helmberger with the description offered by Eva Leah's father of his family's experience:

> While there were several negative incidents during our stay at the hospital, there was no difference in the level of care and attention that we received once the consent form was signed. The chaplain, the patient representative,

a nurse, and the procurement coordinator all found ways of being supportive. Everything we needed, from a hug to a cup of coffee, was available. We
couldn't have been treated better.

☐ Dimensions of Compassion and Kindness

Difficult to define, yet easily recognized, "compassion is the virtue of being
moved to action by the sight of suffering. . . . It is a virtue that circumvents
thought, since it prompts us immediately to action. It is a virtue that pre-
supposes that an answer has already been found to the question 'What
needs to be done?'" (Hauerwas, 1994, p. 11).

Much like mystical thinking, compassion belongs to a dimension of life
that circumvents thought and resists scientific analysis. Curiously, the
mystical, illogical thinking that confounds the scientific community, and
which is considered a hindrance to the organ procurement programs, may
also account for its success.

The very notion that individuals could be notified that their once perfectly healthy loved one has died via new and easily misunderstood criteria, that medical personnel are asking to take that loved one's organs and
put them into a compatible stranger, even as the survivors are experiencing heart-wrenching pain, is unfathomable and remote from any logic.
That from only 10,000–12,000 eligible candidates (Youngner & Arnold,
1993), 5,791 families consented to organ donation is beyond comprehension; just short of a miracle (UNOS, 1999).

Rarely do these makers of near-miracles indicate that they donated because it was the right thing to do. Instead, they report that they donated
because of compassion for other families who might be facing the loss of
their loved one, because donation offers some solace, some sense of meaning (Bartucci, 1987; Holtkamp & Nuckolls, 1993; Pelletier, 1993; Savaria et
al., 1990; Stocks et al., 1992). People donate because they are generous,
kind, loving, concerned, life-affirming individuals.

Some trauma experts believe that attributing meaning to a loss is essential to grief resolution, that some explanation or a personal healing theory,
must be developed (Figley, 1989; Gilbert, 1997; Taylor, Lichtman, & Wood,
1984). Organ donation may readily provide a healing theory for many
donor families.

As Eva Leah's father states: "The only thing worse than the death of our
beautiful daughter would have been to miss the opportunity for her death
to bless others. We're grateful for that."

However, restitution—bringing something of value from something tragic—has always been thought of as part of the recovery phase of grief (Simos, 1979). With donation, the donor family may miss the process of developing meaning because the value, the exquisite meaning derived from organ donation, is established before the family has even commenced their mourning. In addition, the organ donor's family may struggle to accept another paradox: The act of giving that brings meaning, also confirms the death of the loved one. "Bittersweet—at best," as one donor mother observed.

Donor Family Trauma and Ongoing Support

It is within the hospital setting, when the death of their loved one becomes a timebound reality, that a donor's family members first confront trauma-driven grief. Here in real-life experience, many must also confront various aspects of organ donation and brain death that appear far different from mere abstract rumination.

The medical process itself may be potentially stress producing, resulting in secondary victimization (Redmond, 1989). However, the impact of the hospital experience is determined by the perception of this experience by the donor family. "If the mourner perceives the world as providing support for mourning, that perception is an extremely positive factor." Conversely "to the extent that a perceived lack of . . . support constitutes a concurrent stress or crisis, in itself a high-risk factor, the mourner is further disadvantaged" (Rando, 1993, p. 495).

The power to further traumatize suggests that there must be ways to forestall such further traumatization and thereby enhance the probability for natural bereavement. While agreeing that violent or sudden deaths can be a powerful risk for the development of traumatic stress responses, Stamm (1999) offers a challenging conclusion when she alleges that "many people remain fairly intact after psychological trauma as long as their environment restores a sense of trust and safety" (p. 32).

The hospital and organ procurement staff have an unparalleled opportunity to begin the long process of restoring the donor family's sense of trust and safety. The task of restoring that trust and safety is as simple and as complex as meeting the needs of the family during that window of opportunity between the event that brings them to the hospital and the time they leave. During that time, every effort must be made to reduce or eliminate further aggravation of the original trauma.

Support will continue to be pivotal to the well-being of the donor family. Options for community support should already be in place and offered to the family before they leave the hospital (Willis & Skelley, 1992). Written information regarding appropriate referrals to bereavement specialists or support groups within the community should be offered to all organ donor families. Even with a scarcity of time and limited human resources, there are ways to maximize efforts to provide ongoing support for donor families. "Ways may be found to encourage relatives, colleagues, and friends to offer not just an immediate visit, but an extended time of greater support" (Horowitz, 1997, p.137). Horowitz outlines a number of points to help relatives and friends provide extended and effective social support for traumatized individuals. Some of those points have been adapted specifically for the donor's family:

1. Protect the mourners from excessive stimulation. In the acute phase of response to the loss, family members should be advised to avoid driving, operating machinery, or engaging in other activities that might require alertness.

2. Encourage the members of the family to tell their story, even if they are emotional. When possible, encourage this debriefing prior to sleep. There is some indication that sleep and dreaming alters the meaning of this event to the self. Sanctioning emotion is helpful; this may be especially important for male members of the family. Emphasize the social connections that are available for the family.

3. Help those exposed to the trauma to avoid excessive replays of the event via radio and television coverage. Telling one's own story of the events is quite different from seeing and hearing excessive repetition of that event. Children, especially, may have trouble separating the television screenings from the actual event and should be protected from exposure to such media coverage.

4. Provide respites for the family members. Individuals should be encouraged to engage in some other activity or some distraction that will provide moments of respite. Care for young children by a trusted adult might provide support for the child and respite for the grieving adult.

5. Understand that a trusting relationship, even if it is new and temporary, is the best way to restore trust and reduce fear. Use that relationship to give the family member something to do or to offer guidelines for coping. During the early days of grief, it may be necessary to be more directive when helping the traumatized family.

6. It must be remembered that family members are still vulnerable. Deeply traumatized individuals may appear no different than those who are

caring for them. They may sound lucid and intact. However, this facade of normalcy may be masking intense emotions that can erupt as great searing grief, remorse, or diffuse rage. Traumatic deaths often trigger a need to blame, which may be directed to those attempting to help.

7. Assurances attesting to the "efficacy of the self" should be used. Those assurances need not be elaborate. A gentle "You can do this" combined with "You are not alone" may provide hope and comfort. Believing in their own power to survive—even when individuals question whether they want to survive—increases a sense of confidence for traumatized individuals.

8. The experience associated with donor-family grief is, by definition, complicated. Those within the family's social network must understand that the stress response may continue for months, a year, or even more. Expecting individuals within the donor's family to return to pre-event levels of functioning within a few weeks, or even a few months, is unrealistic. Friends and relatives who can remain accepting of fluctuating emotional responses will provide the most effective support.

9. Information concerning professional and self-help groups should be readily available for the families of donors. Often relatives and friends can remind family members of these important resources when needs arise.

10. When the members of the donor's family become distressed because of lack of communication from the recipient, others within the natural support system might be helpful by reminding them that there are a myriad of reasons when the recipient chooses not to correspond; that this is not a reflection on the donor but rather a personal choice of the recipient that may be founded on rational circumstances.

11. Any confusion about the concept of brain death may be discussed first within the family system. Written material that explains the diagnostic criteria used by health care professionals may be given to a more distant family member who could share this information with the survivor. When the less emotionally-involved friend or family member gains an understanding of brain death, he or she can prevent distortions or misunderstanding about this event and the criteria used to determine this diagnosis.

☐ Closing Thoughts

The hospital and organ donor procurement organization staff are positioned to meet the needs of organ donor families immediately before, during, and following the donor's hospitalization. Some risks related to trauma-driven grief may be reduced or even eliminated when those needs are met. Transplantation focuses on ongoing life; part of the family member's ongoing life involves living with their decision and knowing that the decision was best, not only for the donor program, but also for their family.

As these families leave the hospital experience, they must confront their loss and what that loss means to them. Trauma changes people. It leaves some individuals more dependent, forces others into caregiver roles, and creates financial burdens; families are forced to make adjustments as relationships are reassessed and reassigned. Redefining their relationship with their loved one is a major part of that change.

Murray (1996) speaks to this issue:

> We could choose to take family relationships seriously at this time. If we did, we might find the survivors forced suddenly and drastically to redefine their relationship with the newly dead person. When we ask the family members if they will agree to donate the organs of their newly dead son or daughter, sister or brother, they might make this decision as one of the crucial, telling and final acts with which they will accomplish that redefinition. (p. 120)

Redefining the relationship with the loved one is only one of many tasks awaiting the organ donor family as they experience the aftershocks of traumatic loss.

CHAPTER

Trauma-Driven Grief and the Organ Donor Family

When life is no longer an option for a loved one, transplantation provides a way for survivors to turn a personal and familial tragedy into a remarkable gift of hope for other desperately ill individuals. In an unparallel fashion, organ donation and transplantation affirm our humanity. But this particular opportunity to celebrate life while experiencing loss is rarely as simple as it sounds.

While the technical aspects of transplanting organs are no longer considered difficult, the emotionally charged process of obtaining those organs remains a major problem. As the deeply grieving, often traumatized family is left to deal with sudden, unexpected loss and its sequela, aspects of organ donation also influence the family's grief.

Because there is a paucity of formal studies on this form of grief, this chapter will present an overview of donor family grief from three perspectives: (a) clinical knowledge about the donor family experience, (b) current knowledge about the process of organ donation, and (c) trauma-driven grief. Derived through some form of trauma, often carrying an overlay of post-traumatic symptoms, the donor family's experience will be viewed through the lens of post-traumatic stress.

☐ Risk Factors for Post-Traumatic Stress

The organ donor's family may experience some or all of the known risk factors for post-traumatic stress responses as defined by Rando (1993):

1. Sudden and unnatural death
2. Violence or mutilation
3. Preventability or randomness
4. Loss of a child
5. Survivor's personal encounter with death
6. Multiple loss

Most cadaveric organs are obtained from young, previously healthy, persons who have been fatally injured in accidents, have committed suicide, or were the victims of homicide. Other organ donor deaths may have been less violent but are just as sudden, unexpected, and usually premature. The manner in which most donors die (suddenly, without warning, often in a violent, sometimes mutilating, random, and preventable manner) as well as the object of that loss (usually someone's child) sets the stage for post-traumatic stress (PTS).

Not all donor family members experience PTS. Traumatic deaths, which make up the population of donor deaths and which constitute a "stressful life experience that can produce a situation ripe for traumatic stress response, may or may not lead to a traumatic stress disorder" (Stamm, 1999, pp. 3–19) depending on the perception of the person who is experiencing the trauma.

☐ Defining Characteristics of Post-Traumatic Stress

Defining characteristics of post-traumatic-stress response—numbing, rage, anxiety, guilt, and intrusive reactions—are often observed in the donor family's response to their loss.

Numbing

Psychic numbing is at the heart of post-traumatic stress. Rando (1993) calls this response a "symbolic death as a defense to avoid permanent physical or psychic death" (p. 584). The fact that emotion is lost while cognition is retained has critical implications for the organ donor family. Numbing, abetted by denial and disbelief, may even be a pivotal component of the family's reaction to the trauma that allows them to consider the option of organ donation.

According to Horowitz (1997) this "numbness is not simply an absence of emotions; it is a sense of 'benumbed'" (p. 26). Individuals often describe the feeling as being wrapped in layers of cotton. This experience is not unlike other forms of emotional blunting, the difference being a matter of degree. However, this numbness is not necessarily characterized by a state of torpor such as that seen with deeply depressed individuals.

> Bre and her husband, Dan, were stopped at a traffic light when a man approached their car. When Dan refused the man's request for money, the man drew out a gun and reached across the passenger side of the car where Bre was sitting and fired four shots, fatally wounding her husband.

> She describes the subsequent numbness: "I'm zoned out. I can't feel. I know something is wrong but I can't connect it to anything. I know Dan is dead—so am I. I remember the shooting but there's no feeling to go with that memory."

When there is an absence of overt signs of something wrong, the survivor's family, friends, and colleagues, as well as the individual's professional support system may misinterpret the meaning of this absence. The survivor may drive away the ones he or she needs for support and comfort by treating them with indifference. Failure on the part of the professional caregiver to recognize this benumbing response may lead to inappropriate diagnosis, or at the other extreme, inappropriate expectations.

Rage

Beneath the numbness resides enormous frozen affect, preserved until the mourner can deal with an intensity of emotions that are often beyond the scope of human imagination. Rage, a common response to a sudden and especially violent, preventable death is a frequent familial reaction. Men are often characterized as being hesitant or unable to express emotions, even as they demonstrate anger and rage. Forgetting that anger and rage are powerful emotions is a common mistake. Rage, combined with the intense need to blame or to make someone suffer for this monstrosity—both appropriate responses to extreme loss—may be so intense that security rather than psychological intervention is required.

Anxiety

Anxiety is another cardinal component of post-traumatic stress reactions and is by definition always present to some degree (Rando, 1993). Feelings of anxiety are a quality of mind that gives the bereaved a sense (and sometimes the appearance) of being all over the place. Anxiety on the part of the donor family member may have many sources, including confusion about brain death, reappraisal of the decision to donate, or the disposition of the loved one's organs. Each source must be identified and worked through. Some anxieties will respond to education about the grief experience or issues related to the donation experience. Other forms of anxiety involve deep existential and philosophical issues that will yield only to considerable time and effort on the part of the survivor. Anxiety of all sources benefit from the support of a trusted caregiver.

Guilt

Members of the donor's family experience guilt in much the same way that other mourners would. The perception that one missed clues that could have prevented the death or the irrational belief that one was somehow responsible for an unpreventable death are often part of the donor family's grief presentation. Guilt regarding consent to donate may be another part of the donor family member's clinical presentation, especially if that family member harbors doubts about the soundness of their decision to donate.

Guilt may be camouflaged as anger when the deceased was neglected by the family or when the family perceives some unfulfilled responsibility to the deceased. Frequently, the medical profession and organ procurement organization receive the projected guilt from those family members who cannot tolerate awareness of their own complicity. "By punishing the 'guilty' ones, family members attempt to assuage their own unconscious guilt" (Cerney, 1993, p. 34).

Intrusive Repetitions

Intrusive repetition is a phenomenon that plays a paradoxical role as counterpoint to the phasic numbing found within post-traumatic stress. Intrusive responses alternate with periods of denial and numbing to facilitate necessary restabilization after contact with overwhelming trauma (Rando, 1993). Individuals may experience these intrusive repetitive reactions as thoughts and images of the event, nightmares, recurrent obsessive thoughts, feelings related to the original event, compulsive verbalizations of the story of the trauma, recurrent expression in artistic productions, patterning in interpersonal relationships, and somatic responses to stress (Rando, 1993).

For the donor's family, these intrusive repetitive reactions may include all the events surrounding the traumatic death of a loved one as well as those experiences that are unique to the organ donor family experience (i.e., the cognitive dissonance related to brain death, fear of mutilation, and suffering relative to the donation or reappraisal of the decision to donate).

☐ Sudden and Unnatural Death

The sudden death of a family member is incongruous. It is also a major risk factor for complicated mourning (Rando, 1993). Sudden death, with its unique characteristics is discordant and out of place in the mindset of the family left to mourn. Many sudden deaths are characterized by violence, violation, and volition. The grief of an organ donor's family is often, although not always, influenced in varying degrees of those elements. However, the death of the organ donor is always distinctly unnatural. Brain death criteria alone does not account for that distinction. The unique or unnatural aspect of the donor's death is further amplified by the reality that parts of the donor's body continue to sustain life elsewhere, perhaps in several locations, within the bodies of one or more people.

Defining Characteristics of Mourning Sudden Loss

Rando (1993) offers a redaction of bereavement issues that influence the grief of families who mourn the sudden loss of a family member (pp. 555–557). The following characteristics have been adapted to the needs of the donor's family.

The Assumptive World of the Mourner Is Violently Shattered

One overshadowing aspect of all sudden losses is that fundamental assumptions about life tend to implode. Because the death is sudden, there is no time to prepare or reevaluate belief systems. "Control, predictability, and security are lost, and the assumptions, expectations, and beliefs upon which the mourner has based her life are violated" (p. 555).

For the donor's family, this breach of one's assumptive world influences not only beliefs and expectations about life, but also about death. Certain assumptions about the death experience must be reconfigured for those unfamiliar with brain death. Even those who intellectually understand and accept the medicolegal criteria for neurological death report a degree of cognitive dissonance when lifelong assumptions about the death experience are challenged. Acceptance of and belief about brain death are often compromised when reality confronts theory.

The stunning impact of the event and the shock to the mourner's psyche leaves the mourner unable to absorb the vital information that his loved one is dead. No matter how often or how well the situation is explained to him, it makes no sense. The mourner cannot fully grasp what has happened.

The donor's family must contend with all the natural phenomena present when a loved one dies suddenly, then confront features of nontraditional death such as the mind-bending complication that the person who is dead appears to be breathing. The loved one is being aggressively maintained, medically speaking, and in spite of being dead, he or she often looks amazingly well. This scenario must have some impact on the human psyche.

Troubling questions may arise in clinical practice when a family member feels that he or she had not accepted the death of her loved one prior to making the decision to donate. Working through acceptance after the fact of donation opens the door for reconsiderations about the actual death as well as the family's decision to donate.

The Family Members' Capacity to Cope Is Diminished

An unexpected death is an assault on the human system, causing the mourner's adaptive and coping abilities to dysfunction. The donor family's ability to manage, which is determined in part by each family member's health and stamina, may be compromised (Cerney, 1993). Deciding for or against organ donation, especially when the wishes of the loved one are not known, may create lateral stress just when the family's capacities to cope are most limited.

For many, organ donation long has been considered an effectual factor in helping the donor's family cope with loss. Indeed, the mantra of most "organ procurement specialists is that organ donation helps a family deal with its grief" (Batten & Prottas, 1987, p. 44). Other surveys (Bartucci, 1987; Batten & Prottas, 1987; Pellitier, 1992; Savaria et al., 1990) support the claim that organ donation brings comfort and solace to many families. Within the act of organ donation these families found, if not a sense of meaning, at least a sense of redemption. The comfort derived from knowing that others were spared a grief such as their own must be considered one of the most remarkable aspects of organ donation. However, there is a distinct difference between receiving comfort from donation as opposed to donation improving the coping capacity of an individual. Caregivers and family members must understand that it is possible to derive a sense of comfort from an act of altruism while recognizing that that act did not lessen the pain or strengthen the ability to cope.

Some might argue that organ donation increased rather than lessened their pain. These individuals disagree with the sing-along version about the value that organ donation brings to the traumatized donor family. Journalist Hayes Johnson describes his less positive response to the donation experience in a 1992 editorial.

> The neurologist's words were so shocking I simply couldn't comprehend them. "Your sister is brain dead. I feel obligated to point out that she would be an excellent candidate for organ donation."

> And so began the most devastating and confusing day of my life.

> Within 12 hours, I would call all the family members back home to Vicksburg, Miss., to mourn the loss of our brightest star; Jennie Katherine Johnson, killed in a car accident. I would inform my mother, critically injured in the same accident, that her only daughter was dead.

> And I would give permission for an organ procurement team to take the heart, liver, kidneys, and corneas out of my 18-year-old sister's body before unplugging her from a ventilator.

> It was April 13, 1986. I was 25.

> The recent furious legal and ethical debates over Baby Theresa forced me, unwillingly, to face memories I wanted to leave buried with my little sister.

> Finally, a six-year standoff with my feelings has ended. For the first time I can admit to a lot of bitterness, not just at Jennie's death, but also at the process that converted her so swiftly and almost casually from loveable college freshman and aspiring artist into a human organ farm.

> I'm talking about the darker side of organ donation. It's much more complicated than any news story can convey.

> I still don't remember who put the idea in my head that organ donation was one of the few ways to make some sense out of a senseless horror. I just know that somewhere in the middle of the craziness, I latched onto that concept.

I had another recurring thought: Maybe Jennie wouldn't be as dead if part of her lived on in someone else's body. I saw that same one-two thought process echoed in words printed throughout the media during the Baby Theresa ordeal.

The child's family and doctors said it. Lawyers pleaded it. A court case and legislation were built on it. But I can tell you it's faulty thinking.

The fact that a loved one's heart keeps beating in another person's chest doesn't lessen the blow you feel from the loss. And nothing can ever explain untimely death, whether it comes to an 18-year-old or to an infant.

Yet, the experts in the field of organ donation and transplantation will let you fixate on those two concepts—making sense of tragedy and creating a sort of living memorial to lost loved ones—in order to win your support for organ donation.

For a long time after my sister's death, I had nightmares about allowing the mutilation of her body. I even began to have doubts about the doctor's claims that she had been brain dead, and that she could feel no pain while they took away her vital organs. These reactions hit me like aftershocks for years.

Beyond such irrational fears there also is a cold reality most donor families must face.

Once this act of human kindness is completed, so is your usefulness in the transplant world. Except for the collection of reusable body parts, the whole of transplant science is geared toward organ recipients.

Their right to privacy overrules a donor family's right to know who received the organs. Any communication between recipient and donor family has to be initiated by the recipient. In our case, there apparently have been no attempts by any of the six people who got my sister's organs to contact our family.

Six months after the accident my mother made a quixotic journey from Mississippi to Richmond, VA—where a young man received my sister's heart—in hopes of locating the recipient.

She found the right hospital, but never made it past staff members who refused to give any information for fear that it might upset the recipient's family. They made it clear they thought her mission was more than a little morbid.

After recovering from her injuries, my mother went back to college to become a social worker, determined in another way to make good out of bad.

One of her pet projects now is to establish a support network in Mississippi for organ donors' families.

She has made me swear, however, that when her time comes to join my sister, I will not allow anyone to take her organs. I won't.

For my part, I carry a driver license that lists me as an organ donor. They can have my whole body if they want it.

But when I'm gone, I don't want anyone standing around trying to explain how death got cheated a little on the day they took a piece of my flesh and planted it in someone else.

I want experts to take the time to explain all the negative sides of organ donation to the people I love. Then I want those loved ones to say goodbye and get on with their lives. It's time I did the same. (1992)

Symptoms of Acute Grief Following Sudden Loss Appear More Intense and Persist for a Longer Period

Grief following sudden loss may include intense anger, guilt, helplessness, and death anxiety. Vulnerability, insecurity, the need to understand, and the desire to affix blame and responsibility, compete with confusion and disorganization. The bereaved is often obsessed with the deceased (Rando, 1993). Shock, numbness, feelings of hopelessness, intense sadness, self-blame, desolate pining, and yearning round out the litany of emotional responses to sudden loss. The persistence and intensity of such emotions often demoralize the mourner and exhaust the natural support system.

The organ donor's death is both the same as and different from other deaths. The same may be said for the grief that follows. While the same intense and prolonged anguish associated with any sudden loss is present, the content of donor family grief may differ because of the unique experiences found only within the organ donation experience.

Closure is missing because of unfinished business and lack of time for goodbyes. When death is instantaneous, the lack of closure leaves the mourner feeling robbed and anguished. The nature of the organ donor's death often allows some time between the trauma and the declaration of brain death that may be used to attend the task of unfinished business and may provide a measure of closure. Health care professionals must be instrumental in creating a safe place where donor families have an opportunity to address this task and express final goodbyes.

The mourner often engages in obsessive reconstruction of events related to or leading up to the death. This behavior is the mourner's attempt after the fact to gain some control and predictability, to place events in some logical progression (Rando, 1993). This repetition often helps the mourner grasp the reality of the event and thereby to facilitate acceptance.

While this process may further enable the mourner to grasp the reality of what has happened, it may also afford an opportunity for the mourner to take on the responsibilities for missing cues prior to the death. "Problems with guilt can ensue, as can difficulties if the mourner's focus on the past and her attempts to grasp and make sense out it interfere with current functioning or persist too long" (Rando, 1993, p. 556).

When the hospital experience was perceived as negative or when the needs of the donor's family were not met, these issues become part of the mourner's obsessive reconstruction. There is a risk that the donor's family members may become fixated on negative events that could have been avoided. As the mourner laments peripheral and preventable aspects of a major trauma, less energy is directed toward the more legitimate, essential, and exhaustive tasks of mourning.

Some donor family members have indicated that this reconstruction often feels incomplete. As one mother stated: "There are pieces of the puzzle that are missing; parts of my son that I cannot account for." Reconstruction of events may lead some family members to search out the recipient of those missing puzzle pieces.

Sudden Loss Produces a Sense of Profound Loss of Security and Confidence in the World

Yalom (1980) claims that the notion, "It can't happen to me or to mine" is often used by people to cope with the uncertainties of life. Sudden loss tends to shatter this primitive, albeit effective, defense. Without this protection in the mourner's life, he or she may become "rigid, compulsive, frightened, or overprotective in her attempts to defend herself" (Rando 1993, p. 556).

Families faced with the sudden loss of a loved one tend to focus on the current surround rather than on the total life experience. This propensity to focus on the immediate events and relationships at the time of the death may cause the mourner to over-focus on negative aspects of the relationship and circumstance rather than viewing them within the larger context of their total life experience.

This preoccupation with the present surround of sudden death may be of particular concern to the donor's family because so many organ donors are adolescents or young adults who died at an typically turbulent age that can be characterized by conflict and unsettled relationships. When the adolescent died while engaged in questionable or risky activities, the focus on current events and relationships may become a major therapeutic issue. In circumstances of suicide, which is the second leading cause of death for this age group, the family is nearly always left with difficult questions surrounding their loved one's death and their relationship to the victim just prior to death.

The Mourner of Sudden Loss Is at Risk for Post-Traumatic Stress Response

Rando (1993) states that, "implicit traumatic aspects of sudden death can add an overlay of post-traumatic stress symptoms that intensify the mourning experience" (p. 557).

While the suddenness of organ donor deaths place their family members at risk for post-traumatic stress, there are other factors that may heighten that risk. Many donor deaths involve violence, mutilation, preventability, or randomness, and in 70% of the cases, the parental loss of a child. When these risk factors are experienced in combination, expectations for uncomplicated mourning may be unrealistic.

Clinical evidence also suggests that confusion regarding brain death and the realization that parts of their loved one continue to sustain life, as well as other specific factors related to organ donation may constitute added risk for post-traumatic stress for the donor family member.

Types of Sudden Loss

Usually sudden loss brings to mind accidents, homicide, suicide, or other sudden and unexpected events that involve some external force. However, unexpected deaths may also come about as the result of a sudden somatic event.

Sudden Somatic Events

These deaths do not usually involve violence or any form of mutilation, but they retain a sense of trauma in that they are usually considered premature, unexpected, sudden, and in some cases, preventable. These factors may make deaths that occur from sudden somatic events equally traumatic for family members who are left to mourn. An example of this form of trauma might be the cardiac death of a 32-year-old male. For his family, this young man's death can be as traumatic as his accidental death would have been. When a 24-year-old woman collapses with a cerebral aneurysm while being fitted for her wedding gown, the family may be decidedly traumatized. Or when a 15-year-old honor student succumbs to an acute asthma attack, there is no question that her family may perceive this death as traumatic—not just because of the mode of death but also because of the object (a young person) and the prematurity of the death. A large number of organ donors die from sudden, unexpected, somatic events.

Accidental Deaths

Accidents are the leading cause of deaths among all persons between the ages of 1 and 37 (National Safety Council, 1998). This statistic corresponds with the age and mode of death for most organ donors. Accidents are sudden, often violent, preventable, mutilating; sometimes they may involve a child and can include more than one family member. All these characteristics constitute a significant risk factor and contribute to "confusion, anxiety, incomprehensibility, bewilderment, self-reproach, depression, and overwhelming states of psychological and physical shock" of the surviving family members (Rando, 1993, p. 511).

Accidents that are deemed preventable (e.g., drunk driving, negligence) further injure the survivors. Yet, unpreventable accidents carry their own type of stress when there is no one to blame and no appropriate place to direct anger. In such cases, those individuals who are in closest proximity, even those who are attempting to help (e.g., health care professionals, OPO staff, family, and friends) will suffice as targets for anger or rage.

Homicide

According to Rynearson and Geoffrey (1999) death by homicide presents at least three peculiar features that differentiate it from other deaths. First, homicide is violent, forceful, and sudden; second, this form of death is a violation, a transgressive act; and third, homicide involves the intentional act of another human being. Perhaps more than any other death, a homicide "dispels the comforting belief that there is protection from violence and inhumanity. Death in this instance is not 'fair' or peacefully accepted" (Rynearson, 1988, p. 218).

Intense fear, rage, sorrow, and aversive homicide-related thoughts as well as other overwhelming levels of affect may characterize the mourner's grief when a loved one has been murdered. When death comes via a deliberate act, there is a need to affix blame and mete out punishment. There is often a sense of wildness and rage that accompanies the mourner's grief. The dissolution of lifelong assumptions leaves the mourner searching for reasons and causes in an attempt to restore the moral order of the universe in terms of responsibility, blame, and punishment. The mourner strives to regain control and meaning that will provide a sense of safety.

The mourner's rage may be funneled into elaborate fantasies for revenge and contemplations about ways to make the murderer suffer. Such thoughts can come to govern the life of the mourner (Rando, 1993, p. 544). They also may be seen as adaptive.

Anger and the desire for revenge are part of the survivor's struggle to live. By attacking the victimizer, the survivor is energized and for at least a brief period of time is able to escape the realm of inner deadness caused by the homicide (Rando, 1993). According to Lifton (1979), these emotions and the accompanying images of revenge "can also be a way of holding onto a psychic lifeline when surrounded by images of death" (p. 176).

How does the donor's family, whose loved one has been senselessly murdered, relate to donation? How can the enraged, revenge-seeking individual express comfort or solace gleaned from the knowledge that another lives while their own died in such a senseless, preventable, and possibly random fashion? When the mourner's assumptive world has been shattered with a shotgun blast or other violent means, how does he or she perceive the keeper of her loved one's body parts? Is it possible that the deep and abiding anger might spill over to other relationships and be directed toward the hospital, the OPO, or perhaps even to the recipient?

Definitive answers to those questions are not available at this time. However, the longevity and normalcy of homicide survivors' responses further complicate the risks.

> Homicide survivors may present symptomatic behaviors characteristic of post-traumatic stress disorder (PTSD) up to five years following the murder of a loved one. This becomes a normal range of functioning for this distinct population. (Redmond, 1989, p. 52)

Much like the parental loss of a child or loss via suicide, homicide generates a bereavement response that produces a significantly pathological appearance (Rando, 1993). Health care providers and mental health workers must avoid inappropriately labeling this bereavement response pathological.

Fifteen percent of all murders are committed by a family member (Rando, 1993). This is a decidedly complicating variable. When family members identify both with the perpetrator and the victim, the wrenching grief, rage, and desire for retribution are so confusing and overwhelming that it cannot be fully assimilated. Complications may be inevitable when the next of kin, who signs the consent form for donation, is also the perpetrator. A variation on this topic will be discussed further into this chapter.

Suicide

Most bereavement literature agrees that suicide is one of the most difficult deaths that can confront the human family. Many authors claim that grief following a suicide is the worst kind of bereavement experience (Rando, 1993, p. 523; see also Cain, 1972; Strobe & Strobe, 1987; Worden, 1991). This difficult death and the resulting mourning places the survivors at greater risk for physical and mental health problems compared to individuals bereaved due to other causes of death (Rando, 1993). While there are some challenges to this conclusion, there is no argument about the "distinctive aspects of a death by suicide" (Rando, 1993, p. 523).

When the loved one chooses to die, those who are left to mourn must contend with the sequela of sudden loss plus those distinctive aspects related to this form of loss. Those aspects may include heightened anger, guilt and shame, the search for understanding, strong familial and societal reactions, and the need to reframe the death in more acceptable terms.

Shneidman (1972) offers a fitting metaphorical observation:

> I believe that the person who commits suicide puts his psychological skeleton in the survivor's emotional closet—he sentences the survivor to deal with many negative feelings and more, to become obsessed with thoughts regarding his own actual or possible role in having precipitated the suicidal act or having failed to abort it. It can be a heavy load. (p. x)

In addition to dealing with their own reactions, the individuals are left to deal with the reactions of the extended family as well as those of society. The survivor may gyrate between anger, guilt, and shame; each emotion casting its own shadow on his or her grief. This grief, forever laced with unanswerable questions, often leads to guilt and self-blame.

Occasionally, blame is bounced around the family, from member to member. At other times a person is singled out as the scapegoat. Self-blame and blaming others may serve to avoid placing the anger more appropriately: with the deceased loved one. Even when anger characterized the relationship between survivor and the deceased prior to the suicide, many individuals find it annoyingly difficult to sustain any anger toward the deceased following death. Anger does, however, come intermittently. One heartbroken mother, whose son had killed himself, responded to the request for organ donation by saying, "Yes, take them; give them to someone who wants to live." For this mother the comment became a therapeutic issue. However, it could have remained a benign comment, accepted for what it was: an angry statement made in an emotionally charged moment.

Haunting questions that plague survivors of suicide often foster a strong sense of abandonment. A sense of rejection may settle on the mourner's grief. A mother lamented that rejection with this observation: "Loving my son was much like trying to fill a sock with a hole in the toe with sand. Nothing I did or said was enough. In the end, he even rejected my efforts."

When someone chooses to die, there is an intense need to understand. "Why, that question mark twisted like a fishhook in the human heart," (De Vries, 1961, p. 243) takes on a unique and multileveled meaning for those who are left to mourn a chosen death. These questions have to be asked. Mourners usually do not expect answers, for the questions are much deeper than any answers could be. The therapeutic healing comes from the exploration, not from attempts to supply superficial answers. The inability to understand this form of death often feathers into the desperate need to make sense of the loss. "If I can only understand, perhaps I can accept." Eventually acceptance of what cannot be understood, acceptance of the unacceptable, must come for survivors of suicide.

Ironically, the need to deny this mode of death is often as strong as the need to understand. Family members will go to extraordinary lengths to deny what Lazare (1979) terms a "socially unspeakable loss" that generates a conspiracy of silence and fosters social withdrawal. Family members will often attempt to avoid social stigmatization by omitting the cause of death from the obituary, falsifying insurance forms, and lobbying to have death certificates changed. Yet, even in their denial, family members may struggle with guilt and self-blame for the very act that they refuse to recognize.

Secondary Trauma of Media and Legal Involvement

Losses that involve violence attract media and legal attention. The intrusion of the media into the mourner's private world often becomes yet another violation.

Media Involvement

The tabloid mentality of journalism may place the bereaved family's grief into the public arena at a time when they are most vulnerable. Repeated televised viewing of the crime scene, groundless and premature speculations regarding the death, and the exposure of personal family information further compound the family's trauma and complicate their mourning. Both media and legal systems may siphon off attention and energy from the primary task of mourning, creating additional long-term problems for the survivors by delaying or inhibiting legitimate grief reactions.

The media may further complicate the donor family's grief in other more subtle ways. Often the media will investigate a high-profile recipient or donor, opening the door for a breach of privacy that may not be welcomed by either the recipient or the donor family.

Legal Involvement

Difficult to navigate in the best of times, the legal system may challenge the family who is already emotionally overextended. When the donor family becomes involved in this system following the death of their loved one, the difficulties are not only magnified but may be cruelly distorted.

In my clinical experience, three separate homicide cases have involved defense attorneys who argued that their client did not actually kill the patient but that organ donation was responsible for the donor's death. The defense argued that the patient was breathing when he was taken into the operating room and not breathing when he came out, that death occurred in response to the removal of the life-support system following surgical removal of the patient's vital organs. This particularly cruel indifference represented secondary trauma for the families, and in two of the three cases noted above, it exacerbated doubts about their role in consenting to donation.

Medical professionals who contend that the current debate over brain death is of little significance have not considered the implications for survivors who must sit through such hearings in a courtroom. When the debate shifts from the operating room to the courtroom, or when the debate is handed from physicians and ethicists to the hands of a competent attorney who has a vested interest in defending his client, it will be the donor's family who covers the cost.

☐ Preventability or Randomness

There are usually serious repercussions when a mourner believes that the loved one's death could have been prevented. The notion that a death could have been prevented carries an implicit charge that for some reason it was not prevented. The missed opportunity to have avoided this type of death increases it absurdity. "The mourner tends to cope better if the death is construed as unpreventable, whereas the perception of death as preventable appears to increase the duration and severity of grief and mourning" (Rando, 1993, p. 513).

The issue of preventability, so inextricably linked with accidental death, is also a prominent theme for those who mourn the death of a relative by homicide or suicide. These deaths did not have to happen.

Homicides may also involve randomness, which further complicates the mourner's grief. The reality that a loved one died simply because he or she was at the wrong place at the wrong time brings a certain existential terror that sabotages one's protective illusion of control.

For many, it is preferable to believe that one has some control over events, even indicting oneself for allowing the event, rather than choosing to believe that such hateful things can happen in a random world. Self-blame and guilt may seem a high price to pay for maintaining a sense that the world is safe enough to inhabit. Yet, it is the price many people appear willing to pay.

☐ Violence and Mutilation

When death involves violence—as is the case with homicide and suicide and most accidents—there are massive feelings of horror, shock, helplessness, vulnerability, and threat (Rando, 1993). One of the most curious aspects of violence is that it appears to stimulate generalized aggression on the part of the victim. Problematically this aroused hostility conflicts with a sense of conscience and often leads to feelings of guilt or shame (Horowitz, 1997). The hostile family member may be left to deal with not only the loved one's death, his own anger, and the need to blame, but also his feelings of guilt and shame related to his aggressive feelings.

Preoccupation with a Loved One's Suffering

When deaths are particularly violent or mutilating, mourners often report recurrent and intrusive distressing recollections, including images, thoughts, or perceptions. Surviving family members may be preoccupied with issues of suffering. Persistent contemplation about what the death was like and questions such as "Did the loved one know?" "Was she alone?" "Did she call out for me?" offer a haunting backdrop for the survivors of such deaths. Imagined scenes of the loved one's suffering often shadow the mourner. Rando (1993) suggests that these imagined scenarios are often "far more painful for mourners than it actually was for the deceased" (p. 513).

A poignant recollection of such imaging is shared by a family member:

> We held hands weeping aloud when we should have been asleep; mother and daughter mourning together the deaths of husband and daughter; sister and father. I spoke first: "I cannot erase the image of the plane disassembling in the air. Did they know they were going to die? Were they terrified? Did your sister call out for us?" For a while there were only sobs in answer to questions too awful to even contemplate. Quietly then, my daughter spoke. "However much they suffered, Mother, it was but a moment compared to our suffering." (Holtkamp, 1991)

The donor family often struggles with the multiple traumas of violence and mutilation. First with the original trauma of the fatal event, then the extensive, mutilating, and aggressive efforts undertaken first on behalf of the donor, then on behalf of preservation of the transplantable organs.

Youngner (1996) describes organ donation as involving "the mutilation of dead bodies" (p. 52). Wolf (1991) reports that fear of disfigurement is a common theme among donor families. In a study conducted by Australians Donate (1999), when participants were asked their reasons for choosing not to become an organ donor, more individuals indicated concern over disfigurement (13%) than concerns about not really being dead (4.8%) or the fear that "doctors won't try as hard to save me" (4.0%).

Even donor family members who intellectually accept the concept and consequences of brain death, are often afraid that their loved one will suffer pain as the result of donation (Cerney, 1993). These family members may struggle with recurring images of the loved one's suffering and with distressing fantasies of the violence and mutilation forced upon them. When the donated organs are deemed medically unusable (postoperatively) or if, for any reason, the organs are rejected, the donor family's grief may be exacerbated by their disappointment and the reality that they and their loved ones were subjected to donation-related procedures without the anticipated beneficence.

> Eva Leah's brother speaks to the question of reappraisal and doubt related to fear of mutilation: "At first I thought organ donation was a wonderful way of remembering Eva Leah. But then I began having nightmares about her body being cut up and different parts being scattered across the United States. I worried that we might have acted too soon, that she might have felt pain."

While the prevalence of such thoughts in connection with the donation process itself remains unknown, clinical evidence indicates that such preoccupation is not uncommon and may become a therapeutic issue.

☐ The Loss of a Child

Donated organs most often come from individuals who are young enough to leave behind grieving parents. Rando (1986) suggests that, "the loss of a child through death is quite unlike any other loss known" (p. 6). When a child's death is sudden, preventable, random, and violent, as is the case with most donors, the course of bereavement is further complicated by the traumatic mode of the death. Response to even the threat of the loss of a child will be intense from the moment parents become aware of the crisis.

The uniqueness of this loss is characterized by the intensity and duration of the impact on the parents and on other family members.

> Research has documented that compared to other types of bereavement, parental mourning is particularly intense, complicated, and long lasting, with major and unparalleled symptom fluctuations occurring over time. (Rando, 1993, p. 611)

While studies are not conclusive, there is strong evidence indicating that in the third year of bereavement there may be an intensification of the grief experience (Pine & Brauer, 1986). Upsurges of expressive grief during the parent's third year of bereavement represent unique facets of this loss (Rando, 1986). Sanders (1986) reported an extended length of the shock phase of parental mourning, lasting into the second year of grief. This does not mean that parental grief continues to escalate, but rather that there may be pockets of intense grief over time that should not be considered pathological.

Such upsurge of grief in the absence of pathology was eloquently demonstrated for the American public during a televised interview with President George Bush conducted by Sam Donaldson in the fall of 1999. During the interview to promote Bush's new book of personal letters, Donaldson played a brief home movie depicting Bush's small daughter playing happily on the front lawn, shortly before she died at age 4. Visibly shaken, the president wept as he watched the film and tried to comment on the event that had occurred 41 years earlier.

Former President Bush effectively demonstrated an important paradox about the parental loss of a child: Parents may have great grief and go on to live loving and enormously productive lives.

The intensity and duration of parental grief is based in part on the unique bond between parent and child. In our culture, we are personally and socially accountable for the welfare of our children. It is our duty and joy to bring them safely to adulthood. When tragedy destroys what one was so essentially responsible for, parents are multiply victimized.

We are victimized by the realistic loss of the child we love, we are victimized by the loss of the dreams and hopes we had invested in that child, and we are victimized by the loss of our own self-esteem. Not unlike the survivors of concentration camps, we cannot comprehend why we did not die instead. (Kliman, 1977, p. 191)

The bond between parent and child is so strong that the death of that child may be perceived as a personal assault on the parent. Whether parents perceive the death of their child, by any means, as a personal encounter with death that threatens their own survival, warrants close attention.

☐ Survivor's Personal Encounter with Death

When one family member survives and the other is lost, common questions may reflect the guilt experienced by the survivor. "Why did I survive while my loved one died?" or "Why did I not help him survive?" are questions that imply that the survivor has no right to be alive (Horowitz, 1997; Rando, 1993).

Donor family members must often contend with survivor guilt portrayed against a backdrop of vivid images of violence, mutilation, and horror that complicates the mourning process. The risk for traumatic stress response is heightened when the survivor, who also experienced a personal encounter with death, was exposed to graphic scenes of violence, or bears some responsibility for the death, or if suicide or homicide was involved.

The degree of personal danger experienced by the survivor may influence the intensity of the emotional response. However, personal encounters with death need not be limited to actual geographical presence at the scene of the trauma. The vivid imagination and speculation frequently used by survivors to relive the event is often enough to generate complications. With or without a serious threat to the survivor's life, there will be a need to relive the event in order to gain mastery of the trauma (Rando, 1993).

☐ Multiple Loss

By definition multiple loss is traumatic (Rando, 1993). Automobile accidents, as well as domestic and random violence, occasionally claim the lives of multiple family members. Therefore, this particularly tragic death scenario is not unfamiliar among the families of organ donors.

Within the hospital setting, a family who loses more than one of its members, or who lose one member and must also concern themselves with the surviving but injured relatives, may require special attention and support. When several members of a family are involved in a tragedy, numerous variables enter the clinical picture that may complicate the responses from survivors and overwhelm their overall coping ability.

The overwhelming nature of and the unavoidable strain caused by multiple loss is often more than the family and the extended social support system can manage. It is not uncommon for supportive resources to be exhausted long before the grief is. Those who are attempting to help are often traumatized by those same deaths and the overwhelming devastation that follows.

☐ Family Dynamics

Traditionally, the family has been the primary support when one of its members was in need. Figley (1986) considers the family and the natural support system in general important resources to emotional recovery following a traumatic loss. This observation is valid in spite of normative changes within the family system.

Diverse Family Units

As previously noted, the tendency to refer to the donor family as though it is a traditional and unified system is misleading. Indeed, the traditional nuclear family may no longer be the only typical American family. Divorced parents, single parents, warring factions, plus estranged and blended families all constitute family units. Conflict among these units or even among members of one unit may create complications that require additional support, understanding, and patience on the part of the caregiver. However, even highly dysfunctional families may be drawn together to offer one another support in the wake of a common loss.

Varying Perceptions of the Same Event

Although members of a family may experience the same event, they tend to appraise stressful situations quite differently (Fulton & Fulton, 1971). These variations may be attributed to personal sensitivity, interpretations, and vulnerability. The physical and psychological status of the bereaved person and their relationship to the donor, the circumstances of the death, and the individual's support system influence the total experience.

> Personal differences in mourning styles, idiosyncratic courses of bereavement, non-identical needs, and the loss of different relationships despite the death of the same person all can complicate the individual family member's coping, the family's reorganization process, and the systems dynamics and ability to survive the loss. (Rando, 1993, p. 377)

Individual responses within a family system are also determined by how the donor's death fits into that individual's psychosocial framework, their personal expectations, and responses generated by those expectations (Cerney, 1993). Added to these manifold variables are the various opinions and responses to organ donation that may color the mourner's experience. Because of these individual variables, each family member's perception of the stressful event must be considered independently.

While family support is a valuable asset, problems may arise when family members suppress expressive grief out of fear of upsetting one another; or irrational demands are placed on one another (Rando, 1993). The value of family support must also be balanced by the likelihood that members will displace blame, anger, or other hostile feelings onto another member. It would seem that families have the capacity to provide comfort and healing or to reek havoc and create further aggravation of the primary trauma.

Even when harmony exists, family members are seldom fully united in either their perception of the events or the courses of action to be taken following the death. Yet, critical decisions, including the decision to donate the loved one's organs, must be made during this time of heightened emotions and vulnerability. Because the family will influence the mourner and vice versa, it becomes problematic when the more aggressive and verbal family members attempt to persuade the next of kin to make decisions that would not have been made under other less stressful conditions. Choices that are made during severe stress or under duress may be subsequently regretted or at least reconsidered, thereby complicating the individual's grief response.

Complications are bound to surface when family members disagree about the decision made regarding donation. Although the next of kin has the authority to decide for or against donation, extended family members may disagree with that person's decision. The custodial parent may have the legal right to make the decision, exclusive of the other parent's input. While organ procurement organizations are generally hesitant to proceed with donation when one parent objects, it is still legal, in some cases, to require only one parent's consent. These examples of conflict about organ donation are indicative of situations that might provide fertile ground for subsequent complications to take root within the mourning process.

There may be numerous variations of family conflict over organ donation that are not yet uncovered because surveys about the donation experience are generally sent only to the designated next of kin, thereby excluding other members of both the nuclear and extended family.

Secrecy About Donation

Denial or secrecy of the cause of death (e.g., suicide) is "known to produce severe family and individual pathology" (Rando, 1993, p. 530). Secrecy about organ donation may create similar problems within the family system.

Communication between family members is a key element in determining the impact of a death on the family. The emotional costs of keeping the donation a secret may exact a heavy toll on family members' psychological, social, and physical well being.

> In particular, the secret and the fear that the truth will be discovered form the basis for a weighty conspiracy of silence, foster reluctance to share grief and feelings about the death, and aid in the development of strained relationships. . . . (Rando, 1993, p. 530)

When the consenting family member withholds knowledge of their decision to donate from other family members, this secrecy has surprising and often harmful consequences much like those described above by Rando.

> Even prior to John's death as the result of cardiac arrest at age 32, Jennifer had known that her husband wanted to be an organ donor. However, his widowed mother and his siblings could not even bear the thought of donation. When Jennifer made the decision to donate without their knowledge, she did not realize how far-reaching the consequences would be. John's brother and sister had a vested interest in reviewing the autopsy report, which revealed certain genetic aspects of John's heart condition. However, the autopsy report would also reveal the secret donation. Jennifer's refusal to share the autopsy report led to strained relationships between her and her husband's family.

While the strained relationships were difficult, the more critical risk centered on the noninformed family members discovering the donation on their own. Secrecy always adds tension to an already emotionally charged event. Trauma-driven grief needs no further complications.

Family Member Liability

There can hardly be a more lethal variable influencing a family's grief than the culpability of one of its own members for the death of the loved one. When a family member is responsible for the loved one's death, his or her relationship with that family member may be annulled; the loss may be recognized but not the mourner's grief. Deliberate involvement, particularly if the death involved a helpless child, may generate a form of disenfranchised grief that denies even the perpetrator-mourner's right to grieve.

Shelly's story poignantly illustrates disenfranchised grief within a donor family system when there is family member liability:

> Shelly was beautiful, talented, well educated. Jared, her boyfriend had moved in with her over a year ago. Her family was not happy about her decision, but Shelly was in "love" and thought their working relationship was good; not perfect, but good. She worked nights as a critical care unit nurse; he worked days. They took turns caring for Shelly's 4-year-old son, Sam.

> One evening Shelly was called to the ER. Jared met her and told her that Sam had fallen. Doctors told her gently that her little boy was brain dead. They also told her that it was no accident. The police told her the same thing. The extended family who had arrived at the hospital said they weren't surprised. Stunned with disbelief, Shelly was steadfastly defensive of her boyfriend. She wanted her son to be an organ donor. Shelly's mother, an attorney, argued that she wanted the boyfriend to be an organ donor. At that point, the scene got nasty.

> The doctors were angry; nurses and police were angry; Shelly's family was angry. They blamed Shelly as much as Jared. Yet, they blamed themselves as well. Each raged against their own sense of helplessness and failure to prevent this outcome. Shelly became the target for all the frustration and the collective guilt of everyone involved. The loss of little Sam was all too obvious, but Shelly's relationship with her child was annulled; her grief went unrecognized amongst the rhetoric. Support was withheld as penalty for her "complicity." Her isolation was further established by legal counsel who advised against all conversation about the event pending litigation against Jared.

When guilt is in response to actual liability, "the guilty response to the stressor event may, in part, need to be completed by acts that compensate, show remorse, and increase social acceptance by acts of contrition" (Horowitz, 1997, p. 142). When the guilty party is also the next of kin, he or she may perceive some sense of absolution by organ donation while the rest of the family may feel only increased anguish because of what they perceive as the additional and unnecessary plundering of the child's body.

Rando (1993) presents an excellent review of the need for and the complications of grief for an abuser who dies; however, there is scant information about the grief of the individual who deliberately, purposefully causes the death of another. It is as though "what we cannot speak about, we must pass over in silence" (Wittgenstein, 1961).

However, a pivotal question remains to be answered: Do killers ever mourn their victims? The answer is yes. Character flaws or mistakes made in moments of passion seldom protect individuals from grief that may be just as searing as any other. Addressing that grief in a meaningful way and caring for the mourner "without validating the abuse or lessening the culpability of the perpetrator" (Rando, 1993, p. 476) may be exquisitely challenging for the caregiver.

☐ Closing Thoughts

The possibility of an overlay of post-traumatic stress symptoms on the donor family's grief is real. The risk of that possibility increases when death is sudden, preventable, random, involves violence or mutilation, when such death involves a child, or when there is multiple loss. Organ donations come from just such traumatic deaths often producing a trauma-driven grief that leaves shocked and benumbed mourners in its wake.

For some there is little question that donation provides the solace of knowing that something of value came about within the context of their loved one's death and donation. However, there are strong indications that organ donation may constitute another risk factor that portends complicated or traumatic responses from some mourners. One particular complication may involve an aspect of donor family grief that has no parallel: the extension of life of the donor's body parts.

The Organ Donor Family and Recipient Relationship

The characteristics of sudden, traumatic loss provide a backdrop for the donor family experience. The trauma-driven grief of the donor's family is further colored and toned by contextual variables related to the donation of their loved one's organs. There may be serious risks associated with any one of these many variables. With only clinical observations and the knowledge of the impact of traumatic loss to guide us, we must explore a particularly sensitive aspect of the donor family's experience.

When a family member becomes a donor, there will be at least two variables found within the grief of the donor's family that are not found in the experience of any other mourner. First, each organ donor family must come to terms with the neurological death of their loved one and the cognitive dissonance that often accompanies it. Second, the donor family members' grief must incorporate the knowledge that somewhere parts of their loved one's body continue to sustain life. Throughout earlier chapters, we have dealt with the former; the time has come to turn our attention to the latter.

In her article, "Legal Framework for Organ Donation and Transplantation," Sylvia Rodgers (1989) poses a provocative question that continues to resonant throughout the transplant community. "When donor families make an anatomical gift, they are voluntarily giving the gift of life and a gift of hope. Do they have the right to know who receives the gift?"

(p. 846). There is considerable polarization among those who are pondering that question today.

The purpose of this work is not to take sides in this vigorous debate; that would be all too easy. The purpose of this work is to explore the questions surrounding donor family contact with the recipient from a trauma-driven grief perspective. Questions of concern are not whether there should be any contact at all between the donor family and recipient and their kin or whether it should be open or limited and select contact. Within the scope of this work, concern will center on the emotional consequences of donor-family–recipient contact, or the lack thereof, on the traumatized organ donor family.

☐ The Donor Family's Need to Know

Both the donor family and the recipient often express a strong interest in knowing about the other (Fox & Swazey, 1992). Some have observed two critical considerations regarding the donor family's perspective on the subject: "[T]he natural curiosity (and perhaps need) of many donor families to learn about the outcome of their 'gift of life' so as to confirm the soundness of their decision to donate and as a constructive contribution to their coping with grief "(Corr et al., 1994, p. 627).

From the recipient's perspective, Caine and O'Brien (1989) contend that there "are few patients [recipients] who do not experience overwhelming feelings of gratitude towards the donor family and a great desire to let that family know what their generosity of spirit has meant to them" (p. 389).

While these statements mirror clinical experience, it has not yet been proven that communication with the recipient is uniformly constructive in helping the donor family member deal with his or her grief. Furthermore, it seems unlikely that the need to confirm the soundness of their decision or the natural curiosity on the part of the donor family fully accounts for the drive that compels some donor families to find their loved one's recipient and to become involved in their lives.

Conversely, the recipient's need to associate the life-saving gift with a human image and to express appreciation is but a portion of the recipient's often compelling desire to meet the donor's family. Fox (1996) contends that "the desire to learn specific details about the donor also derives from recipient's anxiety about the individual and social attitudes that may have been transposed into their bodies along with the transplanted organ" (p. 254).

The medical community has always been discomfited by the tendency that "on some level below consciousness, recipients experience anthropomorphic concern about whom they have become so closely associated with in this more-than-anatomical way—about the gender, ethnicity, race, religion, education, and social class of the donor, along with his or her moral character and way of life" (Fox, 1996, p. 254). Donor families reciprocate with a keen interest in those who sustain a part of their loved one (Fox & Swazey, 1992).

One reason for this keen interest is "that on preconscious and unconscious levels, [donor families, recipients, and their families] feel that something akin to the transfer of psychic and social as well as biological qualities of self to the other has taken place" (Fox, 1996, p. 256).

The exhortation to care for one another is a value that is shared by many. The core concept of most major religions promotes the giving of oneself for the good of others. Perhaps these long-held values further explain the strong bond that develops between the donor, the recipient, and their families. There is a sense of oneness experienced by recipients and donor families that can be greatly enriching, emotionally and spiritually, for both (Fox & Swazey, 1992). This sense of oneness may also enrich caregivers and others who are more peripheral to the transplant experience.

However, for many others, this experience only presents more troublesome questions about the wonder of this union and its long-term effects on members of the donor's family. While recognizing the spiritual aspects of this gift and the sublime meaning of what is exchanged, the caregiver must not be blinded to the more disturbing, shadowy sides of this new connection.

The juxtaposition of this exquisite gift, filled with literal and figurative meaning, against a backdrop of desolate human sorrow is a seldom-recognized aspect of one of the most sociologically intricate and powerfully symbolic events in modern medicine. Contributing to the emotionality of the donor family experience today is the driving need of many donor families to make contact with *their* recipient.

Although this psychologically intricate, powerfully symbolic and emotionally charged need for donor families to meet the recipients may be based on many factors, the motives of the donor's family members are fueled by two acknowledged aspects of traumatic loss: compulsive inquiry and the search for that which is lost.

Compulsive Inquiry

Rando (1993) reminds the caregiver of the need to recognize "the crucial importance of the mourner's compulsive inquiry into events surrounding the death, the need to assign blame and responsibility, and the search for meaning" (p. 541). Compulsive behaviors serve as a form of self-protection, and each "is intricately related to the need to restore control, predictability, and a sense of justice and order in the world" (p. 541).

Rynearson (1987) speaks of unnatural death involving a variable combination of violence, violation, and volition. He stresses that each is associated with a compensatory psychological response. For instance, violence may precipitate post-traumatic stress, violation generates victimization, and volition results in compulsive inquiry. Clinical experience suggests that compulsive inquiry is a strong presence in the grief of many donor families regardless of whether their loved one's death involved volition. The following story illustrates such compulsive inquiry.

When their child was killed in a single-car crash, the coroner's report indicated a strong odor of alcohol permeating the interior of the car. The parents were distressed because they believed that their daughter did not drink alcohol. "Their need for information was so great that they consulted a spiritualist in hopes of gaining information as to the exact circumstances surrounding the death, a strategy used by 2 other parents" (Kachoyeanos & Selder, 1993, p. 44).

This strong and obsessive need for information occurs independent of antecedent psychopathology or an ambivalent relationship with the deceased. These obsessive inquiries are not necessarily reflections of unconscious conflict, but appear to be the psychologic consequences of overwhelming affect and weakened defenses (Rynearson, 1987, p. 86). Obsessive inquiry is an attempt to make sense of the absurd reality that families are forced to make.

Clinical observations suggest that some organ donor families may extend this compulsive inquiry to events surrounding the donation and post-donation. Often donor family members refer to "parts of the puzzle that are missing" while others note their persistent sense of "something that is incomplete or left undone." This lack of closure and sense of incompleteness often fuels compulsive inquiry regarding events taking place post-donation, including attempts to gather information regarding the recipients of their loved one's organs.

Searching for That Which Is Lost

There is a period of searching and yearning for the deceased, even under normal conditions, that may last for months or even years. The disbelief that death has occurred and an urge to search for and recover the lost person are intrinsic features of normal mourning (Bowlby, 1989). "The searcher still commonly believes, or half-believes, that the dead can be found and recovered" (Aberbach, 1989, p. 7). Bowlby offers ethnological evidence that human and animal responses to loss always involve the urges first to recover the lost object and then to scold it. This response appears to be part of the human being's coping repertoire, even when the separation is known to be permanent—death (Rando, 1993).

Rando (1993) contends that "despite interpretations to the contrary, urges to find, recover, and reunite with the loved one and the feelings and behaviors accompanying these urges—anxiety, yearning, anger, protest, searching—are not pathological" (p. 105); rather, it is a biological and psychological adaptiveness as a response to separation.

The searching behaviors of bereft parents are often more intense than those associated with other types of losses (Gilbert, 1997). This observation may reflect the intense sense of responsibility felt by parents to "bring their child safely into adulthood" (Holtkamp, 1991). In spite of the seemingly useless acts of searching, it *"may serve a vital function in enabling the bereaved to make his peace with the dead"* (Aberbach, 1989, p. 7; emphasis added). Curiously, one donor's mother echoes the sentiment of many others with her observation about making peace with the dead: "We hope that others realize that as we donor families find a piece of our lives [i.e., the recipient], we come to have more peace in our lives" (Anonymous parent, 1995).

The longevity of such yearning and searching for the dead—with complicated mourning that search may never end—may also have peculiar implications for the donor's family because there is an external reference for their search: the recipients of their loved one's organs. For the organ donor's family, who is searching for the lost loved one, the recipient may be seen as a link between the mourner and that which is mourned.

☐ The Theory of Linking Objects

Valmir Volkan (1981) states, "We use objects to represent our psychological wishes and struggles. For instance, children carry teddy bears and security blankets (technically known as transitional objects) as they get to know themselves and their environments" (p. 81). Other objects, such as rosaries or worry beads, may offer the illusion of absorbing our anxiety. Jewels may be used to bolster our self-esteem, club emblems and insignias absorb our anxiety about belonging and longing for acceptance. Just as these objects work to ward off various anxieties, Volkan claims that linking objects may be used to absorb conflicts about loss.

The mourner invests a linking object (usually inanimate) with the ability to maintain the illusion of external contact with the deceased where the mourner can accomplish a magical reunion. Externally sustaining a relationship with the deceased through the linking object allows a mourner to create "functions to save him from the pain of mourning and *of letting the dead die*" (Volkan, 1981, p. 336; emphasis added).

Types of Linking Objects

Rando groups Volkan's linking objects into the five categories listed below.

1. A personal possession of the deceased's (e.g., clothing, or a watch)
2. A gift from the deceased
3. Something of the deceased's used to extend senses or bodily function (e.g., a camera—an extension of sight)
4. A realistic representation of the deceased (e.g., a photograph)
5. Something that was at hand when the mourner initially learned of the death or saw the body—in other words, something that could be considered a "last minute object" (e.g., the record that was being played when the mourner received notification) (Rando, 1993, p. 127).

Objects such as these are not to be confused with mementos or keepsakes that are benign in nature. Defining the difference between mementos and linking objects may rest in that hard-to-describe area between choice and compulsion (Volkan, 1981). Another definitive difference is that mementos or keepsakes are not usually imbued with magical powers of connection—linking objects are. Symbolically, linking objects stand for aspects of both self-and-object and form a "symbolic bridge (or link) to the representation of the dead" (Volkan, 1981, p. 20).

The belief that the object can provide a meeting place for a reunion of the mourner with the one he mourns may be adequate motivation for its establishment (Volkan, 1981), and because the object is used to keep the grief externalized, its whereabouts is crucial to the mourner, who jealousy guards it. More importantly, "if something happens to the linking object so that it can no longer absorb the grief, the mourner is deprived of his or her defense and painful emotions can come crashing in" (Volkan & Zintl, 1993, p. 24). This aspect of a linking object has immediate and obvious relevance to the donor's family members who attempt to use the recipient as a link to the donor.

According to Rando, linking objects as defined by Volkan (1981) are "tokens of triumph over the loss and . . . they mark a blurring of the psychic boundaries between the mourner and the one mourned. It is as if the representation of the two persons, or parts of them, merge externally through the use of these objects" (Rando, 1993, p. 127).

Volkan and Zintl (1993) describe a linking object as psychologically hot for the mourner because it revives some conflict about the loss and what the loss took from him. Volkan continues by describing how we "re-create the relationship in the external world, to recapture the vitality and the *conflict*" (p. 80) through the use of linking objects. When the linking object provides a psychological meeting ground for a reunion between the mourner and the one mourned, the mourner may seek to restore the lost love and then eventually resolve the ambivalence that characterized his relationship with the deceased in her lifetime (Volkan, 1981). These observations are particularly thought provoking if applied to a donor family's relationship with a recipient.

"Linking objects play the song of the relationship. Ironically, they also keep mourners from adapting and moving on with life" (Volkan, 1993, pp. 80–81). The pathological aspect of linking objects resides in the premise that when the mourner has an external reference (i.e., the linking object) the painful work of mourning remains unresolved.

Living Linking Objects

Continuing bonds with the deceased are known to exist. Klass, Silverman, and Nickman (1996) describe bereaved individuals who actively experience the continuing presence of their loved one. Except in cases where pathology is apparent or was present prior to the loss, it is not considered unusual when otherwise intact mourners report seeing, hearing, feeling, or smelling their deceased loved one. These events act as a connection to the deceased and appear to be meaningful and comforting to the survivors. However, when these continuing bonds are personified rather than internalized there may be additional risk for aborting the mourner's grief. Personification may be established with an inanimate or living object.

Volkan (1981) acknowledges that a living person may serve as a linking object and describes a replacement child as such a link between a mourner and the child mourned. According to this theory, "replacing a child with another allows the parents partially to deny the first child's death. The replacement child then acts as a barrier to the parental acknowledgement of death, since the real child exists, who is a substitute" (p. 319). This living replacement child becomes the "embodied meeting place" (p. 321).

The death of a loved one places the bereaved family under severe stress and when individuals are under such stress the capacity of the secondary-process or rational thinking is attenuated and primary-process thinking, a magical type of thinking, breaks through. "Primary-process thinking is carried out more through pictorial, concrete images; representation by allusion or analogy is frequent; and *a part of an object may be used to stand for the whole*" (Youngner, 1996, pp. 34–35; emphasis added). A part of the donor does continue to contain life in another human being. Could this part be used to stand for the whole?

As noted elsewhere, donor families feel that some kind of transfer of psychic and social attribute and biological qualities of the donor takes place during transplantation. Since the recipient literally contains a part of the deceased loved one, would that recipient be perceived as an embodied meeting place? Fox and Swazey's (1992) description of a sense of oneness that donor families, recipients, and their families often experience may intimate a form of union between the parties. Might the recipient become an "embodied meeting place" (Volkan, 1981, p. 321), or serve as "a symbolic bridge between the mourner and the deceased" (p. 371), or even "mark a blurring of psyche boundaries between the mourner and the one mourned" (Rando, 1993, p. 127).

Is it plausible that a recipient might, perhaps, rekindle the song of the relationship with its vitality and the conflict? Is it possible for the recipient of the loved one's organs to be a representation of the two persons or parts of them? The obvious complications for the recipient that might arise from being used as a place of reunion between the mourner and the one mourned are overwhelming. But what are the consequences for the family members of the organ donors?

Is it possible that on an unconscious level a donor family member might imbue the recipient with magical powers of connection with the deceased? Might it be imagined that the donor family could invest the recipient with "power to maintain the illusion of external contact with the deceased and with which the mourner can magically accomplish reunion" (Rando, 1993, p. 124)?

We do not know; but there could hardly be a more appropriate phrase to describe a recipient than a "token of triumph over the loss." While Volkan believes the recipient may serve as living linking object, he cautions that we "would need to conduct in-depth psychodynamic interviews with members of donor families, or have some of them in psychodynamic psychotherapy in order to 'prove' that [these clinical observations] are correct" (V. Volkan, personal communication, February 22, 1995).

Hypothetical complications materialize into reality if the donor family member uses the linking object (the recipient) "to recreate the relationship in the external world, to recapture the vitality and the *conflict* of the relationship." If the conflict within the pre-morbid relationship of donor and donor family member collides with the "rage against those who are exempt" (Horowitz, 1997, p. 20; emphasis added), the song of the relationship—so much a part of the linking object relationship—may be less than harmonious.

While Volkan (1981) and others (Rando, 1993; Worden, 1991) contend that the use of linking objects is pathological in that they delay or inhibit the mourning process, the pivotal questions for organ donor families may center on the two variables which separate linking objects from mementos or keepsakes: Is the family member's attachment to the recipient motivated by choice or compulsion, and how much magical power does the donor family member assign the recipient?

A definitive answer about the use of recipients as linking objects is not available at this time. However, when compulsive inquiry, fueled by searching behaviors, is ignited by an individual's inability to accept the death of his or her loved one, the risks appear staggering.

☐ Donor-Family–Recipient Communication

According to Fox and Swazey (1992), it was not unusual during the early years of human organ transplants for medical teams to reveal the identities of the donors of cadaver organs, their recipients, and their families to one another. These individuals were often provided with details about each other's backgrounds and lives. The thinking at that time reflected the physician's belief that the participants in transplantation—both the givers and the receivers—were entitled to such information.

Moreover, the physicians believed that such information would enhance the meaning of the transplant experience for the recipient and recipient's family while affording the donor family some degree of consolation and a sense of completeness. With increased clinical experience, transplant teams became uncomfortable about "the way in which recipients, their kin, and donor families personified cadaver organs, and about how many of them not only arranged to meet but tried to become involved in each other's lives as if they were indebted and related to one another (Fox & Swazey, 1992, p. 37). The earlier sanctioned interactions became major factors that led most transplant units to establish a policy of anonymity and confidentiality that persisted until quite recently. Many members of the transplant community continue to believe that it was in the best interest of both donor families and recipients not to meet or even communicate.

Although the policy of anonymity and confidentiality was primarily intended to protect donors and recipients against some of the side effects that such transplants can engender, there is the possibility that the policy of anonymity may have helped transplant teams to maintain emotional stability by insulating them from the stories of the donors and the tragic ways in which they died (Annas, 1988, as cited in Fox & Swazey, 1992). Anonymity also protected the transplant teams "from close encounters with the animistic, magic-infused thinking about transplanted organs in which the givers and receivers of cadaveric organs often engage" (Fox & Swazey, 1992, p. 43).

Throughout the 1990s opposition to the anonymity protocols of most organ procurement organizations came under strong criticism, primarily from a small but vocal group of organ donor families. The demand of open communication between donor families and recipients affirmed the observation that "donor family members often feel a strong need to search for the person in whom a part of their close relative continues to function and to sustain life" (Fox, 1996, p. 256). Like the early physicians, family members of donors were saying that it would offer "consolation and a sense of completeness to the donor family" (Fox & Swazey, 1992, p. 37) to have updates on the recipients and to even have access to the recipient.

Current Trends

The current trends are well defined in a news release on July 27, 1997, by a task force led by the National Kidney Foundation (NKF). The news release revealed specific guidelines for communication between donor families and recipients. Margaret Coolican, chairman for the National Donor Family Council, stated: "The guidelines are based on the belief that donor families and recipients have the right to choose whether they wish to communicate with each other, and health care professionals are in a position to make these opportunities available to both parties" (p. 1).

Considerable thought and preparation went into developing these guidelines, which are quite thorough. Presented here is the abbreviated version of those guidelines taken from the National Kidney Foundation's July 1997 news release.

National Communication Guidelines

At the time of consent to donation, health care professionals should offer an opportunity to donor families and transplant candidates to receive follow-up information about the donor or recipient at a designated time after transplantation.

Special attention should be paid to the wishes of those who do not want to receive such follow up information. They should be assured that all personal information will be kept confidential.

Donor families and recipients who do not wish to receive information should be informed by health care professionals that they can change their decision on this matter and obtain additional information at any time in the future.

Within one month of donation, health care professionals should provide donor families and recipients who wish to receive it, a written report confirming which organs and tissues were procured and information on age, gender, geographic region, occupation and family information, along with cause of death or illness.

If the intended recipient is unwilling to accept written communication, health care professionals should retain it in their files and inform the authors that their communication has not been forwarded for this reason.

If members of donor families and transplant recipients wish to disclose their names and/or addresses in order to communicate directly via phone, e-mail or in person that disclosure should be accomplished by mutual agreement of both parties. Direct communication should take place without the assistance of the health care professionals, unless they are wanted by the participants.

These voluntary guidelines are intended to provide transplant and procurement professionals basic systems for providing information to donor families and transplant recipients and establishing methods of allowing donor families and transplant recipients to communicate with each other. (p. 2)

☐ Risk Factors Related to Lack of Communication

The National Guidelines for Communication are both thoughtful and thought provoking. Yet, when viewed from a bereavement perspective, one intricate question in this process remains unsettled: How do families cope with the knowledge that the recipient is unable or unwilling to communicate?

Perceived Lack of Appreciation

Clinical experience suggests that donor families frequently perceive this unwillingness to communicate as a lack of appreciation for or an insult to the donor.

> When Trudy was told that the recipient of her son's heart had declined written communication, she was devastated. "He has my son's heart," Trudy wailed, "How could he [the recipient] refuse to write or even read my letters?"

Human error may also foster a sense of being unappreciated. A donor parent addresses this issue:

> Why aren't transplant recipients encouraged to acknowledge donor families? Three years ago, we donated our daughter's organs and tissues and were frustrated as letters we wrote went unanswered. After a year we learned that our letters had not been forwarded! Fortunately a caring coordinator sent them. The heart recipient responded immediately, and now we enjoy a wonderful friendship. Had this not been the result, we could all bid farewell. We still hope to hear from the other recipients and wish them good health and happiness. (Anonymous parent, 1995)

The suspicion that the donor's gift was not appreciated may receive curious reinforcement through the media. Appealing cases that involve a donor family member being united with the recipients of her loved one's organs are often thought to be good promotion for organ donation and, one might add, a boost for television ratings as well. While pictures of this donor-family–recipient meeting are relayed on national television, thousands of other families across the country, much like Trudy and her family, are left to ponder: "That donor family gets to meet their recipients and we didn't even get a thank you card from ours." This perceived lack of appreciation further traumatizes the donor family and may even contribute to ambivalence regarding their decision to donate. Even well-thought-through guidelines for donor-family–recipient communication cannot guarantee equity.

Privacy Issues

Media efforts to promote organ donation and boost ratings are not necessarily wrong or harmful, but some dramatic appeals have had a curiously unexpected and significant impact on organ donor families. When the donor family or the recipient declines to communicate, either may experience undue pressure to oblige the other, and the gift they once believed that they had given or received anonymously becomes a media issue rather than a private matter. Such breached confidentiality may compromise the well being of either party.

> The newspaper article reported the story of John, a man in his mid-50s who had received a heart transplant two months earlier. John wanted to meet the donor's family. He made impassioned pleas in the newspaper and on local television. The heart donor's wife, Joy, had known from the beginning who had received her husband's heart and chose not to have any contact.
>
> A year later, on the anniversary date of his transplant, the newspaper and TV channel did a follow-up story of John and his first year with his new heart. His sincere pleas to meet with his benefactor's family were even more intense. Joy called to ask if this man's health depended on communication with her and her family. When she was assured that it did not, and that she must do what was right for her and her family, she responded: "I'm glad he's well. I understand he's grateful. But that's all I need to know. I don't want a relationship with this man. I want to grieve for the loss of my husband and then get on with my life without additional complications."

To the outside observer, this problem may seem easily resolved; it was not. It's seldom easy when one party's needs conflict with the needs of another. Intrusive media coverage in the name of the public's right to know or to boost ratings may have ominous overtones for all trauma families. However, for organ donor families this intrusion may have far-reaching consequences related to their right to privacy, boundary issues, and other unique concerns that impact recovery from their loss.

Perceived Lack of Closure

Donor families may speak of a lack of closure attending their grief. Some have summoned the courage to speak about this matter and share with great honesty their subterranean feelings, their grief and their need to meet their loved one's recipient. One courageous mother eloquently shares such thoughts in a public presentation:

> David . . . my youngest son was 19 when his lung collapsed. The doctor said he thought [David] might have Marfan's Syndrome. We were told that, if

this was the case. There was nothing that could be done for him, just not to expect a long life.

Just short of his 21st birthday, he slipped into a coma. A week before he died, he said, "Mum, if anything happens to me, would you just make sure I'm brain dead . . . and if there are any body parts they need, let them have them because once I'm brain dead I won't need them any more."

That has weighed very heavily on me ever since because I was never given the opportunity to be sure for myself. I had to take the doctor's word that he was "brain dead."

At first, it was a great comfort to us all that David's kidneys and liver were able to be used to help give 3 other people a chance to live and have a healthier life.

But as the numbness of David's death wore off and was replaced by emptiness I began to feel the pain of not having completed the circle of life. BIRTH . . . LIFE . . . DEATH . . . BURIAL . . . of the whole *person*.

I'm no longer able to touch my son, but there are parts of him still here and I'm not allowed to have any contact with them. I feel fragmented. Incomplete. There are pieces missing and I can't find them.

I've kept in contact with the [procurement] coordinator over the years, and have had a "thank you" note from one of David's recipients *for which I will be forever grateful.*

Late last year I rang the coordinator and asked her to find out how all of David's recipients were, because I had a feeling one was not well. She rang me back and told me one chap was going through a particularly rough patch but the others were doing very well. My mind was never off him. I worried about him, but felt lost, inadequate because there was nothing I could do to help him.

Just prior to Easter this year, I suffered quite severe chest pains for several days. I thought I was having a heart attack. That was followed by deep depression often sobbing uncontrollably. At the time, I could see no reason for what was happening to me. I felt devastated like I had lost David all over again and I was grieving. I wasn't coping very well at all!

Eventually, I rang my coordinator and told her I was worried about one of David's recipients. I felt he wasn't well and could she please let me know how he was. She rang back the next day to say he had died of a heart attack around Easter but he had had 3 good years, thanks to David's kidney which hadn't let him down and the others were doing very well.

Although I was happy to know that this man had had 3 good years with the help of David's kidney, I felt relieved to know WHY I'd been SO depressed and why I had the chest pains but most of all I had found one of my "MISS-ING PIECES."

You see, when I gave birth to David, I gave birth to a whole person. All his "PARTS" are a part of me and they always will be.

One of David's recipients is now only 4 years old and she will hopefully live a long and healthy life which has made me realize that as long as I live I will always feel there is a part of me missing somewhere out there in someone else. I can't embrace them. I can't share the joys in their life. I can't show them how very happy I am that they're still here. I can't be, in anyway, a part of their lives.

It is an ache that never goes away! An emptiness that can't be filled. A jigsaw puzzle with now 2 pieces missing!

I am incomplete!

—Jeanette Tyers, 1999

A "jigsaw puzzle with pieces missing" and a mother's pain that is palpable. Though problems may arise within the context of donor families meeting recipients, for some individuals, there is also a sense of incompleteness and a lack of closure when they are kept from the recipient. The paradox is stunning: That which is uplifting may also provoke great anxiety.

Fractured Fantasies and the Theory of Equivalency

Some families have reported that in making their decision to donate they had to envision a potential recipient. The fantasized recipient was generally a child of the same sex as the donor (Simmons, Klein, & Simmons, 1987).

O'Neill (2000) originated the term the "theory of equivalency" to describe the assumption by donor families that their loved one's donated organs will be allocated to recipients bearing similar sociodemographic characteristics to those of the donor. This assumption is evident when parents state that they donated so that other parents would not have to experience a loss such as ours. Yet statistics reveal that 75% of donated hearts come from males aged 18–27 years, while the majority of heart recipients are males in their 50s (United Network for Organ Sharing, 1997). Because donated organs in the United States are allocated primarily on the criteria of medical urgency and biological compatibility rather than efficiency or equivalency, disappointments are inevitable.

O'Neill (2000) argues that the theory of equivalency is not limited to equivalent age and may extend to equivalent sex, social class, race, ethnicity, social values, religion, and interests—the same components on which relationships usually are based. The kinds of information sought by the donor family, such as the donor's sex, age, race, height, weight, martial status, education, religion, personal qualities, and life history, may fuel their disappointment when the recipient does not measure up to their fantasized version.

Disappointment is another one of those hard-to-measure dimensions of human life that may be relatively benign or a serious component of grief. Such disappointment may do little to "confirm the soundness of [the family's] decision to donate" and scarcely provides a "constructive contribution to their coping" (Corr et al., 1994, p. 627). Peripheral issues siphon away energy needed to mourn and there are usually consequences for the mourner.

The Age Issue

The debate about allocation of transplantable human organs has been governed by two principles that divide the transplant community. "The first, maximize efficiency, would favor recipients for whom a transplant would ensure the highest chance of living a long and high quality life. The second, urgency of need, favors allocating organs to those who are the sickest and most likely to die" (Caplan & Coelho, 1998, p. 247). There are ethical dilemmas with either principle. Those who are young, otherwise healthy, and who have not already had a transplant would benefit from a policy that favored efficiency. "Those who are older, are at death's door due to the failure of a previous transplant or artificial organ or even a previous xenograft would go to the head of the waiting list on a policy sensitive to medical urgency and patient need" (p. 247). As previously noted, the system in the United States relies more on medical urgency than efficiency.

Caplan and Coelho (1998) offer a curious apologist remark in an attempt to repute the notion that the rich and famous get preferential treatment with respect to getting transplants. Such practice, they claim, compromises a fundamental principle held by the medical community that organ donations are based solely on potential medical benefits without regard to nonmedical factors. Yet, they concur that only those who can pay or have insurance are allowed on waiting lists in the first place. Apparently, the lack of money is not perceived as a nonmedical factor.

Regardless, after a potential recipient has either insurance or enough cash, organs are typed and matched with the sickest individual who would be most likely not to reject that organ. Blood and tissue typing, urgency of need, time spent on the waiting list, and distance between the donor and the transplant center are the only factors that are supposed to be considered in allocation of organs (Caplan & Coelho, 1998).

The method of allocating human organs in this country has a decided impact on many donor families. A donor mother, Elizabeth, shares her thoughts about how this system altered her grief and her attitude about organ donation.

> I had somehow expected the recipient of my 15-year-old daughter's heart to be relatively close to her own age. I had taken comfort from the knowledge that somewhere in the world, when life was no longer an option for my child, another child would live.

> When I learned that my daughter's heart was transplanted in a 62-year-old man, I was crushed. My daughter's heart didn't extend the life of a young person who was standing on the precipice of life, but extended the life of an old man who had already lived four times longer than my daughter—a man who had not particularly taken good care of himself—who had no chance to give this precious gift the long life it might have had if it had been transplanted into a younger recipient.

Hard questions are being asked about allocation. "What if a patient is directly responsible for his or her organ failure? What if a person has abused drugs or alcohol and thereby caused organ failure? What if they smoke or are morbidly obese or have a criminal record? What role does fault play in the allocation of scarce resources?" (Caplan & Coelho, 1998, p. 248). What role does fault play in the grief of the organ donor family?

As noted in Elizabeth's lament, the age of the recipient is not the only variable that may disturb the donor family. There are troublesome and delicate factors related to allocation that must be addressed from a bereavement perspective. Some of these factors may relate to the lifestyle of the recipient, others to race.

The Racial Issue

In this country, there is some polarization between races. We can deny it if we choose, but denial does not change reality. We are imperfect people. And, when individuals have strong feelings about organs staying within their own race, equally strong emotional responses should be expected when they do not.

In spite of the fact that "in kidney transplantation (which accounts for 75 percent of all organ transplants and about 84 percent of those awaiting a transplant), the probability of a match between the donor and the recipient within the same racial group is greater than between racial groups" (Reitz & Calender, 1993, p. 354), African Americans still fear that donation is for the benefit of the White population.

However, "in a 1982 study taken at the [Howard University Hospital Transplant Center in Washington, D.C.], where the patient population is 95 percent black . . . 41 of 47 cadaveric organs (80 percent) used for kidney transplantation were donated by non-blacks" (Reitz & Callender, 1993, p. 354). Interestingly, the study at Howard University indicated there was significant concern over the negative implications of cross race transplants. "A significant number of respondents preferred not to cross racial barriers because they felt the black kidney was superior" (Reitz & Callender, 1993, p. 354).

There was no report related to the response of the 41 non-Black donor families in this study to determine their feelings about crossing the racial barriers.

None of this should matter. Indeed, organ transplantation should squelch any racial bias among us. It should be the great equalizer. Unfortunately, we remain a flawed, biased, and polarized society—and we are foolish to think that denying this issue will lessen its impact on some donor family members' grief. It would most definitely be an issue in some donor-family–recipient contacts, either for the donor family, the recipient, her family, or all of the above.

The expressed interest of the donor family and the recipient and his or her family in the details of one another's lives, the desire to know about the gender, ethnicity, race, religion, education, and social class, as well as moral character of one another implies that these factors matter.

The Diverse Lifestyles Issue

The donor family and the recipient and his or her family do not always share the same reality. People live very different lifestyles. They have different values, different beliefs. A person's belief system helps determine their response to the fault factor.

When a celebrity, who was as well known for his alcohol problem as he was for his talent, received a liver transplant, the publicity surrounding the event allowed the family of the donor to discover that their loved one's liver had gone to this individual.

In his uncle's words, "My 20-year-old nephew died through no fault of his own. He was murdered as he withdrew $20.00 from an automatic teller machine. Now we learn that his liver went to some old, drunken reprobate. That's just not what his parents had in mind when they donated his organs."

Such comments may sound harsh to the bereavement-impaired public. Crucial to comprehending the uncle's reaction is the knowledge that traumatic loss stirs aggressive responses from family members. Homicide generates rage. Rage that the young die and the old live; rage that people sometimes are responsible for their own organ failure; rage at our helplessness; rage at the source; rage at those who could not prevent this loss; even rage against those who are exempt.

The question of differing values may take many forms. Pennington's (1998) article, *Public Information and Transplantation from a Recipient's Point of View*, was intended to point out the unethical attempts by the media to obtain the name of a celebrity's liver donor. In reality it stirred other consternation. "In the case of Linda Machiano ('Linda Lovelace') of 'Deep Throat' notoriety, a tabloid offered $5,000 for the identity of her liver donor" (Pennington, 1988, p. 1037).

It would require little insight or imagination to understand the consternation that a parent might feel upon learning that the recipient of their child's liver is a former well-known pornographic film star. Nor should it be surprising to the caregiver when this issue presents complications within the donor family's grief response.

If we are to recognize and address the reactions and responses of donor family members to fractured fantasies that often accompany the donation of a loved one's organs, it will be necessary to understand the trauma-driven grief that governs those responses. It would be imprudent for policies and procedures to disregard the powerful emotions experienced by the donor family and recipient and the variables that may exacerbate these emotions.

Emotional Instability of Family Members

The premorbid emotional stability and stamina of the donor family member is a significant determinant in how he or she copes with trauma (Cerney, 1993). Transplant candidates are required to undergo a psychological assessment as part of the medical evaluation to determine his or her suitability to receive an organ transplant. There are no such considerations for members of the organ donor's family or for the recipient's kin. Yet, preexisting mental illness, personality disorders, or other dysfunctional characteristics are just as well represented within these populations as they are generally.

Emotional or adaptational problems may not be evident prior to the emotionally vulnerable donor family member becoming involved with the recipient and his or her family. However, when emotional liabilities exist, it should not be difficult for seasoned clinicians to envision some of the complications that might arise when these highly traumatized and emotionally fragile people meet and become involved with one another. The outcome of such a union would be further complicated if the donor family member holds a proprietary attitude toward the donated organ.

The Responsibility to Address Complications

Psychological traumas can precipitate diverse hysterical symptoms such as recurrent hallucinations, emotional outbursts, and other sensory or motor disturbances, even in the absence of preexisting mental illness. A latent period between the occurrence of a stressful event and the onset of symptoms or psychic numbing that is so much a part of traumatic stress may mask serious emotional disturbances. This latency period as well as the recognition that "once symptoms formed . . . there was a remarkable tendency toward reoccurrence or persistence long after the event's termination and its immediate effects" (Horowitz, 1997, p. 15), confirms the need for caregivers and policymakers to consider the labile emotional status of the traumatized donor family.

Each discipline must consider the haunting question that hovers when the specter of meetings between the donor's family and recipient materialize. Who is designated or at least available to help the more vulnerable, sometimes fragile individuals when complications arise?

Whoever claims that responsibility must be aware of the ramifications of communication and contact between the donor family and the recipient. Issues to be explored with the donor family member should include:

- specific motivation for such relationships,
- the basis for such a relationship,
- the status of family member's ability to cope with their own grief,
- the intensity of the donor family member's attachment to the recipient,
- potential complications that might arise if the recipient dies,
- fantasies that might be unmet by the relationship and how the donor family member might respond to such disappointments, and
- the capacity of the bereaved family member to make thoughtful decisions.

☐ Mystical Ideations and the Donor Family

In the earlier days of organ transplantation, the powerful emotions and the human dynamics of the gift exchange were recognized. In spite of some discomfort in the way "donor families personified cadaver organs and about how many of them not only arranged to meet but tried to become involved" (Fox & Swazey, 1992, p. 37) with the recipient's life as if they were indebted and related to one another, health care professionals at least acknowledged these phenomena. "They also took active steps to help donors, recipients, and their families deal with them, often with the consultant help of psychiatrists and psychiatrically trained medical social workers" (Fox, 1996, p. 262).

In some cases, the donor family member may exhibit a proprietary interest in the donated organ. On an intellectual level, the heart of their loved one may be acknowledged as simply a vital body part. This cognitive belief is often held in tandem with a sense that the essence of the donor's self or personhood had been transmitted along with the organ. This less cogent thought process drives close relatives of a cadaver donor to seek out the recipient and, especially with heart transplants, "to relate to this person as if he or she embodied the living spirit of the donor" (Fox & Swazey, 1992, p. 41).

The risk of retaining a proprietary grasp on the donated heart is but one possible complication: The enticement to attribute to this recipient the magical powers of connection, the embodied meeting place for reunion with the deceased, could be irresistible.

In such cases, when the donor family's drive to make personal contact confronts the recipient's overwhelming need to express his or her gratitude and to know more about the donor from whom the organ came, complications may arise not only for the donor but for the recipient as well. They may become enmeshed in a debtor-creditor vise that prevents closure.

Much less attention is now paid to human dynamics involved in the transplantation process. But it is a mistake to assume that because transplantation has become so commonplace and routinized, it no longer evokes the powerful positive and negative gift-associated reactions in donors, recipients, and their families (Fox & Swazey, 1992). Rather, it may be suggested that because physicians are less likely to perceive the psychosocial aspects of transplantation as problematic as previously thought, psychiatrists and medical social workers are less likely to be active members of transplant teams. Because of this trend, the risks involved in tangled relationships between the donor's family and the recipient are less likely to be perceived.

Curiously, some psychosocial aspects of organ transplantation that were once considered problematic are now publicly recognized as moving and inspiring events that affirm the miracles of the gift of life. The need of donor families to meet and become involved with the person who received the loved one's organs is one example of such reverse thought. A romanticized version of such a meeting may be found in Lee Gutkind's (1988) *Many Sleepless Nights*.

> Dick Becker, Richie's father, has never gotten used to the death of his only son, to whom he was so faithfully devoted. . . . This unfortunate and pervasive reality was especially apparent one Sunday in Charlotte, North Carolina, when I brought together, all in one room, Richie Becker's parents, Dick and Sharon, along with the recipient of Richie's heart and lungs, Winkle Fulk and her husband Dave. . . . At the end of the evening, just before we were about to say goodbye and return to the motel . . . Dick Becker stood up in the center of the living room of his house, paused, and then walked slowly and hesitantly over toward Winkle Fulk. . . . He eased himself down on his knees, took Winkle Fulk by the shoulder and simultaneously drew her closer, as he leaned forward and placed his ear gently but firmly first between her breasts and then at her back. Everyone in that room . . . was suddenly and silently breathless, watching as Dick Becker listened for the last time to the absolutely astounding miracle of organ transplantation: the heart and lungs of his dead son Richie, beating faithfully and unceasingly inside this stranger's warm and living chest. (pp. 356–359)

In some cases it appears that donor families and recipients meet to their mutual benefit. Indeed, there is a spiritual quality that is palpable within such meetings. Many individuals are able to accept donation as a gift; recognizing that the organs given in compassion are no longer part of the child or other loved one that has died. These individuals can meet with and communicate with recipients with apparent ease. For others the inability to let the dead die prolongs and complicates an already difficult tragedy.

☐ Closing Thoughts

Clinical observations have reinforced the belief that what donor family members confide in therapeutic settings varies significantly from what they say in public. Obviously, a clearer understanding of mystical and psychosocial aspects of the donor family's drive to become involved with the recipient is required before definitive assessments are attached to behaviors that appear unhealthy or even macabre.

The potential for macabre scenarios will only increase as the latest advances in transplantation become routine. On January 17, 2000, it was reported on national television (Good Morning America, 2000) that a man in France had received a double transplant of both forearms and hands. Any proprietary interest on the part of the donor's family could be devastating for everyone concerned in this remarkable case. The fact that the deceased person's hands and arms live and function attached to another human being surely must have some consequences for the donor's family about which we may only speculate.

CHAPTER

Therapeutic Concerns and Donor Family Trauma

The traumatic death of the donor sets the stage for a host of potential complications. As the donor family drama plays out, the complexities surrounding organ donation assume various roles to provide unique content and substance for their grief. Like other victims of traumatic loss, donor families struggle with the rupture of long-standing assumptions about life—and even about death. Coping strategies are challenged, defenses are overwhelmed, and the family's sense of security may be breached as simple trust vacates when suspicion moves in.

The impact of traumatic deaths that result in organ donation may leave the family member with an overlay of post-traumatic stress symptoms. When such symptoms are present, they must be addressed first in order to get to the underlying grief. This chapter considers the overlay of post-traumatic stress symptoms and the basic working assumptions related to trauma. Common themes of trauma are explored, along with specific themes related to donor family grief. Each topic is examined to determine and explore any content differences related specifically to the experience of organ donation.

☐ Post-Traumatic Stress

The DSM-III considers the defining feature of post-traumatic stress disorder (PTSD) as the development of characteristic symptoms following a psychologically distressing event that is outside the range of usual human experience. The text continues by stating that the most common traumas involve either a serious threat to one's life, a serious threat or harm to one's children, spouse, or other close relatives and friends (APA, 1987).

Two defining features of post-traumatic stress are recurrent and intrusive recollections alternating with a diminished capacity to respond to the external world. Intrusive recollections contain powerful and expansive varieties of responses that include searing grief, intense guilt or anxiety, and rage that may be diffuse or focused. Intrusive material may be referred to as expressive grief while diminished responsiveness is considered psychic numbing. Donor families sometimes use the more picturesque expression of emotional anesthesia. Both responses will need to be worked though in order to reach a point of spontaneous healing.

☐ Working Assumptions Related to Trauma

Basic working assumptions about trauma readily apply to the trauma-driven grief experienced by members of the donor's family. These assumptions, adapted in part from Lindy's (1986) work, will provide a frame of reference for the caregiver as they seek to understand the aftershocks of trauma. With this understanding, the therapist may then prepare the survivor for what has happened, what is happening, and what may happen in the future.

Traumatic death may leave the survivors with an overlay of post-traumatic symptoms. These symptoms are like a blanket covering the mourning.

Defenses, such as splitting and disavowal, are often erected to prevent the feared reinstitution of the state of psychic traumatization. This is a state of over-control; denial has the upper hand and is characterized by psychic numbing (Lindy, 1986). "Psychic numbing is at the heart of the traumatic syndrome" (Rando, 1993, p. 584). In situations of acute trauma, this psychic response is neither voluntary nor conscious. This numbing initially helps the survivor by acting as a protective shield. However, its adaptive quality is lost when it persists.

Intrusive or repetitive reactions may surface when the psychic numbing is breached. These intrusive reactions involve a wide variety of forms. There may be repetitive feelings or obsessional ideas related to the original trauma. Unbidden thoughts, images, or nightmares related to the traumatic event may be emotionally disruptive for the survivor. Behavioral reenactments of portions of the experience are also common. Such reenactments may include compulsive verbalizations about the trauma. The survivor may or may not be aware of the link between the intrusive reactions and the original trauma.

The content of the intrusive phase for donor family members often includes unique material. A donor mother describes the repetitive material that plagued her dreams:

> I was sure I was right to donate Lindsey's organs. It was what she wanted. Yet, night after night I had nightmares about the possibility that Lindsey had not been dead when they took her organs, that she felt pain during the surgery. Nearly every night I am haunted by the grim possibility that maybe, just maybe, she might have lived if I had not agreed to donation.

This mother's repeated nightmares registered her ambivalence about her decision for donation, but the concern about whether the deceased suffered, a natural concern with traumatic loss, is extended to question whether or not the donation *added* to her suffering. Glib dismissal of this fear would be extremely harmful. Patient review of the mourner's understanding of brain death, education regarding neurological death, and gentle reassurances are often helpful.

When speaking of post-traumatic stress there is a tendency to think only of the psychic numbing (denial) and the intrusive phases, however, Lindy (1986) actually outlines three phases: intrusive, denial, and hypervigilant phases. As discussed above, the intrusive phase contains repetitive images, night terrors, and other motor or cognitive forms of intrusions. Numbing, alienation, and estrangement characterize the denial (or, more precisely, disavowal) phase, while the hypervigilant phase represents an oscillation between intrusion and denial. Hyperarousal, startle reactions, cognitive dysfunction, and irritability are some of the efforts used to ward off the intrusive phase during the hypervigilant phase.

Horowitz (1997) describes a latency period that often occurs between the stressful event and the onset of symptoms, as well as the remarkable tendency for these symptoms to recur and persist long after the event's termination and its immediate effects. The latency period, as well as the absence of external evidence of the numbing phase may create a false sense of well being surrounding the survivor. Understanding this characteristic about the effects of trauma is essential for those who effectively intervene on behalf of donor family members and for those within the transplant community who are responsible for developing sound policies that impact these individuals.

> Marty couldn't understand what was happening. For four months she had been actively grieving the death of her youngest son. Then she reported that

she felt "nothing, absolutely nothing. I go through the motions of day-to-day routines, yet I cannot summon up any feelings toward anyone or anything. My friends don't understand. Some think I am doing so well while others consider me indifferent. I've even driven away family members. For months I've felt as though I am the one who is dead."

Marty displayed an attitude toward the death of her son indicative of intellectual acknowledgment of its occurrence accompanied by emotional denial. "To say that emotion is lost while cognition is retained is more or less true, but does not really capture what the mind is experiencing" (Lifton, 1979, p. 175). "Emotional vacancy," a term used by one donor family member, captured the essence of her emptiness.

Even when post-traumatic stress is not present, "the shock that accompanies a sudden death can freeze the mourning process" (Volkan & Zintl, 1993, p. 51). This process must be freed to follow its own course.

The strong affective states associated with the impact of traumatic stressors are naturally occurring phenomena. There is indication that the human psyche usually breaks down the impact of traumatic stressors and their associated affect into manageable states that allow gradual intrapsychic processing (Lindy, 1986, p. 198).

The initial metabolizing process of the trauma is often incomplete (Lindy, 1986). Metabolizing refers to the process by which energy is provided for vital processes and activities and new material is assimilated. For many years anniversary dates and other reminders will stimulate further connections between event and affect. Rather than being metabolized, some reminders threaten to reinstitute the state of psychic traumatization (Lindy, 1986). The intensity of such reinstitution may be alarming for the survivor.

Eventually, reminders of the traumatic experience may take increasingly derivative or more disguised forms. Over the years, the patient loses conscious connection between the stimulus and the memory of the trauma itself. Although the survivor may sense that something is deeply wrong, symptomatic behavior will be attributed to other causes (Lindy, 1986).

The loss of conscious connection between the stimulus and the original trauma has particular implications for donor family members. Media-promoted reunions between donor families and recipients and their families, public appeals for more donors, or academic debates about brain death may trigger intense reactions that had been repressed from the survivor's consciousness. These events often appear to have no direct bearing on the family member's current situation. Sporadically resurrected memories may be attended by strong emotional affect as pockets of grief continue to empty throughout the mourner's life.

Safety is one of the fundamental needs of the human family.

> Yet the very "essence of psychological trauma is the loss of faith that there is order and continuity in life. Trauma occurs when one loses the sense of having a safe place to retreat within or outside oneself to deal with frightening emotions or experiences. This results in a state of helplessness, a feeling that one's actions have no bearing on the outcome of one's life." (van der Kolk, 1987, p. 31)

To experience traumatic stress, the survivor need not be in danger. Individuals may be perfectly safe, yet still be traumatized when a loved one is in danger (Figley, 1986). A sense of danger combined with a state of helplessness always creates anxiety, an ever-present companion for many donor family members.

The survivor becomes particularly sensitive to people and relationships that are unfamiliar with the absurd meaning of the trauma and who might serve to stimulate unwanted traumatic memories without a constructive context for healing.

By definition a stressful life event is one that is not fully in accord with an individual's usual inner working models. Most often, it contains unfamiliar material that threatens the individual's equilibrium and destroys expectations that things will stay the same (Horowitz, 1997). When a loved one dies, the inner model of the survivor must be revised.

This revision may take place in one of two ways: The survivor may adjust their view of the loss so that it becomes consistent with existing assumptions or they may modify existing assumptions (Fowlkes, 1991; Janoff-Bulman, 1992; Marris, 1982; Parkes, 1972). This process takes time and requires considerable cognitive changes that cannot occur all at once. In reality, every time the individual recognizes the discrepancy between the current event and the inner assumptive model, there may be such intense emotional disarray that the completion of a modified assumptive model is never fully achieved (Horowitz, 1997).

☐ The Drive for Meaning

Efforts must be made to redefine the event in order to minimize the threat to the mourner's assumptive world. One effective mechanism used to redefine the event is to attach meaning to the experience (Rando, 1993). For life to be tolerable, the trauma survivor's overall task is ultimately to formulate meaning or significance in the trauma.

Organ donor family members often derive meaning from their experience because of the benefit of donation for others. These family members seem to fit within the category of those who are able to more effectively integrate the experience with their assumptive worlds. However, the achievement of meaning, which is such a popular tag to the value of organ donation, should never be assumed. The act of prolonging the life of another human being serves to provide meaning to the donor's death only if the donor family member perceives it as such. The therapist may assist the family member with the critical search for meaning by remembering that this search may or may not be directly associated with transplantation.

☐ Themes of Trauma

While Lindy (1986) offers working assumptions about trauma and loss, Horowitz (1997) proposes nine themes that are found in the presentations of trauma survivors. He describes these themes as "common problems during the process of working through stressful life events" (p. 17).

Fear of Repetition

Everyone knows about death. The facts are not that difficult to comprehend. But the unconscious portion of the mind that offers protection from overwhelming anxiety also provides shelter from the terror associated with death. Yalom (1980) contends that two beliefs—or delusions—afford a sense of safety for human beings. The first is a belief in personal specialness that cushions one from the harsher realities of life; the second is the belief in an ultimate rescuer who allows us to get close to danger, but who ultimately initiates a rescue. While these beliefs might be categorized as delusions, they represent universal beliefs that, at some level, exist in all of us. The belief that "it can't happen to me" is an effective, albeit primitive, coping mechanism.

When an individual experiences significant trauma, this previously effective coping mechanism fails. In its place is the sure knowledge that if a traumatic event happened once, it can happen again. The obliteration of this illusory coping mechanism can be overwhelming. The anticipation of a repetition of this stressful event may debilitate the mourner even as he or she is struggling to cope with the repercussions of the current events.

Horowitz (1997) claims, "The fear of repetition leads persons to develop a phobic anxiety with any stimulus that can be associated to the previous traumatic event and to engage in a variety of marked withdrawal procedures" (p. 18). The organ donor family may develop phobic reactions to peripheral stimuli that were present during the entire traumatic surround, including the donation experience.

Reactions, such as pounding heart or weak knees or a choking sensation, may be present or there may be a more subdued reaction such as a sense of some nameless foreboding that washes over the survivor. In some cases, donor family members or those who declined donation have reacted to anything remotely related to organ donation with a sense of anxiety. The stimulus could be a television public service announcement, a pamphlet, or bumper sticker about donation, but it can also be a seemingly unrelated event. Linking this anxiety with the fear of repetition often enables the individual to work through anxiety.

Fear of Merger with the Victim

Much like the fear of repetition, the survivor may experience fear of reenactment of the trauma with the self as the victim rather than the deceased. This fear is particularly confusing, for any sense of relief that one's self did not die in the traumatic event is quickly doused in the flood of guilt over surviving.

Guilt or Shame Over Surviving

There is a level of magical thinking present in the common irrational belief that "destiny chooses an allotment of victims, as in the placation of primitive gods through human sacrifice" (Horowitz, 1997, p. 21). If the survivor believes that he or she has escaped at the expense of others, guilt often follows. When the others who were killed were family members or close friends of the survivor, the natural feeling of relief for having escaped becomes very complicated and may require directed efforts to untangle.

Shame and Rage Over Vulnerability

As irrational and unrealistic as the expectation of personal omnipotence may be, it is nevertheless, "a universal hope and sometimes a deeply felt personal belief" (Horowitz, 1997, p. 19). This sense of personal omnipotence is especially observable among bereaved parents who frequently labor under the illusion that they should have been able to protect their children from harm.

Men in particular may feel shame or rage because of their sense of impotence in the face of death. The societal admonitions of a lifetime to be strong, to protect one's family, and to solve problems crash in a heap as men come face to face with death: The great problem of humankind that has no solution. Acknowledging and addressing such problems of inadequacy and recognizing the commonality of such issues represents critical therapeutic milestones for the male client.

Rage at the Source

Any 2-year-old or their parents can vouch for the fact that rage is a natural response to frustration. "One important theme after stressful events is anger with any symbolic figure who can be construed as responsible; however, irrational this may seem" (Horowitz, 1997, p. 19). An example of such irrational anger might be the family member who becomes angry with the doctor who announces the death of the loved one—a version of kill the messenger. The natural reconstruction of events leading up to the death may be played repeatedly by the mourner, searching for clues—for weak links in the chain of events where someone, anyone, could have done something, anything—that would have altered the outcome of this unthinkable event.

When there is clear culpability involved, when there is an identifiable perpetrator of the death, this rage is understandable. Irrational rage is more difficult to understand and to defuse precisely because there is no legitimate target. Laden with moral bias or magical thinking that borders on the ludicrous, irrational rage even may be directed toward the deceased for perceived abandonment, even when he or she did not choose to die.

Rage at Those Who Are Exempt

Rage is seldom more convoluted than when it is directed toward those who are exempt from the aftermath of the trauma.

> If one has suffered a loss, perhaps the death of a loved one, it is possible to feel angry with those others—no matter how sympathetic they may be—whose loved ones remain alive. Such responses range from envy to hatred

and destructive wishes, even though such ideas seem irrational, undesirable, and unthinkable to the person who experiences them. (Horowitz, 1997, p. 20)

Such thoughts may be presented in the form of questions such as: "Why my child?" "Why should the young die and the old live?" or "Why did my child die and yours live?"

> Following the accidental death of her daughter, Marge became one of the most interesting and challenging members of our donor family support group. Well-educated and articulate, Marge thought deeply about everything, struggling to make sense of the senseless event that had claimed her daughter's life.
>
> "If I can understand it," she lamented, "I can accept it. But I can't sort out why a 17-year-old dies and a 60-year-old (the recipient) lives."
>
> Marge is one of the few clients in my clinical experience to express rage against the recipient. It took enormous courage for her to share with such honesty. Yet it was the first step in working through that rage.

Since these feelings of envy or hatred or these destructive wishes often exist for survivors of traumatic loss, including donor family members, it is not unreasonable to believe that they could be directed toward the recipient, especially when that recipient does not live up to the donor family's idealization. However, admitting such less-than-admirable thoughts and feelings toward others is so difficult that the therapist may need to assist the survivor to articulate and explore such unhappy thoughts and feelings.

Guilt or Shame Over Aggressive Impulses

At times, the rage directed at those who are exempt extends to destructive fantasies directed to anyone symbolically connected to the stressful event. When the loved one's death was caused by the deliberate act of another, the mourner may harbor elaborate fantasies of revenge. When violence is a part of the event, the violence itself seems to stimulate aggression. As the survivor recognizes the intensity of his or her aggressive thoughts and feelings, there is often a conflict with conscience and feelings of guilt or shame.

The therapist should understand these natural reactions as attempts to assume some control in the situation or to restore a sense of justice in the world. This rage, with its accompanying thirst for revenge, is part of a critical struggle by the survivor to assert vitality. The natural desire to fight back can be appeased only by the exercise of the imagination. Nonetheless, this exercise helps the survivor escape the realm of inner deadness caused by the victimization (Rando, 1993).

Mourners may be concerned that they are no better than the murderer because of their own rage and murderous impulses. Failure on the part of the therapist to normalize and legitimize these feelings may result in the mourner turning their rage inward or becoming demoralized by the notion that they are as evil as the perpetrator.

Fear of Loss of Emotional Control

With rage and other intense affect threatening to overwhelm them, survivors often fear the loss of control. The fear that one might act out their rage is especially strong when the loved one's death came about by violent means.

> As one father shared: "It was as though someone had to pay for this monstrosity; others had to hurt as I was hurting. I was afraid that if I ever let myself go, I would never be able to stop."

The therapist may offer help with this concern by reminding mourners that releasing strong emotions in small increments may actually defuse the intensity of the emotions, thereby lessening the threat of losing control. Physical exercise may also help dissipate or structure strong emotional reactions.

While the use of a punching bag is sometimes recommended for clients who need a benign way to vent their rage, one member of the donor family support group shared a more innovative method that she discovered to deal with her own anger:

> Sally was the oldest, most gentle, and some say the wisest, member of the donor family support group. When Sally spoke in her soft southern drawl, everyone, from teenagers to bankers listened.

> At that particular session the group topic had been "rage," and everyone except Sally had shared their thoughts and frustrations. Someone finally said, "Sally, I can't even imagine you ever getting angry."

> She smiled in response and waited a moment; Sally's timing was exquisite.

"When my son, Jack died so soon after his daddy, I was so mad I couldn't even talk. I stayed that way for many, many weeks. Then I got an idea. I got an old set of dishes, took 'em to the back yard. I put myself and those dishes about 15 feet from the back of my house.

"For 10 minutes I threw dishes at that brick wall. I would throw and cry and then cry and throw. And when my tantrum was over I actually felt better." Sally smiled, "That is, until I realized I had to pick up all those broken dishes. If you're going to borrow my method, you need to remember to put a big box under where you're throwin'."

Sally's story brought chuckles from the group. Then someone asked Sally if anyone found out about her tantrum. She replied. "Well, my other son saw that huge box of broken dishes in the garage and asked what had happened to 'em. I told him I dropped 'em."

A great paradox of mourning: a group of highly traumatized individuals sharing laughter just after an emotionally charged therapy session that had focused on rage.

Sadness Over Loss

The bitters of grief flavor the trauma that results in the death of a loved one. The absence of the presence of a loved one brings intense sadness, the universal response to death. Just beneath the numbing, just beyond the intrusive imagery and emotions, the forlorn sadness marks time that is now forever altered.

Reassurance of the therapist's availability and accessibility encourages the mourner to draw on the combined strength of this working alliance as he or she struggles with the strong expressive grief of loss.

☐ Specific Concerns Related to the Donor Family Experience

Added to the common themes of traumatic loss, organ donor family members often present in treatment with specific concerns related directly or indirectly to donation. As stated elsewhere, there are basically two components related to organ donation that are not present in other losses: The first is the nontraditional mode of death or brain death; the second, addressed in the previous chapter, is the knowledge that parts of the deceased loved one continue to sustain life in one or more individuals. A common concern, not directly related to organ donation, that frequently impacts donor family is grief: the parental loss of a child. Clinicians who intervene on behalf of donor families must be familiar with the consequences of this unique loss. When certain grief avoidance behaviors begin to lose their potency to ward off intense grief reactions, those behaviors often become part of a family member's clinical presentation. Clinicians may have to inquire directly to learn of these behaviors.

Confusion Over Brain Death

Some of the post-donation ambivalence regarding the decision to donate rests with the population of donor families who state that they did not clearly understand brain death at the time of donation. While a clear understanding of this pivotal aspect of organ donation should be a prerequisite to consent, Batten and Prottas (1987) make an even more striking observation: "Families will donate before coming to terms with their relative's death and without completely understanding brain death. *Being willing to act on the intellectual knowledge of death without its emotional acceptance may, in fact, be what makes donation possible at all*" (1987, p.41; emphasis added).

If the family member had not accepted the loved one's death at the time of consent, this issue may subsequently become a therapeutic issue. Curiously, bereaved individuals who are often counseled against making irreversible decisions during the first 12 months following the loved one's death, are called on to make a momentous and immediate decision regarding the option of organ donation. Some have argued that making a decision regarding organ donation is no different than making decisions regarding the funeral. However, the consequences are decidedly different. Funerals seldom evoke traumatic memories; organ donation may. Some individuals have only fragmented memories of the funeral; donor families often have vivid memories of the hospital and donation experience, as well as living reminders of their decision to donate.

The Parental Loss of a Child

Because most donors are young enough to leave parents behind to mourn, the parental loss of a child becomes a common theme among survivors. These parents and other family members are left to mourn a unique loss that challenges their coping capacities. A survey (NFO Research, Inc., 1999) of bereaved parents revealed that grief following the death of a child touches all, that the age of a parent doesn't matter. The death of a child is devastating, whether it's a young mother with a stillborn child or an 80-year-old father of a 50-year-old son.

The death of one's child has been identified as one of the worst possible events in adult life (Owen, Fulton, & Markusen, 1983; Sanders, 1980; Volkan & Zintl, 1993). Rando (1993) lists the loss of a child as one loss most likely to lead to complicated grief. Raphael and Middleton (1987) describe the loss of a child as a personal disaster, encompassing "shocking, overwhelming personal experiences that test the individual beyond his adaptive capacity and bring major stresses and sometimes changes his life" (p. 281). De Frain (1991) describes bereaved parents as feeling out of control, helpless, and confused. Volkan and Zintl (1993) claim that to have a child "predecease a parent is a monstrous thing. It is the most difficult loss that humans mourn" (p. 97). Figley (1983) contends that when the child's death is sudden and unanticipated with little or no time for parents to prepare the impact is especially devastating. Organ donor deaths are always sudden with little or no time for preparation.

Regardless of how the death of a child occurs it creates a sense that a crime has been committed. Every belief in one's worldview is brought into question, and the parents are sentenced to life without their child.

Uniqueness of Loss

The parental loss of a child is so difficult because it compromises some basic beliefs (e.g., that a child should and can always be protected, that parents should not outlive their children, that there is a natural order to life and a deeply ingrained belief that life should be fair). This sense of unfairness is visceral and dates back to one's earliest days of crying, "That's unfair."

Human beings insist on order. If, for instance, we are confronted with a broken circle, we automatically close it up, making it complete. When confronted with a set of stimuli or a situation that defies patterning, we experience despair and anxiety, which persists until we can fit the situation into a recognizable pattern (May & Yalom, 1989). For parents, that recognizable pattern may eventually be found within the meaning they are able to attach to their child's death.

Search for Meaning

The need of parents to derive some meaning from their experience is exceeding strong.

> Attributing meaning to a loss is essential to grief resolution, and some sort of explanation, a personal or "healing" theory must be developed. The drive to establish a healing theory is so strong that, should the bereaved [parents] attempt to avoid doing so, they will experience repetitive, intrusive images of the loss that are accompanied by strong emotions. (Gilbert, 1997, p. 103)

There is some evidence that parents feel a particular yearning to imbue their child's life and death with meaning. The death of a child is so far removed from our logical sense of order and fairness that even while searching —"half-believing the dead can be found"—for the lost child, the search for meaning will commence.

"Because of the unnaturalness of losing a child, and the sense of guilt and failure it produces, [the search for meaning] is an essential component of the parent grief process" (Rando, 1986, p. 20). The search for meaning in response to the loss of a child is a healthy means of coping for parents. The presumption that there is meaning, however opaque and distant, is an important therapeutic step that frequently offers the parents some solace as they cope with the unfathomable event of losing a child.

The powerful need for meaning is so strong among parents that they may feel pushed to consent to donation.

> [The death of a child is] . . . especially tragic and fraught with problems of meaning. In the face of this sort of death, the grief-stricken family may be forcefully pushed to donate their young relative's organs by their intense need to make redeeming sense out of what they would otherwise experience as morally and existentially absurd. (Fox & Swazey, 1992, p. 34)

Many donor family members suggest that organ donation brought some sense of meaning from their absurd situation. The idea that something of value came from their loved one's death is, to some extent, comforting. Yet, other family members contend that their grief is beyond solace. Clinical observation suggests that both of these sentiments fluctuate over time and vary even within family systems.

Guilt: The Hallmark of Parental Grief

The parent may find that the will to live is severely undermined. Two common fears emerge in tandem: the fear that one cannot survive the death of a child and the fear that one doesn't even want to try. These twin fears may be fueled by the almost intractable guilt found in many bereaved parents. Miles and Demi (1986) outline forms of parental guilt.

- Death causation guilt. This guilt relates to the belief that one or both parents contributed to the death of, or at least failed to protect, the child. This belief need not be based on reality.

- Parental role guilt. This guilt involves the parents' perception that they failed to live up to their own expectations of their role as a parent. Part of that role often entails an exaggerated sense of responsibility for the child's welfare, regardless of what other variables existed. This belief in one's power to protect is illustrated in the comment from a bereft mother: "I felt as though my love alone should have been strong enough to protect her."

- Moral guilt. A surprising number of parents (normal, intelligent, rational human beings) report that their child's death left them feeling that they had been singled out for punishment due to some moral lapse.

- Survivor guilt: Used in this context, survivor simply means that the parent outlived the child. That survival may be perceived by parents as a betrayal to their child. The parent feels it was inappropriate for the child to die first. Something has gone terribly wrong, and since they were ultimately responsible, they are ultimately guilty.

Given the almost predisposition of many parents for feelings of guilt, it is probable that some might experience regrets about their decision to donate their child's organs. It might be helpful to remember that in the minds of some individuals, the idea of consenting to organ donation is comparable to pulling the plug. The significant difference—that the organs were removed *before* the plug is pulled—may further complicate the donor family's grief. Two parents sum up a lament heard frequently in clinical practice:

> I have had doubts that I did the right thing. I find myself wondering if there might have been a miracle if we had just waited a while longer.

> Organ donation seemed the right thing to do but it's been three years and occasionally I think, just maybe, she might have lived if we hadn't given up.

Conflicted Relationship with the Donor

Young people just on the precipice of life make up a substantial number of organ donor deaths. This youthful period of life is often filled with uncertainty and experimentation. Relationships may be tangled, if not conflicted. When a child dies during a period of rebellion or defiance, parents may be left to struggle with considerable unfinished business. This unfinished business may collide with every bereaved parent's need to believe that his or her child's life was worthwhile; that he or she mattered.

Parents of adolescents, those unique human beings that hover between childhood and adulthood, are particularly adept at feeling responsible for choices over which they had little or no control. Assuming responsibility for the consequences of another person's choices—especially for choices that result in death—can often lead to perceived guilt. In such cases the caregiver must help the survivor accurately place responsibility for such behaviors. However, helping the surviving family member recognize distorted boundaries that result in excessive and inappropriate guilt represents only one side of this issue.

The dark humor of emergency units is replete with stories of parents whose child dies as the result of some unsavory activity, yet is described quite differently by that parent. Even with numerous indicators that the youth was engaged in activities that were anything but applaudable, parents may describe this youth in glowing terms.

That's what happened when Jamie's son, Eric, was declared brain dead. A single gunshot wound to his head during a drug induced haze ended a troubled adolescence that included everything from truancy to drug abuse and robbery. Jamie's sobs echoed through the halls as she struggled with the reality of her loss. When she heard several hospital staff talking about the "terrible thing Eric had done" she couldn't make them understand that Eric was so much more than how he died.

As a young child he had been the most loving and generous of her four children. No one in the ER could know about the little boy who loved bedtime stories and said his prayers. Outsiders couldn't know of the hundreds of dandelions clutched in small sweaty hands, only a few people remembered the beautiful essay that Eric had written in the seventh grade about how his mother had worked two jobs to raise her sons on her own. In spite of her work schedule, she had never missed a ball game or school meeting. Eric wrote about how good that made him feel, how much he loved his mother.

It is essential that hospital staff and later mental health caregivers check their own judgments. The patient—no matter who they are or what they were doing at the time of their death—was someone's child. The patient is never just what he seems at the time of his death. The natural tendency, even on the part of the mourner, to focus on the immediate relationship with the deceased must be addressed. The mother's attempt to describe her son in glowing terms must not be stifled, but rather encouraged, for it can become a therapeutic tool in that it can put the young person's death in perspective—as only part of his life.

Duration of Parental Grief

Parental grief appears to last long after the death of the child (Bouvard, 1988; Gilbert & Smart, 1992; Miles & Demi, 1986; Peppers & Knapp, 1980; Pine & Brauer, 1986; Rando, 1986; Rinear, 1988; Rosenblatt & Burns, 1986; Spurgeon, 1984). Effectual therapists as well as organizations providing support programs for donor families must have a comprehensive knowledge of the course and severity of the parental loss of a child if they choose to work with donor families.

Grief Avoidance Behaviors

Alan Wolfelt (1993) opines that "we are faced with an epidemic of . . . grief avoidance response styles" (p. 1). He describes various means of avoiding grief, two of which are relevant to the donor family experience. With the appropriate monikers, The Crusader and The Replacer, these two grief avoidance responses invite certain risks for organ donor families.

Risks Associated with Grief Avoidance

It is usually easy to become compassionate about the causes that beckon the mourner. However worthy the cause, Wolfelt (1993) contends that becoming so engaged prematurely can inhibit and delay the crucial work of mourning.

Avoiding grief for any reason may create a number of negative results:

- Chronic anger, anxiety, restlessness, or poor concentration;
- Conflicted relationships;
- Chronic illness, real or perceived; and
- Chronic low-grade depression.

The mourner herself may be unaware of her own emotional fragility. The comments of noted stage actress Helen Hayes, two years after the death of her husband, speak candidly about this matter:

I was just as crazy as you can be and still be at large. I didn't have any really normal minutes during those two years. It wasn't just the grief, it was total confusion. I was nutty. . . . And that's the truth. *How did I come out of it? I don't know, because I didn't know when I was in it that I was in it.* (Caine, 1974, p. 95; emphasis added)

The Crusader

In defining the crusader, Wolfelt (1993) states that "the crusader is the person who converts his or her grief into over-dedication or premature involvement with a cause" (p. 18). It is easy for organ procurement organizations to become willing accomplices in this particular avoidance behavior because donor family members may seem remarkably intact. Even the individual may not be aware of the confusion that surrounds them, to paraphrase Miss Hayes, "They didn't know when they were in it that they were in it." The cyclic numbing so common in trauma can blur perceptions of how well the donor family member is functioning. It is not easy to recognize whether an individual is ready to participate in crusading activities. Indeed, traumatized individuals often appear superficially intact while experiencing dramatic internal chaos.

OPOs often invite family members to participate in volunteer programs based on four factors: (a) the assumption that the donor family member is intact and in control, (b) that "she wants to do it," (c) that it is helpful for the family member to have something meaningful to do, and (d) that donor family participation is perceived as helpful to transplant programs. The fact that the family member wants to participate is no guarantee that it is in their best interest. For some individuals, premature crusading serves to keep the mourner from the work he or she needs to do. Suzanne's recounting of her experience with volunteering reveals the role of both the OPO and the media in promoting her premature crusading efforts.

Suzanne was only 42 years old. She had recently lost 15 pounds (without trying) and she was sleeping only three or four hours each night—hours filled with nightmares. According to her own reports, her house was a mess and she and her husband were barely speaking.

Suzanne was totally disinterested in anything that once gave her pleasure. She couldn't concentrate and could not remember from one moment to the next what she was supposed to be doing.

Suzanne's feet felt like lead; her body ached, an imaginary cinder block rested on her chest. She audibly sighed her way through each day. Some of those days she thought she heard voices in the hallway. At other times she was sure a car had pulled into the drive. At such times, a burst of energy sent her scurrying to see if someone was there. There never was.

One day when things were especially bad, Suzanne walked up to a total stranger who was standing on the corner and told him all the terrible things that were going on in her life; she kept talking even as he backed away. That same day, she mailed her tax return in the night deposit box at the bank. Then she followed yet another stranger, not to her home but to his.

Suzanne wondered if she might be going mad.

She was not. She was responding quite typically to the death of her only child, Jason. Eight weeks earlier Jason had died in a car crash and became a multiple organ donor.

Nine weeks, three days, and four hours after Jason died, one week after the episode with the bank and the stranger, Suzanne received an invitation to participate in a volunteer training program sponsored by the local organ procurement organization. Donor family members were being trained to go about the community and encourage others to sign up to become organ donors. Part of the reason family members were being asked was because they could speak to the community about how much donation had helped them with their grief.

Suzanne's husband said something like "when pigs fly," but Suzanne was convinced she had found the perfect outlet for her grief. Like other bereaved individuals who fight for various causes such as Mothers Against Drunk Driving, Hospice, or The Compassionate Friends, Suzanne had found a cause. For the next year, she threw herself obsessively [her word] into this program, and for many months it appeared that Suzanne was better able to function and go on with her life—except that apart from her public speaking and local television appearances, she didn't really have much of a life.

Fourteen months after the death of her son, when she was asked by the recipient of Jason's heart to meet, Suzanne reluctantly agreed. After the initial meeting, a national television network filmed an interview with the recipient and Suzanne. The recipient spoke of his overwhelming appreciation for his new heart and Suzanne talked of the value of organ donation in coping with her grief.

Soon after this interview, Suzanne entered therapy with her own assessment: "When I later watched the interview of Jason's heart recipient and saw myself—glazed and wooden, I knew I was in trouble. I have used distraction so effectively," she said, "that I have managed to set aside my pain and focus only on my projects. Now it feels as though I've just begun to grieve. I still can't believe he's gone and yet, I've met this very fine man who claims to have Jason's heart. I'm not ready for that."

When Suzanne had denied her pain as much as she could, her grief gushed forward with all the intensity that had been there when she had left it behind.

Wolfelt (1993) acknowledges that avoiding grief may be in service of surviving. Avoidance activities may be temporary behaviors that enable the mourner to cope. However, when these patterns become rigid and fixed in place there may be consequences for the mourner. The destructive effect of the behavior is typically directly proportional to the degree of avoidance. However, prolonged avoidance of any degree will always be destructive. When we hide our feelings, not just from the world but also from ourselves, the result is always damaging.

While Suzanne's experience may not be typical, it is by no means unusual. This is not to say that all crusading is wrong. It may serve as a means of adaptation. As one donor father stated, "I have time to volunteer and grieve."

Horowitz (1997) claims "action is the prototype terminator of stress states because action changes events" (p. 90). He uses the image of the knight who slays the attacking dragon to illustrate this point: The knight not only slays the dragon, terminates the threat, he also discharges (or changes) the state of his own rage. If, in the donor family member's case, the threat is fear or anxiety this metaphor might fit. Engaging in action activity may lessen the individual's emotional responses, however, the basic threat that aroused such emotions—the absence of the beloved and mourning that absence—cannot be changed by action.

Clinical experience suggests that structuring might be a more definitive term to use when individuals are able to use avoidance responses to achieve some respite from the agonizing pain of grief. Structuring, which is done consciously to avoid the pain and remains flexible and unforced, may be adaptive rather than harmful. Ideally, the respite offered by action would modify the mourner's responses in such a way that the overwhelming emotions would be dosed out over a period of time and therefore become less threatening.

However, there remains a risk related to timing and content of becoming an advocate for organ donation. For individuals to proclaim to an audience that organ donation is helpful in coping with grief within the first few months following a traumatic loss seems disingenuous, extraordinarily like testifying to an outcome at the beginning of a process.

The Replacer

Caregivers recognize premature replacement as possible grief avoidance behavior. Wolfelt (1993) uses the term the replacer, to describe "a person who takes the emotions that were invested in the relationship that ended in death and reinvests the emotions prematurely in another relationship" (p. 16). For the mourner, there is little, if any, conscious awareness that this replacement serves as a means of avoiding the work of mourning. While it is understandable that the mourner would want to avoid the painful feelings related to loss, the mourner must be encouraged to trust herself and others with the truth about how much it hurts.

In spite of the same goal—that of avoiding the painful work of mourning—premature replacement does not necessarily involve an illusion of a magical union with the deceased or provide an external reference for the mourner's grief as does a linking object. It simply may be a question of focusing energy on this new person as a way of negating the full impact of the loss. Whenever the mourner successfully shirks the work of mourning, the consequences are usually problematic.

> I'll not likely forget the first time I saw Matt. He was skipping across a parking lot to greet the man who had received his 15-year-old son's heart. Matt's son had died 18 months earlier and Matt had not wasted time getting in touch with the recipient. They had become great friends, Matt told us as he brought the man over to our group to introduce him. Matt explained that since meeting, approximately six months after the transplant, the two families had become very close. They regularly went out to dinner or a movie, and Matt and his wife had brought baby gifts for the recipient's first grandchild. Matt had even invited the recipient's entire family over for Thanksgiving. It was only when he suggested to his wife that they should move their church membership to the recipient's church, that his wife drew the line. About the same time the recipient fell ill and never recovered.

> With the recipient's death and his marriage strained, Matt agreed to enter counseling. There, he was able to process delayed grief over the loss of his son, as well as the grief related to the death of the recipient whom he had genuinely liked.

The temptation for a donor family member to take the emotions once invested in the relationship with the donor and reinvest it prematurely in a relationship with the recipient is obvious. To the extent that such a relationship is born from a need to avoid confronting the pain of loss, that premature replacement may come at exorbitant emotional costs to the mourner.

The goal of transplantation is to help the desperately ill patient live a normal life. To do this, the recipient must come to think of himself in terms other than patient or recipient. The same may be said about the family members of the organ donor. However, in some cases, donor family members and recipients appear to have an overwhelming need to meet and become involved with one another. The potential for risks within such meetings cannot be ignored.

When the patient dies or rejects the donated organ the donor's family member may experience a double grief—grieving for both the recipient and part of the loved one. When the family assumes a proprietary interest in the donated organs, he or she may experience emotional reactions ranging from disappointment to rage when a recipient is culpable in the rejection of the organ.

When unable to tolerate the painful affect of trauma, or when displaying an attitude toward the loss indicative of intellectual acknowledgement of its occurrence accompanied by emotional denial, the donor family member may be more likely to perceive the recipient as a linking object.

Consider the potential for such complications that are present in Richard Selzer's story *Whither Thou Goest* (1990, pp. 1–21):

"Brain-dead," said the doctor. "There is no chance that he will wake up. Ever. . . . Hannah, it is three weeks since your husband was shot in the head. The only thing keeping him alive is the respirator." [Note the conflicted language: "husband is dead, the only thing keeping him alive."]

Hannah waited for the walls of the solarium to burst.

"I'm asking you to let us put an end to it, unplug the machinery, let him go. . . . But before we do that, we would like your permission to harvest Sam's organs for transplantation."

"Harvest?" said Hannah. "Like the gathering in of wheat?"

"Yes," said the doctor. "That is what we call it when we take the organs. It is for a good cause. That way your husband will live on. He will not really have died. . . ."

"Dead is dead," said Hannah.

A week later she received a letter from the doctor.

Dear Mrs. Owen,

You will be pleased and comforted to know that because of your generosity and thanks to the miracle of medical science, seven people right here in the state of Texas are living and well with all their faculties restored to them. Your husband's liver has gone to a lady in Abilene, the right kidney is functioning in Dallas; the left kidney was placed in a teenaged girl in Galveston; the heart was given to a man just your husband's age in a little town near Arkansas; the lungs are in Fort Worth; and the corneas were used in two people right here in Houston. . . .

Hannah folded the letter and put it back in its envelope . . . without reading the end. There was no need. She already knew what had become of the rest of Sam. She had buried it in the family plot of Evangelical Baptist Church cemetery.

That was three years ago. . . . "Dead is dead," she had told that doctor. But now three years later, she wasn't so sure. For Hannah had begun to have doubts.

. . . she stopped going to the cemetery to visit the grave. It wasn't Sam in that cemetery, not by a long shot. It was only parts of Sam, the parts nobody needed. The rest of him was scattered all over Texas. And unless she had been misinformed, very much alive. And where did that leave her?

Here he is scattered all over Texas breathing in Fort Worth, urinating in Dallas *and* Galveston, digesting or whatever it is the liver does in Abilene. . . .

Hannah could not have said exactly when the idea first occurred to her. . . .

What was instantly made clear—it was so simple—was that she must go to find that man who was carrying Samuel's heart. If she could find him, and listen once more to the heart, she would be healed. She would be able to go on with her life.

The recipient of her husband Sam's heart resisted granting Hannah's request to come and listen to her husband's heart. ("It is such a small thing, really, to ask in return for the donation of a human heart," she had written in one of many imploring letters she had sent.) The recipient finally consented.

The house was in darkness, every shade and blind having been drawn and shut. It had a furtive, tense look which was exactly what she saw on the face of the man standing before her. . . .

Hannah followed him into a small room, a den, furnished with a sofa, an upholstered chair and a television set. One wall was lined with bookshelves. She guessed that he had spent his convalescence in this room.

"It's your show," he said. "How do you want me?" When she didn't answer, he reached up with both arms and pulled the T-shirt over his head.

"I suppose you want this off," he said. Then for the first time Hannah saw on his chest the pale violet stripe that marked the passage of her husband's heart into this man.

"Best I think, for you to lie down flat," she said. "I'll sit on the edge and lean over. . . ."

"How are you going to listen to my heart without a stethoscope? . . ."

"I'm going to listen with my ear. . . . I have very acute hearing," she added, because he looked dubious as though he might call the whole thing off. But he didn't, and lay back down staring straight up at the ceiling and with his arms at his side as though he were still a patient at the hospital waiting for some painful procedure to be done. . . .

Then Hannah bent her head, turning toward the left, and lowered first to her elbows, then all the way . . . when she touched his skin, she could feel him wince.

Oh, it was Sam's heart, alright. She knew the minute she heard it. She could have picked it out of a thousand. It wasn't true that you couldn't tell one heart from another by the sound of it. This one was Sam's. . . . And Hanna settled and gave herself up to the labor of listening. . . .

Selzer leaves the impression that this hour of listening to Sam's heart was enough for Hannah, that she had "at last been retrieved from the shadows and set down once more upon the bright lip of her life" (p. 21). Perhaps.

Hannah may have been one of the fortunate ones. Perhaps all she needed was to make this connection and afterward she would indeed be able to let the dead die. Others have not been that fortunate. But a word of caution for readers who perceive Selzer's story macabre: *Damnant quod non intelligrint*. We must not condemn what we do not understand. When determining what is within a normal range of behavior for donor families, we must remember that nothing about organ transplantation is normal. There is nothing normal about taking organs [spare parts] out of newly dead bodies and transplanting them into gravely ill bodies of compatible strangers. Normal grief under such abnormal circumstances may require radical reorientation and new methods of assessment.

☐ Closing Thoughts

Working assumptions about trauma, common themes of trauma, and those specific to organ donor families enable us to see more clearly some of the risks that may impact this population. It is tempting to believe that because transplantation has become so commonplace, it no longer evokes "the powerful positive and negative gift-associated reactions in donors, recipients and their families that it had in the past" (Fox & Swazey, 1992, p. 44). Making such an assumption would be a grave mistake.

The grief of the donor family has not changed. The compelling need of some donor families to meet the recipient in whom a part of their loved one continues to sustain life and the need of most donor families to know that their gift was appreciated is as strong as ever. Exploitation of the donor family by either the organ procurement organization or the media is wrong. To effect recipient–donor family meetings as a public relations tool or a way to increase ratings is troubling to many and warrants close attention from those who choose to provide mental health care for donor families as well as from those who set policy in this arena.

The study of donor family trauma and loss represents a new field that is being broken; it is difficult ground. While much remains unknown, we must proceed with caution as we attempt to provide effectual care without causing further harm to a particular group of people who, at a time of great vulnerability, reached beyond their pain to think of others.

CHAPTER

Healing Sources for the Donor Family

Amidst the medical advances in transplantation, little concern has been voiced or efforts made to understand how organ donation impacts donor family grief. Decades of neglect must be addressed. In this volume, we have reviewed the surround of organ donation, explored the donor family's hospital experience, established the traumatic nature of donor family grief, examined the unique features of brain death and donor-family–recipient relationships, and reviewed themes and assumptions that characterize trauma and trauma-driven grief. Each of these factors may further complicate the donor family's grief.

This chapter will consider how caregivers might intervene effectively on behalf of donor family mourners. Prerequisites for the caregiver, and ways and means to assist the mourner achieve necessary tasks, will be offered as well as an overview of the role of the organ procurement organization and the family as healing sources.

☐ The Caregiver

In the midst of his argument for commodification of organs, Peters (1998) conceded that "[p]robably some degree of sorrow visits families because a

loved one was an organ donor, and some negative reaction to organ donation will happen from time to time no matter what motivates organ donation" (pp. 202–203). Acknowledgment of the problem is an essential first
step in establishing appropriate care for these families. The second step is
the preparation for caregivers to intervene effectively on their behalf.

The client–therapist encounter is the very heart of grief therapy. It is a
"caring, deeply human meeting between two people, one (generally, but
not always, the patient) more troubled than the other" (Yalom, 1989,
p. 13). In therapeutic relationships with trauma survivors, the line of de-
marcation between client and clinician may dim because the survivor's
concerns are every man's and every woman's because many of their stories, questions, anxieties, and struggles have been, are now, or will eventually be our own. Not everyone faces a traumatic death, but death itself is
everyone's ultimate concern. Working with individuals who have survived
the traumatic death of a loved one requires a delicate balance of objectiv-
ity and insight on the part of the caregiver.

Rando (1993) suggests that individuals who have lost a loved one under
traumatic circumstances fall into two categories: "[t]hose who do not want
to talk about it and those who do" (p. 590). Building a trusting relationship with those who want to talk about it generally proceeds in a typical
fashion. Trauma survivors who use avoidance and postponement, however, will be difficult to engage in treatment. Both categories of individuals
will evaluate the trustworthiness of the therapist.

Entering the Trauma Membrane

Clinical experience with family members of organ donors appears to validate the claim that trauma survivors erect a "trauma membrane" (Lindy,
1986) to keep out individuals who have no understanding of their situation. This membrane serves as an outer shell to guard against persons who
might stimulate painful trauma memories without contributing to the
healing process. Any foreign matter that disturbs the individual's healing
is kept outside the trauma membrane, while those who are perceived as
promoting recovery (or at least who demonstrate understanding) are permitted inside. This explains why traumatized individuals will often gravi-
tate toward others who share a similar loss or trauma. "Usually, fellow
survivors—those who truly know the absurd reality of the traumatic event
or have shared its experience—have a special place of closeness" (Rando,
1993, p. 591).

Nursing staff, auxiliary personnel, and organ procurement coordinators
often develop a unique bond with the donor family based on the shared

experience of the donor's hospitalization. This bond is often dispropor-tionately strong relative to the brief amount of time shared by the family and the professionals. These professionals occupy unique positions from which to offer effective care as they meet the family's needs during and immediately following the donor's hospitalization.

While few therapists have personal experiences that might validate their ability to contribute to the inner reparative process, it is imperative that they demonstrate trustworthiness in order not to be perceived as "foreign matter that might hinder [the survivor's] healing" (Rando, 1993, p. 591). This may be achieved by negotiating certain issues of trust.

Negotiating Issues of Trust

Lindy (1986) and others found that the caregiver might be invited within the trauma membrane if there are successful negotiations of issues related to trust. Those findings revealed that in order for the caregiver to gain entrance into the healing membrane several conditions must be met.

First, survivors need to feel that the caregiver is sensitive to the unique circumstances of the traumatic event and that he or she can be trusted with the survivor's feelings about the experience (Lindy, 1986). For mi-nority groups, a shared reality of life prior to donation is an asset for the caregiver. Rapport building as well as trust often can be accelerated when the caregiver can relate to the donor family member from the same cul-tural or racial reference point. Whether the gift of a shared reality is present or not, the family member will evaluate these questions: Is the caregiver sensitive? Is she perceptive enough to use her sincere imagination to un-derstand my circumstance? Does she care enough to try? Can I trust her with my feelings? Can she relate to me as a human being rather than to the pathology?

Second, caregivers must be genuinely moved by the narration of the survivor's experience in the traumatic event and must be able to commu-nicate this to the survivor (Lindy, 1986). The ability to be genuinely moved by the survivor's story requires sensitivity and the courage to care. In spite of the shock, disbelief, and numbness that cushion the survivor, there ap-pears to be a paradoxical sensitivity that allows them—with extraordinary accuracy—to evaluate those who can and will, and those who can't or won't, contribute to their healing.

Third, there needs to be successful negotiation of the threat of overload, with the caregiver communicating an expectant but noncoercive attitude regarding the traumatic material (Lindy, 1986). The therapist demonstrates trustworthiness by her lack of anxiety in her attitudes toward and interactions with the survivor, when she treats the survivor with respect and allows him maximum control, and when she conveys appropriateness of atypical responses to atypical conditions, avoiding pathologizing the survivor's reactions. Based on trust that the therapist will be there for the duration and emboldened by this sense of support, the survivor may regain a sense of self-efficacy that overrides the sense of helplessness.

Fourth, the working alliance must be consolidated. In Lindy's (1986) report, this consolidation took place when the caregiver identified a neutral event that was manifestly unrelated to the trauma and caused the patient intense affect (rage, guilt, anxiety, etc.) and linked it to aspects of the trauma. The working alliance creates the therapist–patient dyad that "will hopefully form a unit capable of tolerating and digesting more affect-laden memory than the survivor alone can tolerate" (p. 197). While Lindy reports that in his experience the consolidation of the working alliance occurred during the third or fourth session, such predictability has not been demonstrated in my work with donor family members. Working with trauma and loss has never afforded neat and tidy predictable timelines in my experience. While the consolidation of the alliance with the patient does occur when unrelated material is linked in a meaningful way, it may be unrealistic to expect therapy to proceed through tight orderly phases on an inflexible timeline.

Each case brings variegated responses to the experience of trauma. Often the survivor spends considerable energy on protection from the anguishing pain by trying to maintain some emotional equilibrium when the denial or disavowal is breached.

In addition to Lindy's observations about building trust and gaining entrance into the trauma membrane, there are other requisites for the effective caregiver for donor families.

Awareness and Understanding of the Unique Aspects of Organ Donation

The caregiver's trustworthiness will be further strengthened by demonstration of her knowledge of the history and context of transplantation, the procurement process, the family's hospital experience, and the trauma-driven grief that follows. In addition, effective caregivers must be aware of the unique factors that impact on the donor family's trauma: brain death and the knowledge that the loved one's organs continue to sustain life. This awareness will bolster the caregiver's general effectiveness and will enable her to link seemingly unrelated events to the trauma. For example, the mourner's obsessive ruminating about the loved one's suffering or the possibility of mutilation may be traced to the family's confusion about brain death.

Brain Death

The theory of brain death is not particularly difficult to understand when one is not in extreme anxiety. The problem is that individuals rarely have a preneed of understanding this diagnosis.

According to Youngner (1992) the concept of brain death is supported by the following characteristics of patients who are being maintained by medical technology, after they have suffered irreversible loss of all brain function.

1. The clinical diagnosis of irreversible loss of all brain function is relatively easy to make (the exception being newborns and young infants). Competent neurologists, neurosurgeons, or other critical care physicians can make the diagnosis at the bedside.

2. Following brain death, the prognosis is entirely predictable and dismal. Despite maximum efforts, the patient will never regain consciousness, will develop asystole, and will die by traditional criteria usually within hours or days. In no other medical condition can one so accurately predict, not only the certainty, but also the timing of death.

3. "Even if the notion of brain death is not fully accepted, the quality of life in the short time remaining before traditional death is unacceptable. The patient is unconscious and maintained only with maximum invasive intervention" (Youngner, 1992, p. 123).

According to Wikler and Weisbard (1989), the brain death diagnosis is as sure as anything else in medicine. However, even when an individual understands the brain death theory, or thinks he does, the visual cues duel with the intellect. When theory meets reality, the question mark created by this confrontation may reappear throughout the grief process. The therapist must always be mindful of the cognitive dissonance experienced by many family members.

The effective therapist must also understand that caring for these donor-patients and their families "is a demanding and stressful task for health professionals" (Youngner, 1992, p. 124) and the language of donation slips from time to time even among seasoned professionals. For instance, even when accepting the criteria of brain death, nurses "may find themselves comforting such patients or warning them before painful procedures" (Youngner, 1992, p. 124). Understanding this phenomenon as part of human nature rather than a question mark about the declaration of brain death is essential and must be conveyed to the concerned donor family members.

The organ procurement organization is an excellent resource for information about brain death for both the therapist and the family member. These organizations are usually very willing to help in matters that relate to the well being of an organ donor family.

Difficulty may arise for the therapist when he or she holds the same reservations or ambivalence about brain death as the mourner—the same dichotomy in beliefs and values regarding the gift of life and all that it involves. In such cases, the bias of the therapist may so hinder her work with the donor family member that it will become necessary for the therapist either to recuse herself or work through her own disquietude.

The Donor-Family–Recipient Relationship

The therapist should be alert to all possible risks related to the donor-family–recipient relationship, including the use of the recipient as a linking object. When the family member enters therapy with the perception that she cannot find peace until all the parts of the puzzle are found, the therapist must help this individual find closure by coming to terms with the possibility that she may never obtain the sense of appreciation she seeks. Redirecting the client to focus on the essence of the loved one during his or her life often proves beneficial. This may be accomplished by a comprehensive review of who the loved one was, what role that loved one played in the survivor's life, and what the survivor misses most about the loved one. The following narration demonstrates this approach:

Mary had repeatedly spoken of her need to find all the recipients of her daughter's organs. "I can't find peace until I know where every part of her is and how the recipients are," she lamented. "I must find those missing pieces."

Dr. Franklin waited for several moments. She had heard this lament many times before. She decided it was time for gentle but indirect confrontation. "Tell me more about Caroline," she asked, "and tell me what you miss most about this child."

Mary first looked startled that Dr. Franklin had not responded directly to her lament, and then stared at the handkerchief that she had been twisting around one finger. Sniffing loudly, she pulled herself upright and began, "I know every parent says this, but Caroline was special. Everyone adored her.

I believe that people fall into two categories: givers and takers. Caroline was a giver. It seemed as though that's all she wanted to do—make other people happy. I thought that sometimes other people took advantage of her but when I tried to talk to her about that she laughed and said, 'Mom, no one takes advantage of me unless I let them.' That's who Caroline was."

"What I miss most is her laughter and her kindness. She had this laugh that sounded like bells ringing—sometimes soft and gentle, other times with all the stops pulled out. You would find yourself laughing even when you didn't know what was funny. You would laugh just because Caroline was laughing. I do so miss laughing."

For a moment, the room was quiet. Then Mary brightened. "I remember a line from a book when the protagonist's daughter is described as being 'so full of grace, so poised that . . . you could hold her in your outstretched palm and she would balance perfectly' (De Vries, 1961, p. 151). That was my Caroline."

Dr. Franklin's eyes were misty as she spoke. "Such a beautiful way to remember Caroline."

"Better than obsessing about her body parts?" Mary smiled slyly.

Dr. Franklin responded with her own smile, relieved that she had not misread Mary's capacity for insight and reason.

Mary's excessive focus on the recipients of her daughter's organs was not immediately confronted. For a time, these ramblings contributed to processing her grief as she reviewed the events surrounding her daughter's death. Primarily, however, they served to protect the client from the harsh reality that her daughter was truly dead, thereby delaying her emotional acceptance of the death. Some of that protection finds roots in mystical notions that her daughter lived on through the recipient.

Recognition of Mystical Thought Processes

In many ways, the study of trauma and loss has sought to emulate the medical or scientific model that eschews any method of study not based on empiricism. But, issues related to organ donation are often subjective, resistant to reductionism, causation, and explanation. Faith, hope, love, generosity, desires, kindness, and resiliency are internal attributes that only can be observed, not understood, by external behaviors. Throughout this work the issue of mystical thinking has surfaced as part of the human experience. It would be a serious mistake to dismiss this aspect of the donor family member's presentation.

The clinician must be willing to consider the dual nature of human beings, "extraordinary lucidity flanked by preposterous irrationality" (Yalom, 1999, p. 92). By accepting the primary-process thinking that often surfaces when an individual is under extreme stress without immediately confronting it with logic, the therapist will validate the survivor's experience and free her to disclose thoughts, feelings, and concerns that might otherwise be withheld. The hypervigilant client will know if she is offered safe conduct to explore the more subterranean thoughts that often accompany her grief.

To work effectively with donor families, the therapist must readily recognize that the "spiritual, religious, philosophical, and existential issues are critical components of an individual's assumptive world . . . play a large part in the readjustment processes after a loved one's death" (Rando, 1993, p. 433). By entertaining openness to critical components of trauma and loss that are neither quantitative nor cognitive, the caregiver offers the family member something more than mere perfunctory care. This willingness to incorporate material that cannot be quantified, allows survivors to be viewed not as maladaptive coping mechanisms but as resilient human beings with a capacity for courage, hope, and spiritual depth. These elements—always difficult to quantify—aid in the recovery from traumatic life experiences.

Support and the Gift of Presence

The value of time that is spent simply offering support for members of the donor's family is often underestimated. However, at various junctures in therapy, the gift of one's presence may be the most valuable tool the therapist has to offer.

> What we are missing! What opportunities of understanding we let pass because at a single moment we were, with all our knowledge, lacking in the simple virtue of full human presence. (Jaspers, 1951, p. 182)

This virtue of full human presence does not negate nor replace, but rather complements therapeutic skills and techniques. The caregiver's competence must be blended with the gift of one's presence with exquisite timing to reach clients who bring a myriad of unique variables to their presentation that alter the timing and trajectory of each clinical experience.

To address the uniqueness of each experience, the clinician must maintain equanimity and patience while the trauma survivor lurches in and out of denial, in and out of periods of intrusion, all the while recognizing (accurately understanding) that for a period, denial or numbness serves to protect the survivor from dark, anxiety-producing thoughts and images which intrude through the door of grief that appears to have the peculiar habit of opening and closing on its own.

Tolerance of Ambiguity

The caregiver, who chooses to work with organ donor family members, must become comfortable with ambiguous issues and circumstances. The paradoxical life and death nature of organ transplantation will manifest itself repeatedly in therapy. The donor family will benefit when the therapist is able to model the phenomenon of holding two conflicted views, such as feeling deep sadness over the loss of the loved one and genuine pleasure that a recipient is doing well.

☐ Interventions on Behalf of the Organ Donor Family

The surround of organ donation provides fertile groundwork in which certain therapeutic problems could thrive. To effectively deal with such problems, the caregiver must be prepared to provide the donor family member with information about the trauma-driven grief that relates to the loss and organ donation.

Normalizing Information Related to Trauma, Grief, and Organ Donation

Providing information and education about the nature of trauma as it applies to donor families is extremely important in that it reduces fear and anxiety by validating their experience while helping to solidify the therapist–client relationship. The following points may need to be provided and restated throughout the course of treatment:

1. Traumatic deaths can be such a personal catastrophe that even the strongest may experience post-traumatic stress responses.

2. For many individuals, the events leading up to the loved one's declaration of death, the diagnosis of brain death, and the emotional sequelae that follows may qualify as a series of traumatic events.

3. The fallout from the original trauma may include negative experiences during the loved one's hospitalization if the needs of the patient or the donating family were not adequately met or if problems arise regarding organ donations.

4. The aftershocks following traumatic loss are normal and to be expected. These may range from intrusive imagery or nightmares to numbing denial or strong expressive grief.

5. There may be a latency period of months before post-traumatic symptoms appear. There may also be pockets of strong expressive grief and intrusive material after the survivor has experienced relative safety from such affect for long periods of time. Knowing in advance that such strong emotions can reemerge may give the survivor a sense of control and reduce fear and anxiety.

6. Grief and trauma responses often co-mingle and are hard to differentiate. In some cases the responses are the same. For instance, denial and sadness are themes of both grief and trauma.

7. Trauma or grief symptoms may actually get worse before they get better. This intensification of symptoms is normal and temporary.

8. One does not "get over" the traumatic loss of a loved one. The survivor never forgets, but is able to integrate the loss within the total context of life. Traumatic memories that surface in the future may be experienced with greater equanimity if the survivor is able to discern how they are connected with the original event and are therefore part of the normal reaction to a traumatic life experience.

9. Symptoms of traumatology may vary among individuals. Not everyone will respond to the same event the same way. Perceptions, relationships, personalities, age, gender, and personal philosophy of each person will influence the course and trajectory of that individual's response to trauma.

10. Even in the midst of great personal tragedy, survivors often bring something of value from the traumatic experience. Early in the grief experience, suggesting that good may come from devastating loss may sound

treasonous to some survivors; for others this possibility is met with hopeful courage. Such encouragement must be always delicately timed.

11. Because organ donation is predicated on the loved one's death, it is understandable that the donor's family may have ambivalent feelings about the experience. Negative feelings, whether based on legitimate or perceived issues, are valid and acceptable. Ambivalence about the donation or negativity related to the procurement process does not necessarily negate the value of the outcome. Organ donor families may be helped to understand that ambivalence about organ donation is not unusual.

12. Donor family members may experience a wide range of thoughts and feelings about the recipient of the loved one's donation. Neither intense curiosity about or disinterest in the recipient are necessarily unhealthy.

Working Through Trauma

The psychological recovery from the impact of catastrophic events almost always entails the survivor working through both trauma and loss. When traumatic loss is related to the death of a loved one, the reactions of the survivors are closely related to those found in complicated mourning. "One of the most important tenets of treatment in complicated mourning involves the need to work through its various aspects. . . . The repetition required in this working through process must be respected by the caregiver. It cannot be eliminated" (Rando, 1993, p. 384). The concept of working through does not negate the value of structuring the work of trauma or loss. Respites from the emotionally demanding work of mourning are often considered adaptational.

Responding to the Basic Assumptions About Trauma

The basic assumptions about trauma noted in the last chapter readily apply to the trauma-driven grief of the donor family. Responding to these assumptions also has significant import for the caregiver because each assumption produces an entrée for intervention.

1. The caregiver must understand that when there is an overlay of posttraumatic symptoms those symptoms must be addressed in order to

get to the mourning beneath (Rando, 1993).

2. The caregiver must clarify the defenses and prepare the individual for the underlying affect states such as helplessness, rage, guilt, and shame.

3. The caregiver must reassure the survivor that the highly-disturbing states such as searing grief, remorse, or rage are lessened and less likely to occur if the mourner is surrounded by supportive companions (Rando, 1993). Conversely, the survivor must also understand that intense expressive responses are acceptable and may serve to exhaust the pain of loss.

4. Understanding the latency period that often occurs between the stressful event and the onset of symptoms is essential for those who effectively intervene on behalf of donor family members. This component of traumatic grief as well as the risks of donor families experiencing capricious episodes of strong expressive or intrusive grief should be of interest not only to clients and caregivers but also to organ procurement organizations. This aspect of trauma-driven grief must receive critical consideration by those within the transplant community who are responsible for developing sound policies that impact on these individuals.

5. The clinician and the client's family must understand that strong affective states associated with trauma may be so intense that it is not only difficult to experience but stunningly difficult to witness.

6. The caregiver must help the mourner clarify topics that may belong to earlier traumas that have been activated by the current trauma. When stressful events occur, earlier residual losses from the past may rush forward to complicate present issues (Rando, 1993). Multiple sequential losses that have occurred in rapid secession may severely threaten the survivor's capacity to cope and may require additional support.

7. The caregiver must bear in mind that the survivor "remains vulnerable to entering a distraught state of mind, even in states of safety and months after the event" (Rando, 1993, p. 597). Neither the survivor nor his or her family may be prepared for such distress after a period of restored good functioning. It is helpful to provide the donor family with information about alternating phases that occur within the stress syndrome.

8. The client and the client's family must also be helped to understand

over time that certain stimuli that cannot be readily connected with the original trauma may bring up memories accompanied by surprisingly strong emotional affect. This material is robbed of some its potency when the mourner is able to connect it with the original trauma.

9. The caregiver may help the survivor regain a sense of trust. It is a dreadful thing to lose one's faith in personal safety; to feel as though one has been severed from all moorings and set adrift in a hostile world provokes extreme anxiety. By being available and accessible, the caregiver furnishes an alliance that can be trusted by the survivor. This trust may represent the first step in rebuilding the survivor's confidence that the world is safe enough to be inhabited.

10. The caregiver must be able to gain entrance into the protective bunting that cushions the mourner from further trauma.

Assisting the Mourner Achieve Necessary Tasks

The initial goal of therapy appears deceptively simple. "Therapy is an effort to remove the blocks to an essentially spontaneous healing process" (Rando, 1993, p. 602). However, to do this the therapist must assist the survivor with a number of essential tasks.

Establish a solid caregiver–mourner unit to serve as a temporary cohesive self that can tolerate affect in stronger doses of affect than the mourner could alone.

Identify and work through painful segments of the trauma into manageable doses. This is not as easy as it reads on paper. Expressive grief is raw and chaotic by nature. Pain must be met with empathy, fear and anxiety encountered without panic. In an attempt to meter out doses of emotions, the clinician also must guard against shutting down the mourner's affective state. Avoiding this dilemma can be accomplished to some extent by reminding the mourner of the clinician's availability, accessibility, and acceptance.

Clarify defenses such as disavowal or splitting that overlays affect states including rage, helplessness, guilt, anxiety, and sadness. The caregiver should be aware that rather than alternating between reality and denial there can be, through an ego-split, denial at one level and reality testing at another, both going on at the same time (Simos, 1979). This can be confusing for everyone—the caregiver, the family, and the survivor.

Dissect and process each memory, identifying and feeling each attending emotion. Caregivers must be sensitive to timing intervention aimed at getting the mourner to express affect. Denial of an intolerable reality serves a purpose. This is treacherous ground for the novice or insensitive caregiver. There are not now and never will be statistical guides or rules of timing. The caregiver must be a listener who follows leads from the bereaved as they approach the pain of grief. Both caregiver and mourner should remember that denial is not a stage that one passes through and never experiences again. When the bereaved person returns to denial as a temporary coping strategy, this needs to be respected.

Identify intrusive material. Caregivers must inquire specifically about intrusive qualities that the mourner may be hesitant to describe on his or her own. Labeling and respecting such material validates and normalizes its existence and frees the mourner to verbalize or otherwise express feelings attached to this material.

Clarify topics that may belong to earlier traumas that have been activated by the current trauma. When stressful events occur, earlier residual grief from past losses may rush forward to complicate present issues (Rando, 1993). Multiple sequential losses may severely threaten the survivor's capacity to cope.

Recognize that the mourner has complete latitude to discuss negative attitudes and experiences related to donation. With safe conduct assured, the client may be able to resist the intimidation to squelch negative feelings relative to his or her personal experience with the phenomenon of organ donation. As stated elsewhere, the mourner may benefit from assurances that negative experiences do not necessarily negate the value of the loved one's gift.

Review the traumatic experience, along with attending thoughts and feelings, to help rob the experience of its potency. Details about how the individual learned of the trauma, how they got to the hospital, their experience once they arrived at the hospital, the process of declaration of brain death, and consent to organ donation should be included in this review.

Mourn the secondary losses connected with the original trauma. This is an essential part of the donor family experience. In addition to the familiar physical and psychosocial secondary losses associated with trauma and loss, there are unique secondary losses that impact the organ donor family. When the donor's organs are deemed medically unsuitable following consent, the family may experience a sense of loss relative to the missed opportunity to bring value from their loss. The rejection of the organ by the recipient or the death of the recipient may be viewed as secondary losses. These losses and their meanings must be identified, processed, and worked through.

Focus on developing new skills or strengthening skills that were overwhelmed by the trauma. Healthy coping skills must be available to the individual in order to avoid becoming mired in denial or grief avoidance behaviors.

Explore issues related to self-held concepts of worthlessness, incompetence, shame, or guilt. This exploration is an important part of intervention on behalf of the donor family. Feelings of helplessness and powerlessness may be countered with positive experiences, interaction, and activities that will support self-worth, personal mastery, and connectedness with others. When appropriate, help the donor family link with larger organizations such as the National Donor Family Council or bereavement support groups, such as The Compassionate Friends. These associations can help the mourner feel connected. Being part of these groups or working for change on behalf of others with similar traumatic experiences can help to reduce the sense of victimization and isolation of the family member.

Learn to tolerate solitude. While support is a vital variable that assists in the mourner's recovery, it is also important that the survivor eventually learn to tolerate the solitude that will allow freedom to express the full range of emotional responses to the trauma.

Accept responsibility for one's behaviors. When the mourner is actually liable for the tragedy or some part of it, he or she must be encouraged to make amends to the extent possible and in ways that are appropriate. Legitimate guilt must be addressed and remorse measures should be adopted to make up for transgression that led up to the trauma (Horowitz, 1997).

Relinquish any sense of perceived or exaggerated responsibility that results in inappropriate guilt. False beliefs about one's responsibility for the trauma must be challenged and clarified. Caution must be exercised when addressing the struggle with perceived guilt. Guilt helps minimize fear, thus becoming a temporary coping mechanism. As long as the guilt is serving a purpose, attempts to rationalize will likely be rebuffed. When the ego is less fragile and other coping skills surface there will be enough time to address the guilt. Guilt may take a strange turn when family members cannot tolerate their own complicity in the trauma or when the donor had been neglected by the family. Projected guilt may take the form of anger toward health care professionals or the organ procurement organization. Strong protests about the medical incompetence or negligence on the part of health care personnel must be assessed with the possibility of misplaced self-incrimination from the family.

Identify guilt related to organ donation. If the donor had not stated his or her desire to be a donor prior to death, family members may exhibit guilt related to their decision to donate their loved one's organs. This guilt may be explored through ascertaining more information about the donor's basic personality—Was he generous? Thoughtful? Would she have chosen to donate? What would she say about the decision? While describing that individual, it may be possible to connect the attributes of the deceased (kind, caring, would-give-you-the-shirt-off-his-back, always-doing-something-for-someone) with the exquisite gift of donation. This exercise may also draw the mourner back to the outcome of donation rather than fixating on the process. Often parents gain a peaceful confidence regarding their decision as these questions are explored and find comfort in concluding that donation was an appropriate memorial to their loved one.

A note of caution is in order: Generally, mourners tend to idealize their loved one and may need to be encouraged to mourn the whole person. However, individuals who choose to donate represent a skewed section of the population that tends to be outwardly directed, generous, and kind. The exercise of describing the loved one (the donor) can be enormously comforting if it is handled with care and should not be discouraged. Even when the donor had been engaged in unsavory behavior at the time of death, the mourner may be helped to remember the individual from years past or to fantasize about what type of individual he or she might have become in the future.

When the next of kin regrets deciding to donate based on negative events related to the donation process, the disposition of the organs, or dismay over information gleaned post-donation, the issues must be acknowledged, respected, and worked through. Occasionally, the family member simply needs accurate information about various aspects of the donation, the care the donor received, a clarification of the time of death, or additional information about the process of declaring brain death.

Clarify any confusion related to the diagnosis of brain death. Even when family members felt knowledgeable about this concept predonation, they may reconsider after the fact of donation and need reassurance.

Identify the context of uninformed consent. This is a difficult issue. When the family's concern is related to a specific issue that was misrepresented and misunderstood prior to donation, education and reassurance may be helpful. If the family member believes they were misled about who would benefit from the donation, families may receive some solace from modifying their expectations. The following story may help place fractured fantasies in the proper perspective.

A mother felt deeply disappointed when her 15-year-old son's heart went to a 60-year-old man. Her hope that the heart would have gone to a young person with a long life ahead of them was shattered. Seven years later the recipient and his wife were among 40 people who attended a meeting of residents in their retirement community. A deranged gunman walked into the meeting and began shooting. The recipient later described hearing a voice tell him, "You can take this guy. You can get there before he turns that rifle on you. Do it!" Like a teenage linebacker of his high-school football team, this older-man-with-a-young-heart, launched into a flying tackle and brought down the 300-pound gunman in a heap, then pinned him down until others could help. Two individuals were killed, but the 60-year-old man received credit for preventing the deaths of 40 other people in the room. All the while his gifted heart never missed a beat. (Elliott, 2001)

This story is unusual but may be used to explore the reality that it isn't always easy to assign value to a particular life and what that life might accomplish. In some cases, family members may dismiss this type story as further evidence that while some families receive information and appreciation for the gift of donation, others receive little or none. The clinician must evaluate each client's potential response individually.

Encourage story telling. Mourners should be encouraged to tell their stories, not just of the trauma but stories about their life and the life of the loved one. Brody (1987) claims that suffering is alleviated by the meaning one attaches to one's experience. The primary human mechanism for attaching meaning to particular experiences is to tell stories about them. Stories seem to relate individual experiences to the explanatory construct of the society and culture and also to place the experiences within the context of a particular individual's history (Brody, 1987, p. 5).

By resisting the urge to structure the client's energy prematurely, the clinician helps the mourner place the loved one's death in perspective with life rather than within just the death surround. Seemingly unrelated stories also may provide important information about the mourner's previous coping skills and other assets that are not readily apparent within the raw emotional context of trauma-driven grief.

Create meaning from the traumatic experience. While some families perceive organ donation as a means of bringing meaning to their tragic loss, the clinician should never assume that this is true for all families or even all members of one family. Even if the act of donation serves to bring meaning from the death, families may need to bring other good from what was hateful in their experience.

Reformulate life assumptions. It is often helpful for the client to explore previous assumptions about life and how those assumptions might now be modified. Many of those assumptions (e.g., I will die before my child; we would grow old together; good things don't happen to decent people; etc.) were deeply- but not necessarily consciously-held aspects of the survivor's coping strategies. These assumptions must be examined and modified to fit the new material in the survivor's life.

Explore spiritual issues. To the degree that belief systems are compromised by the traumatic loss of the loved one, the donor family's grief may be compounded. When individuals lose moorings that once anchored their lives, they may become fragile and without hope. Myths, mystical thinking, and faith bond the body to the soul. Religious faith may not always be rational, but it is often sustaining for millions of people.

While there is opposition to addressing spiritual issues within the therapeutic setting, it seems peculiar that a client, who should be free to talk about anything in therapy, could not speak of that which means the most. Primarily, the clinician's task is to listen, to clarify the client's presentation, and help draw meaning from his or her own faith. It is certainly not the time to deconstruct a personal belief system or to challenge mechanisms that help families cope with a world that appears erratic and unpredictable.

Techniques for Processing

The caregiver may help the mourner confront affect and experience emotional expression and catharsis by using the following techniques.

Empty chair, role play or role reversal such as that used in gestalt therapy. This technique is particularly helpful as a means of addressing unfinished business. When the intentions of the loved one was unknown at time of donation, the family member may also address the question of organ donation in light of what the donor might say in response to the mourner's doubts about the decision.

Rituals as an active form of grieving. Rituals offer donor families the opportunity to interact and respond to the memory of the loved one. There is value in acting out or engaging in purposeful behavior that honors the loved one. Rituals may give individuals permission to express their emotions in a way that is timebound and sanctioned so that even those who are resistant to expressive grief may feel free to respond. Organ procurement organizations frequently have memorials and other special events that celebrate the life of the donor as well as his or her gift to others. Rituals that include the entire family promote unity and solidarity in the face of individual grief. Rituals do not have to be dramatic to serve the purpose of connection. They may be as simple and personal as taking flowers to the cemetery or remembering the loved one's name in prayers. Whether elaborate or simple, the ritual must have meaning for the participant in order for it to be effective.

Writing letters to and from the deceased. Like the empty chair or role-reversal techniques, writing letters to the deceased allows the mourner to address unfinished business. People who are more comfortable writing their thoughts and feelings rather than speaking them may especially benefit from this technique. The mourner must be ready to perform the role of the deceased in response to the mourner's letter. Accurate timing combined with a trusted therapeutic relationship often brings emotional expression and catharsis.

Keeping a journal. Keeping a journal gently forces thoughts and feelings out in the open rather than contained within. Because a journal is private, the mourner has absolute freedom of expression without consideration of how others might respond. Journaling also forces the mourner to complete thoughts that might have remained fragmented and unchallenged. Journals are also helpful in that they provide written documentation of the journey through grief. The mourner is able to look back at earlier experiences and observe progress from his or her own notations. This awareness may increase a sense of mastery and offers encouragement to continue.

Morning pages. Those who find writing in a journal too formal or who resist the idea of writing, have another option. Julia Cameron (1992), author of *The Artist's Way,* suggests the use of morning pages as a means of removing blocks to creativity. This daily exercise involves writing three pages of longhand notes reflecting stream of consciousness. These thoughts may be positive or negative, hopeful or despairing. There is no right way to write and grammar is not an issue. The individual simply writes whatever comes to mind. Within the midst of this seemingly pointless activity, rambling thoughts and feelings may become more cogent, issues clarified, and insights gained.

Cameron (1992) claims that these pages represent blocks to the individual's creativity. For the mourner, the pages may represent blocks to creative expression, procession, or resolution of grief matters. Morning pages require practice. But, if the mourner is willing to persevere, this technique can become a powerful tool when used appropriately and with professional guidance. Cameron claims that by persistent practice of this exercise one may come in contact with an unexpected inner power. Thus empowered, the mourner may discover that she is equal to her life and to her loss.

Vicarious expression of grief through stories or movies. When deeply traumatized individuals, who have initially dealt with their experience through denial and emotional numbing, enter treatment they often report that those defenses were penetrated while watching a movie or reading a particularly moving story about another's grief. A wife of a donor expressed such an experience.

> I thought I was doing admirably well. I had not cried since the day after my husband's death, four days after he had been shot and killed while we walked to dinner. For weeks I've felt nothing. Then, while watching a movie about a beautiful love story where the husband dies, I lost it. I felt like I was never going to stop crying. My friends didn't know what to do with me, so they sent me here.

Literature review. Literature, especially classic literature, tends to express unchanging aspects of the human existence. Literature communicates perdurable truths that bridge all ages, cultures, genders, and status, to explain what it means to be fully human and bereft. For example, after the execution of King Charles I, Father Cyprien de Gamache made the following remarks: "A great philosopher says that moderate afflictions permit the heart to sigh and the mouth to lament, but that very extraordinary, terrible and fatal accidents fill the soul with stupor, which renders the lips mute and prevents the actions of the senses" (Oman, 1936, p. 181). Father de Gamache was describing a truth about the benumbing quality of great trauma long before traumatology became a field of study. When the time is right, some donor family members may benefit from viewing their personal trauma from the perspective of loss through the ages as portrayed in literature.

Professional intervention for organ donor families is not the only mode of healing. It may not even be the most effective. Because support plays such a crucial and pivotal role in managing trauma-driven grief, others may be better positioned to offer that support.

☐ Organ Donor Procurement Organizations as a Healing Source

As noted earlier, procurement coordinators are positioned to offer ongoing care for the organ donor family. Since the mid-1980s, organ procurement organizations have made efforts to address the emotional needs of donor families both during and following consent to donation. While OPOs view bereavement aftercare programs as a public relations tool, most programs have made applaudable efforts to address the needs of the donor family, thereby reducing the risks associated with their grief. In view of the harsh reality that health care agencies are being asked to do more with less, it is commendable that so many organ procurement organizations are making the effort to address the emotional needs of those who make the miracle of transplantation possible.

Types of Aftercare Programs

Some aftercare programs are quite comprehensive, while others consist of a simple gesture, such as a referral service. The type of program chosen by the sponsoring agency will be determined in part by the area served by that agency, population density, ethnic make-up, and resource availability within the area.

Providers of these services must be ever mindful of the limitations inherent in such efforts. Aftercare programs generally offer ongoing support, information, education, and a forum for discussion. Support programs do not and should not offer therapy.

The Aftercare Coordinator

By their commitment and attitude, those chosen by the organ procurement organization to provide bereavement support services will influence the effectiveness of the entire program as well as the welfare of the donor families served. Whether this individual is recruited from within the sponsoring organization or hired to provide bereavement care on a contracted basis, the following criteria must be met:

1. In order to maintain equanimity, the specialist must have come to terms, to the extent possible, with death and grief.

2. Effective listening skills and the ability to respond appropriately are a must.

3. The coordinator must be able to exercise sound judgment and awareness about limitations. Making appropriate referrals is an important part of the program. The specialist must know how and when to do this.

4. Both the aftercare coordinator and the sponsoring agency must have a strong commitment to this program. Bereavement programs involve hard, demanding work. All too often, administrators underestimate the consuming nature, relative to both time and emotions, of a well-implemented aftercare program.

5. The aftercare coordinator must recognize the obligation to serve as a donor family advocate, not as an apologist for the OPO or a promoter of organ donation. To be successful, the aftercare program must be implemented in a way that assures families that their needs are paramount.

6. To respond appropriately, the coordinator must be knowledgeable about trauma-driven grief. In order to reassure the family member and to normalize the mourner's experience, he or she must also understand the normalcy of acute grief.

A Brief Review of the Grief Process

Since the goal of any intervention on behalf of the mourner is to remove blocks to an essentially spontaneous healing process, which is natural, normal, and necessary, the bereavement coordinator must have an understanding of what this process entails.

The grief experience involves emotional, cognitive, behavioral, and social reactions on the part of the individual who experiences loss. The individual typically moves through five responses: (a) avoiding the loss, (b) acknowledging the loss, (c) allowing the pain associated with the loss, (d) accommodating the loss, and (e) achieving restitution. The action verbs used to describe these responses indicate movement; when movement doesn't take place or is delayed, complications may arise.

Avoiding the Loss

Denial, shock, and disbelief characterize the initial reaction to loss. It is understandable that individuals would wish to avoid the painful reality that a loved one is dead. Initially, shock and denial serve to protect the mourner from the full impact of the death. These features serve a useful purpose as they naturally regulate doses of the reality for the mourner to process.

Acknowledging the Loss

Acknowledging the loss of a loved one involves accepting the reality that a loved one has died. This acceptance is a process, not a once-and-for-all-time event. Accepting the loss on a cognitive level may occur when the next of kin signs a consent form for donation or when making funeral plans. But acceptance takes a deeper form—when a widow sits across the breakfast table facing her husband's empty chair or when a widower goes on his first date after 30 years.

Allowing the Pain

Experiencing and expressing the pain of loss has a healing quality. Strong expressive grief is a universal form of grieving and is characterized by tears, anger, protest, anxiety, deep sadness, guilt, the fear of going crazy, loneliness, hypersensitivity, frustration, a sense of hopelessness or helplessness, as well as searching behaviors aimed at finding and recovering the lost love. Even simple grief may carry an intensity of affect that is startling to the unseasoned caregiver. These strong affective responses to loss are a natural occurrence. They are usually self-limiting, although as with trauma, the initial expression of grief is usually incomplete and will revive when reminders, such as anniversary dates, favorite songs, birthdays or holidays occur.

During this period, the mourner may also experience regression or ambivalence. Regression may be evidenced by the inability to think in a cogent fashion, dependence, sickness, or by the use of more primitive coping skills such as denial or self-medicating. Ambivalence is often demonstrated by a twofold response from the mourner. Within the same conversation, the mourner may voice the fear that she cannot go on with her life, followed by the lament that she does not want to go on with her life. Ambivalence may be evidenced toward other aspects of the grieving process as well.

Accommodating the Loss

It takes time to adjust to the world without the deceased. It requires that the mourner determine who she is without the loved one through whom she once filtered her worldview. This is a time of change and discovery while the mourner reevaluates and reformulates her assumptions about life. She will also modify her relationship with the deceased, not by forgetting, but by extracting the essence of the loved one and incorporating those attributes into her new identity. To a great degree this modified relationship with the loved one is based on memories.

While the survivor finds new roles, new directions, and new sources of gratification, her new life will be greatly influenced by her past. The clinician and the client must understand the promise of paradox in that one may relinquish the past while remaining indebted to it.

Achieving Restitution

Some believe that in order to achieve closure to the painful experience of loss the mourner must bring some form of restitution from the loss. In an effort to regain emotional equilibrium, the mourner may unite the past, present, and future by bringing something new, something of value from the grief experience.

When a loved one dies, there is an interruption to life, a blow to self-esteem, or a loss of meaning in life (Simos, 1979). It is imperative that continuity is restored, that damaged self-esteem be repaired, and that a sense of meaning be restored. Retrieving the lost loved one would be a way to achieve these tasks, hence the searching behaviors already discussed in this work.

Forms of restitution are as varied as life itself. It may be described as symbolic, such as monuments, statues, endowments, or charities established in the name of the deceased or in naming a child after the deceased. Investing in new relationships with others or a deepening of relationships with other family members may also constitute restitution. Investing energy in a social or religious movement or in a worthy cause is another example of restitution that helps restore self-esteem and reduces a sense of helplessness and isolation. Restitution may also be achieved through creativity. Creativity is meant to apply to all efforts to bring new things into being, which may include the new identity of the mourner, and new ways of overcoming loss.

This brief overview of grief is offered for less seasoned or less formally trained caregivers with the understanding that it does not cover the multifarious responses to loss. Printed words on paper cannot convey the essence or flavor of grief, nor is grief ever as tidy as it appears in writing. Phases, responses, and behaviors will overlap and sometimes compete with one another for attention from the mourner. For example, the mourner may experience pain in the midst of valiant attempts to avoid it. In a state of disbelief, the family may plan a funeral or sign a consent form for donation. They may even question their ability to withstand the loss, while stating they cannot believe "this has happened." In order to render effective care, the clinician always must avoid attempts to fit the mourner into an established protocol rather than treating the mourner as a unique human being.

One of the most effective aspects of an OPO aftercare coordinator's work is to provide education for the organ donor family, for it is often the family that serves as the primary healing source for the survivor.

☐ The Family as a Healing Source

Traumatic events are usually sudden and unexpected, with "limited or no time to prepare, to devise and rehearse a plan of escape, identify a method of coping, or prevent or avoid the catastrophe" (Figley, 1986, p. 41). One of the most significant elements of trauma is a perceived threat of danger, either for ourselves or for someone we care about very deeply. When the event is both sudden and dangerous, it can also be emotionally overwhelming.

"There is little doubt that the family, plus the social support system in general, is the single most important resource to emotional recovery from catastrophe" (Figley, 1986, p. 40). The family provides a critical support system to individuals before, during, and after the traumatic event. This does not mean that the family can always prevent the complications associated with trauma, even if they are the critical first line of defense. The family may recognize the need for professional care before the survivor does and can be enormously helpful in locating professional resources when such care is necessary.

Following the traumatic event, the family's role in recovery is unparalleled, and the extent that the mourner believes that she has others to rely on for practical and emotional assistance greatly determines his or her recovery (Figley, 1986). It may also be suggested that in many cases family members have a general entrance pass though the trauma membrane.

Major Ways of Family Support

Figley (1986) suggests that family members and other natural support systems offer support in five major ways: emotional support, encouragement, advice, companionship, and tangible aid.

1. Emotional support is the comfort, love, affection, and sympathy that the family shows to the survivor.

2. Encouragement is "the praise and compliments offered by a supporter. It is the extent to which we are inspired by the supporter to feel courage and hope, to prevail" (Figley, 1986, p. 43). Courage is contagious. By demonstrating it and talking about it, the survivor's own courage expands.

3. Advice is useful information given for the purpose of solving a problem. Advice based on close-up knowledge of the problem is not only helpful in practical ways, but may also further bond the survivor and the supporter.

4. Companionship "is simply time spent with the supporter, doing things that are perceived to be mutually enjoyable. It is the extent to which

we don't feel alone" (Figley, 1986, p. 43). This function may offer the survivor a much-needed respite from the arduous emotional strain of the trauma. Distraction provided by companions helps to structure the work of coping with the aftershocks of traumatic loss.

5. Tangible aid is practical help provided by the supporter. It may involve physical or financial assistance. Someone assuming temporary responsibility for some burdensome task is often a welcomed form of support. Practical and financial aid is an important (and seldom spoken of) aspect of providing support for traumatized individuals.

Antidotes for Post-Traumatic Stress

Families may actually serve as an antidote to post-traumatic stress (Figley, 1986). They do this in four major ways:

1. Detecting symptoms,
2. Confronting the problem,
3. Recapitulating the traumatic events, and
4. Resolving the trauma-inducing conflicts.

Detection of Symptoms

Individuals living within a household are aware of everyone else; there is, to some degree, similarities of disposition and temperament among the family members. From this closeness emerges sensitivity to the moods of one another. Family members are usually the first to detect when one of its own is experiencing emotional problems.

Confrontation of the Problems

Family members are in key position to urge and help the survivor confront the problem. Clinicians may spend countless hours establishing rapport and trust with the survivor, which will enable him or her to identify and confront specific problems. Figley (1986) rightly claims that the family already has trust and rapport, as well as greater access to him. Families are generally better prepared to help the client and can do so in less time.

Recapitulation of the Catastrophe

Families may assist the survivors by encouraging them to reconsider the traumatic events, a process known as recapitulation. Because of the accessibility of family members, the survivor may turn to them to reconstruct the events surrounding the trauma. These individuals may also help the survivors recall additional aspects related to the trauma or clarify information (Figley, 1986). On occasion, a family member may even help reframe a situation or correct distorted perceptions of guilt or rage. The family's ability to provide this support is especially important for the donor family member who may have trouble recalling new information related to the patient's care, the declaration of brain death, and the particulars about organ donation.

The family also has the capacity to further aggravate the negative events of a poor hospital experience as well as the ability to reframe the situation in a more generous light for the distraught survivor. It is the immediate and extended family that can offer consolation to survivors who are disappointed that donation was not an option for their loved one; others in the support system may not even recognize this factor.

Resolution of the Trauma-Inducing Conflicts

Both Figley (1986) and Horowitz (1997) agree that the family can be useful in helping the survivor work through his or her traumatic experiences and conflicts. The critical role of a family member is that of facilitator. By encouraging the survivor to talk about the traumatic experience, the involved family member may also clarify distortions, contribute insights, and offer alternative perspectives relative to the original trauma and its surround.

Empathy: The Family's Achilles' Heel

While recognizing that some families have the capacity to further aggravate the survivor's trauma, there is ample support of Figley's (1986) claims about the value of family and natural support systems. A caveat is warranted. The effectiveness of the family system is based on love and empathy. Empathy is a critical attribute of interpersonal competence and effectiveness. But this empathy may render family members "vulnerable to the consequences of their assistance by the very mechanism that makes them so effective: their strength as well as their Achilles' heel is empathy" (Figley, 1986, p. 48). The paradoxical reality finds that those most effective at ameliorating traumatic stress are also susceptible to being traumatized in the process.

Education and Care for the Donor Family

Helping the trauma survivor may best be accomplished by providing support for the family: (a) by educating them about how the trauma is affecting each family member, (b) explaining how the behavior of family members may be reinforcing or exacerbating the difficulties, (c) educating the family members about the immediate and long-term consequences of the trauma, and (d) sharing new strategies and new skills with the family to help them cope with the trauma.

It should be noted that in conflicted, dysfunctional family systems that often seem to thrive on chaos and crisis, more than education would be required to prepare the family to effectively support the survivors. Nevertheless, "attention to the health and vitality of the family system, may provide a powerful stress-coping resource" (Figley, 1986, p. 52) for traumatized donor family members. It is through education and supplemental consultation with organ donor families as a whole, that we may provide the most effective care.

Particular issues that might arise within the context of donation must become part of that education. Strategies for preventing some of these complications and new skills for addressing others should be made available to individuals whose loved one became a donor and for those who care for these individuals.

This education should begin before the organ donor family leaves the hospital and should be directed toward the extended family, friends, and other natural support systems. Organ procurement organizations are positioned to provide education for donor families immediately following the death of the donor.

Normalizing Information About Trauma

Rando (1993) states that education about trauma and its consequences is exceptionally important. Part of that education should include information to normalize "feelings, thoughts, impulses, behaviors, and experiences that cause anxiety or fear of losing one's mind" (p. 593). An adaptation of the normalizing information outlined earlier in this chapter would be helpful for extended members of the donor's family as they attempt to intervene on behalf of the survivor.

1. Trauma is such a catastrophic experience because of its suddenness that it can produce symptoms of post-traumatic stress in almost anyone.

2. For many individuals, the events leading up to the loved one's declaration of death, the diagnosis of brain death, and the emotional sequelae that follow qualify as a series of traumatic events. Some psychological aftershocks just before, during, and after the donor's death are normal and to be expected. These aftershocks may present in various forms, including intrusive imagery, numbing, rage, guilt, or other strong affective responses.

3. Fear of the loss of control of emotions may be particularly difficult for some family members. This reaction does not mean that the mourner is going crazy, but does indicate that there are important issues to work through. By releasing emotions over time the chance of losing control is lessened.

4. Symptoms usually get worse before they get better. This is often difficult to hear. The mourner must understand that the intensification of symptoms is normal and temporary.

5. The symptoms that accompany traumatic loss may never go away completely but the individual will be able to deal effectively with them. Reminding the survivor of the long-term presence of the other family members can be reassuring.

6. Family members may have some negative feelings about experiences connected with organ donation, however, ambivalence about donation does not negate all its positive value. Organ donor families may be encouraged to accept such ambiguity as normal.

7. Donor family members may experience a wide range of thoughts and feelings about the recipient of the loved one's donation. Intense curiosity about or disinterest in the recipient is equally normal.

8. No thoughts or feelings about the organ donation experience are off limits. On the contrary, an honest review of those feelings contribute to the care and recovery of survivors whose loved one became a donor. Families should not hesitate to seek professional help if necessary.

☐ Closing Thoughts

Some organ donor family members experience intense and complicated trauma-driven grief that warrants professional intervention. Professionals who provide such care must have a working knowledge of trauma as well as an awareness of the surround of organ donation that may exacerbate, complicate, or soothe the intensity of such grief.

The organ procurement organization is positioned to provide initial supportive intervention and also provide normalizing information to the family who often plays a pivotal role in supporting the mourner. Professional intervention, informal support, and family support aid the donor family as they move toward spontaneous healing. All must remember that intervening on behalf of highly traumatized individuals is demanding work.

> [It] . . . demands an openness of mind to what is observed and what is unseen, what is known and what is implied, to the logic and to the irrational, to the concrete and to the symbolic, to the practical and to the mystical aspects of life. It calls forth in the helper the poetic as well as the scientist, the personal as well as the professional, and it bridges the gap between helper and the one who needs help. In recognizing the universality of loss and grief, we come to appreciate the commonality of all peoples. Loss removes barriers of race, color, creed, religion, sex: it is a leveler. (Simos, 1979, p. 250)

As helping professionals we must become aware of our own blind spots that might prevent us from seeing the mourner clearly. We must understand that when we are hurting we cannot listen well to the hurts of others. Yet, by having problems and successfully overcoming them, suffering and finding healthy relief from that suffering, we are able to help others find healthy solutions to their suffering (Simos, 1979). Then as we care for the donor family we may share in the remarkably complex and creative process of loss and healing.

CHAPTER

The Quest for Knowledge About the Donor Family: An Unending Adventure

Transplantation and organ donation forces the biomedical world to confront the whole person: the physical, psychological, social, and spiritual being. Within this arena of life and death, we become startlingly aware of human values, beliefs, and concerns that often resist being reduced to mere analytic study. Organ donation and the grief that follows are real life events, not theories or hypotheses.

Yet, we live in a world that encourages avoidance of real life issues. Our culture prefers to dwell on that which is positive and life affirming without claiming the attending sorrows. While organ transplantation is about life, it is also about trauma and loss. Without that loss and the inevitable grief that follows, the transplant enterprise would collapse. Regardless of the remarkable strides made in the clinical technology associated with transplantation, the extent of the psychological impact of organ donation on surviving family members remains uncertain.

The quest for knowledge has been called "an unending adventure at the edge of uncertainty" (Bronowski, 1995), an appropriate commentary on the status of the work we have undertaken. For what is currently known about the trauma-driven grief of donor family members marks only the beginning of an unending adventure. A brief review will summarize both the adventure and the uncertainty.

☐ The Donor Family Experience

As noted in the preface, my consistent response to transplantation has been, "What about the donor family?" We know a bit more about these families now than when that question was first asked. We know, for instance, that donors tend to be young, leaving behind mourning parents or young families. Their deaths are sudden, often violent, mutilating, and sometimes preventable. While the loss may or may not be perceived by the donor family member as traumatic, both the nature and the object of the loss places the survivor at high risk for post-traumatic stress responses.

By extrapolating what is known about the content and trajectory of post-traumatic stress responses, it is obvious that the themes of trauma characterized by Horowitz (1997) and the treatment suggestions offered by Figley (1986), Rando (1993), Lindy (1985), and Horowitz (1997) are appropriate for traumatized donor family members. Yet potential complications unique to organ donor family experience are also obvious to the seasoned clinician. These unique experiences, including the neurological death of the donor, the meaning derived from donation, and the knowledge that parts of the loved one live on in other human beings, have enormous import to the donor family's grief.

Neurological Death

As noted throughout this work, the concept of brain death is troublesome for a number of reasons. Primarily, the family of the donor candidate may understand cognitively that their loved one is dead but the visual cues (chest moving up and down, good color, urine output) may cause cognitive dissonance. Regardless of how medical staff or the family feel about the term brain death, it is, without question, a nontraditional, if not unnatural, way to die. And it is a necessary prerequisite in order for the patient to become an organ donor.

Organ Donation and Meaning

Studies have consistently indicated that most families who consented to donation believe that it offered some degree of comfort. They perceived this act of altruism as a means of restitution, a way of bringing meaning from the traumatic loss of the loved one. Gaining a sense of meaning is important for all bereaved individuals; however, it is particularly essential for parents to find meaning when their child dies (Figley, 1989; Fox & Swazey, 1992; Horowitz, 1997). While donation may serve that need, there is also the risk that in their desperation to attribute some meaning to the trauma, parents may be particularly vulnerable to the suggestion of donation. Two fault lines blemish the concept of donation as a form of restitution. The first concerns the preconception rather than the development of meaning attached to organ donation. The second concerns the reality that even if meaning is derived from this act of altruism, it comes so early in the grief process that family members may need to find alternative ways to develop a healing theory to pave the way for personal transformation.

"Transformation occurs when the client's own interpretation of the good coming from negative events is respected" (Hyer & Brandsma, 1999, p. 140). It must never be assumed that all family members perceive donation as comforting. Indeed, for some individuals donation is considered a complication to their grief and many point to the lack of closure in knowing that parts of their loved one live on—not as comforting, but haunting.

Donor-Family–Recipient Connection

There appears to be a compelling need for many donor families to know about their loved one's recipients. However, for some donor family members, organ donation remains peripheral to their grief. They feel no attachment to or proprietary interest in the donated organs. For them, there was no personification of the loved one's body parts, nor was there any animistic, magic infused thinking about the transplanted organs which so many of the givers and receivers of cadaveric organs often engage (Fox & Swazey, 1992).

For some donor families, a simple note of appreciation and updates on the recipient's condition are sufficient. For other family members, there is a desire for two-way written communication with the recipient. But for some, nothing short of open, face-to-face involvement with the recipients will suffice. The lack of closure reported by families because of knowing that part of their loved one lives on in another human being can represent a secondary trauma.

While there is no empirical data to support either the claim that donor family grief is facilitated by contact with the recipient of their loved one's organs, or the claim of others that this intense contact may actually be harmful, there is an abundance of anecdotal information supporting both sides. The problem with donor-family–recipient contact is precisely that we don't know the ramifications of such relationships.

Even if some may be helped by such a meeting, how would one know who would be helped and who would be harmed? Who decides who is suitable to be placed in contact with whom? What is this person's training? Will he or she be available should something go wrong? How does policy on this matter impact bereavement?

☐ Education as a Form of Prevention

Drawing on the public health paradigm of primary, secondary, and tertiary prevention of disease, Rynearson and Geoffrey (1999) suggest tentative recommendations for caring for individuals who have been traumatized by the homicide of a loved one. Similar preventive recommendations might also prove useful for the organ donor family.

Primary prevention is aimed at elimination of the disease. There is no generic or proscriptive way to eliminate sudden death, although eliminating violence is becoming an urgent public demand. But to some degree, the complications that arise out of the lack of preparation or appropriate care for the donor's family can be prevented.

Secondary prevention focuses on early intervention within high-risk populations. There is some indication that depressive and anxiety disorders that often attend traumatic loss respond positively to early intervention, augmented with judicious use of medication and combined with ongoing psychotherapy (Rynearson & Geoffrey, 1999). Such treatment may be appropriate for at-risk donor family members.

Tertiary prevention stresses early rehabilitation and education to "minimize chronic disability and relapse during recovery from a disease" (Rynearson & Geoffrey, 1999, p. 127). In response to trauma and loss, tertiary prevention would include individual and group psychotherapy, mutual support groups, and educational material aimed at reducing or preventing long-term impairment or escalation of early dysfunctional responses.

Specific Prevention Needs

There are a number of lapses in the present process of procuring organs for transplant where pre- and post-donation intervention might be helpful in preventing unnecessary complications to the donor family's grief.

Preneed Decision Regarding Organ Donation

Many complications relative to donor family trauma could be prevented or reduced if each person decided preneed whether or not to be an organ donor. This decision should be discussed with family members and also be in written form. As critical as this simple gesture might be, it would be meaningless to the family's welfare unless the decision was made with the donor candidate's full understanding of the realities of organ donation.

Preneed Education to Assure Informed Consent

McCullagh (1993) contends that the rapid progress of medical technology seems so complex that decision making is "retained with the medical community, often within one specialist group within it" (p. 3). He believes that when the human subject becomes an object to be used—as when a patient becomes a donor—decision making must include community.

> [It is] essential that the issue of reification of the individual, the grounds for undertaking it and the subsequent uses to which the human object may be put require the fullest community consideration attainable. This can only occur if sufficient detail about the relevant medical situations is made available to a wider audience. (McCullagh, 1993, p. 3)

Maximizing dissemination of information is essential not only in the context of formulating general community responses, but also in specific instances when a family must make decisions about the possible use of a member as an organ donor. "The *informed* nature of any consent to such usage is essential if it is to be regarded as a valid authorization" (McCullagh, 1993, p. 3).

Deciding to be a donor is not enough. This decision must include what parts of the human body the potential donor is willing to donate. To do this the individual must have adequate information to discern the differences between organ donation and tissue donation. These are very different procedures and informed consent to organ donation would not adequately cover the donation of human tissue.

To the extent that the donor family feels it was misled or believes after the fact that their consent was not informed, complications may emerge within the therapeutic setting. These complications might be prevented or reduced if adequate, accurate information is assimilated prior to need.

Address the Conceptual Disarray Surrounding the Concept of Brain Death

"The history of determination of death on the basis of the condition of the brain has been interconnected with the history of organ transplantation. Any explanation of the former requires some familiarity with the latter" (McCullagh, 1993, p. 1). At the present time, explanations are not always consistent and are never quite as simple as they may seem.

Physicians have been trained and laypersons have long held that while there is life, there is hope. Life was defined by a heartbeat. All this changed forever with the first successful human cardiac transplantation on December 3, 1967, and the debate over the criteria and concept of death continues to the present time.

Confusion about brain death among health care professionals, based on the inconsistencies of clinical diagnosis and clinical criteria, is also influenced by differing philosophical, cultural, and spiritual definitions of death (Ott, 1998). One of the most pressing areas within the realm of organ donation is the need to clarify the conceptual disarray surrounding the concept of brain death.

Ott (1998) argues that the "moral, philosophical, and spiritual aspects of the brain death debate may preclude clear empirical answers" but "the debate must continue and we must strive for public and professional consensus" (p. 22). This call for continued debate is academically admirable, but troublesome, for the debate itself carries the potential to harm family members who were led to believe that brain death was absolute and unequivocal.

Both pre-donation education and a consensus on the concept of brain death would create greater trust among those who consent to organ donation thus reducing doubts and regrets post-donation.

Explore Potential Risks Associated with Donor-Family–Recipient Relations

Donor-family–recipient communication and contact may constitute the most complex and emotionally-charged issue facing organ donor families. Attempts to assess this issue in an honest and forthright manner have been compromised by political and vested interests and considerations.

In lieu of formal studies regarding the impact of donor-family–recipient interaction on the long-term grief of the donor's family, various real and hypothetical scenarios must be considered when policies and procedures relating to interaction between the two parties are being explored or developed. It has been observed that "difficult cases . . . are notoriously bad foundations for good rules" (Corr et al., 1994, p. 629). Perhaps. But ignoring the difficult cases would be shortsighted. Policies and procedures that govern donor-family–recipient communication may have enormous impact—either for healing or for harming—on donor family grief. Preventing or reducing further complications of the donor family trauma may be achieved only when the many variegated voices are heard and taken into consideration.

Improve Hospital Care for Donor Families

Because organ donors experience sudden but not instantaneous death, there is some time between the fatal trauma and the declaration of brain death, during which the individual receives emergency care and is placed on a ventilator. While most of the drama of this activity takes place within an intensive care unit, the anxious family maintains vigil in the waiting room. This period of time affords the family opportunities to process some of the necessary tasks associated with the impending death of their loved one. How this time is used may either facilitate or complicate the survivor's mourning.

When the patient becomes a potential organ donor, the family may, in many cases, receive superior care from a number of sources, including the representative of the organ procurement organization. In this anxious time of waiting, families may be assisted as they begin to accomplish tasks related to the impending death of the loved one. Some trauma-related complications can even be avoided if the family members' needs were met during this time. Organ donor family members should never be further traumatized by insensitive care from hospital or OPO staff.

Educate Extended Family Systems Regarding Trauma and Loss

Providing education about the process of trauma and loss may be one of the most effective strategies for addressing the needs of donor families. Verbal or written information should be offered to the primary mourners as well as to the extended family prior to their departure from the hospital. Guidelines for helping the donor family members cope in the early days of grief should be augmented with the reminder that this support will need to be ongoing.

Organ procurement organizations began offering bereavement support programs for donor families in the mid-1980s. With the increasing sensitivity to the devastating sequelae that follow traumatic loss, the number of these programs has increased to include most organ procurement organizations. The basic aftercare program may include written material, telephone support, and support groups, as well as memorials that honor the donors.

> This universal need for support following loss and the lack of such support in the modern world offers the transplant community an opportunity to provide ongoing care for the donor family that makes an influential statement to the entire community. For just as the donor's gift honors important human values, so does offering the donor's family compassionate assistance in coping with the patient's death and the subsequent bereavement process. (Holtkamp, 1997, p. 315)

These programs are an excellent beginning of caring for the organ donor's families.

Provide Professional Intervention for Donor Families

While support is critically important for donor family care, support alone will not ameliorate the more serious complications found in the aftermath of traumatic loss and organ donation. Trauma-driven grief, with its periods of latency followed by disruptive intrusions, often warrants professional care. Cerney (1993) suggests that "[i]t may be more appropriate to provide psychological consultations to the family" (p. 32). The lengthy latency period as well as the cyclic numbing and intrusive phases of posttraumatic stress that may erupt long after typical support programs have ended may necessitate professional intervention.

Organ procurement organizations could be a vital link between traumatized donor family and the professional caregiver by offering appropriate referrals and, in some situations, providing financial support for such care.

☐ Care for the Caregiver

The impact of providing care for organ donor families is another neglected area of research. The lack of attention that has been paid to the long-term impact of caring for potential donors and their families on medical personnel "contrasts with the considerable effort that is currently being expended in order to counteract any attitudes, held by the relatives of *potential* donors, which might inhibit their participation in donation" (McCullagh, 1993, p. 82).

Procurement coordinators, intensive care nurses, and other health care givers must become aware of their impact on the trajectory of donor family grief. They must also recognize the problems and anxieties experienced by caregivers who assist these families. While attending the donor and the donor's family, the caregiver may experience high anxiety and threat, increased vulnerability, heightened insecurity, intensified feelings of helplessness, and a strong sense of loss of control (Rando, 1993).

The emotional cost of caring for donors and donor families must be recognized by those with positional power to address such issues. Caring for the caregiver is as much about reverence for life as is caring for the recipient, the donor, and the donor's family.

☐ The Need for Study

As previously noted, formal studies that address the impact of the organ donation experience on the trauma-driven grief of family members are virtually nonexistent. Various surveys and research efforts directed on behalf of the organ donor family were either nonspecific to trauma, covered insufficient numbers, yielded limited response rates, or were conducted by organizations with a vested interest in the outcome of such studies. An even more worrisome quality about current research is the underlying motivation. McCullagh (1993) claims that "virtually all medical study of the families of donors seems to have been motivated primarily by a wish to influence relatives to consent to organ transplantation" (p. 83).

Serious attention must be given to specific factors found within the donor family experience. The death of the recipient, or increased postdonation awareness of invasive procedures involved in organ removal, second thoughts about donation from the heart-beating donors, disquietude related to brain death issues, and disappointment about recipient response are only a few of the known risk factors that donor families must navigate. These emotionally-charged issues must be explored from a trauma and loss perspective.

While apparent deficiencies in current research do not invalidate consistent findings that many donor families perceive donation as comforting, as bringing something of value from something hateful, and as preventing another family from experiencing the loss of their loved one, a disquieting dichotomy remains between the positive outcomes of these studies and what is observed in clinical settings (Holtkamp, 2000; McKissock, 2000). There is no clear explanation as to why some family members find organ donation comforting and meaningful while nightmares, excessive guilt, and regrets about the donation experience haunt others.

Problems Associated with the Study of Donor Family Grief

There are inherent problems related to the study of the trauma-driven grief of donor families. Batten and Prottas (1987) tentatively question the place and the validity of research in the midst of tragedy. These same authors believed that their response rate of 61% still left room for doubt about the characteristics and opinions of those who do not respond. A more troubling aspect of current methods of study is associated not only with low response rates, but with the limited types of respondents. Most surveys are sent only to the next of kin, effectively eliminating a more rounded response that might reveal conflict within the family system as well as more negative responses to donation.

There is a need to find systematic ways to:

- Increase the percentages of respondents willing to speak of their experiences,
- Include members of the extended family in formal and informal studies,
- Develop a nationwide database,
- Conduct studies that are free of vested interests, and
- Consider the impact of policies on the emotional health of current and future donor family members.

Efforts to assess any negative fallout from donor-family–recipient contact must also be developed to care for those who become enmeshed with recipients and their families in relationships that may become painfully complicated by the creditor–debtor aspect of the unparallel gift of life. Addressing this issue will be anything but easy.

Empirical Reductionism vs. Qualitative Observation

Noted physicist Niels Bohr (1989) stated: "The opposite of a true statement is a false statement, but the opposite of a profound truth can be another profound truth." Organ donation and the grief that follows are filled with such paradox: life and death, joy and sorrow, complications as well as comfort. Yet the most complex paradox of all may be the intertwining of the scientific and the nonscientific, the rational and the irrational, within the field of transplantation and organ donation.

After 40 years in the field of transplantation, medical sociologist Renee Fox (1996) has concluded:

[S]cientific and medical progress does not catapult us beyond the reach of those areas of our being where nonlogical perceptions, compelling images, reified symbols, and tenacious myths reside. Quite to the contrary, such progress may even generate new forms of scientifically shaped magic. (p. 258)

The motivation to donate and the subsequent emotional response are rife with magical thinking, with irrational thought processes. To understand the grief responses emanating from the unique circumstance of organ donation, researchers must first recognize that the messier, less-than-articulate world of mystical or primary-thought processes and the new forms of scientifically shaped magic will not respond well to current methodologies of study. Underestimating this reality will simply compound the problem.

Empirical study sees rational order in the world with one fact leading to another.

By finding certain truths, empiricists believe it will be possible to discover general laws that explain how the world operates. Their concern is with prediction and verification based on external observable phenomena that can be objectively measured. (Klass, Silverman, & Nickman, 1996)

Bruner (1990) claims that such "mechanistic views of science and of the world permeates all aspects of the psychological sciences." Such cold mechanistic landscapes may be less than adequate as we attempt to address the needs of the organ donor family.

Mourners resist being painted by numbers. They possess the innate knowledge that the values of love, trust, hope, resiliency, faith, compassion, altruism, and grief are not realities that can be fully conceptualized by clinical evaluation. The processes of real life cannot be readily compartmentalized, and lists that make sense and are of great value to the clinician may actually dehumanize the mourner.

The belief that scientific study is free from the contaminates of subjective and cultural belief, or of personal bias bears closer scrutiny.

The immunological concepts and vocabulary associated with organ transplantation and the rejection reaction have richly illustrated . . . how much more than strictly scientific material is coded into the precepts and the language of modern Western medicine. This would not be a revelatory insight were it not for one of the positivistic assumptions on which our medicine is based, namely, that because it is so highly developed scientifically and technologically it is *not* imprinted with cultural beliefs and values the way tradi-

tional and folk medicine systems are. We have a rational tendency to suppose that, although our medicine emanates from our empirical and theoretical knowledge, our techniques and our mode of thought, it is relatively
uninfluenced by our world view. (Fox, 1996, p. 257)

Fox (1996) concludes that such supposition is far from true. Within the
realm of organ transplantation, we have encountered emotionally charged
symbolic and anthropomorphic meanings that we apply to our bodies and
their parts that are decidedly influenced by our worldview. Many of these
encounters have challenged our empirical and theoretical knowledge. We
are pressed to recognize the equalities of mind, personality, character, spirit,
and soul so identified with our corporeal selves as we accommodate the
knowledge that various parts of a deceased loved one continue to sustain
life in another human being.

New ways of assessment and new guidelines for perceiving what are
normal responses from donor families must be developed. To do this, we
must consistently remember that organ donation itself is not natural or
normal. Indeed, "some would argue that there is something wholly unnatural about taking a body part from one person and putting it into another living human being" (Caplan & Coelho, 1998, p. 10).

Attempts to view organs as just spare parts to be recycled "rather than as
living parts of a person . . . that resonate with the symbolic meaning of our
relation to our bodies, our selves, and to each other" (Fox & Swazey, 1992,
p. 207) epitomize biological reductionism that may have sinister implications for how we perceive ourselves as human beings and our connectedness with one another.

Psychological reductionism may be equally threatening to the effective
care of the organ donor family for "persons cannot be reduced to their
parts so that they can be better understood" (Cassell, 1991, p. 43). It is in
our best interest to remember that, "reductionist scientific methods, so
successful in other areas of human biology, are not as useful for the comprehension of whole persons" (p. 43).

The Value of Case Studies

"To see truth in the round, we need many angles of vision, many voices of
varied experiences" (Palmer, 1990, p. 12). Case studies provide those many
angles of vision that have proven particularly helpful for explaining areas
of a field of practice that have not been well-researched and conceptualized. Stories allow the trauma-driven grief of organ donor families to be
seen within its surround. The roundness of stories may allow caregivers to
rely less on empirical studies that bring such familiar comfort. From sto-

ries, the caregiver may derive deep, rich, and detailed information as they listen and learn from the many voices of varied experiences.

☐ Resiliency and the Organ Donor Family

There is a quality to individual responses to trauma, and to organ donation, that remains unaccounted for. This quality emerges from the human spirit. Hard to define, impossible to adequately describe, the human spirit is both extraordinarily fragile and astonishingly resilient.

Cassell (1991) claims that "the profession of medicine appears to ignore the human spirit" (p. 43). Yet, this attribute may account for the more optimistic and peculiarly paradoxical note sounded by Rynearson (1988) in regard to trauma—more specifically to the parental loss of a child to a brutal and purposeful murder. While the risks associated with this unspeakable trauma are real and undeniable, Rynearson draws attention to those who somehow cope with the synergism of their tragedy. "The quiet courage and resolute optimism that are normally maintained [by these parents] are a marvel . . . and represent a resiliency we should celebrate and try to understand" (p. 215).

In another work, Rynearson and Geoffrey (1999) refer to the capacity of individuals to find some meaning in the tragedy as a dynamic of resiliency, and contend that attempts to initiate or reinforce such dynamics in therapy are warranted. Although most people who have experienced a traumatic loss will follow a spontaneous time-limited recovery, "there has been no systematic research to define, measure, and explain the elements of resiliency that facilitate this process of recovery"(p. 114). While the quest for empirical answers to what is basically a spiritual process may be frustrating, the organ donor family has much to share about the role of meaning, restitution and resiliency in recovery from traumatic loss.

☐ The Paradox of Recovery

The quest for greater understanding of the donor family experience requires a clearer vision of what recovery from trauma might mean. Recovery is generally thought of as moving successfully through the grieving process by accepting the reality of the loss, allowing the healing pain to be experienced, accommodating the changes that must be made in order to adapt to the world without the loved one and achieving some degree of restitution by various self-satisfying means. Recovery means that the mourner is able to redirect energy toward others and toward the future. When the capacity to invest in love and work and play is reestablished, recovery is thought to have taken place. While accurate, those descriptions of recovery are not particularly satisfying and can easily be interpreted by some to mean that grief actually has an end point.

Another explanation is offered:

> To understand recovery, we must first understand the consuming quality of grief. The nature of the emotional scarring of grief is so strong that though there be a yearning for peace, even that yearning is half-hearted. Deep within, we secretly suspect that our pain may be our last link with our beloved and we are loathe to let it go. Only when the time comes that we can finally pry ourselves away from the hurt, will we discover that the pain has hollowed out a place for a different kind of relationship with our beloved, and cleared the way for new life.

> Here we begin to recognize the reality that great truth, that the entire mourning process abounds with contradictory statements or situations that are nevertheless true. We wish to cling to our hurt even as we plead for release; we embrace new life only when we are finally able to accept death.

> In the upside down world of sorrow, we discover that "going crazy" may actually keep us sane, and that weakness becomes strength when we allow ourselves time to heal. In the end we discover, to our dismay and to our delight, that losing ourselves in service to others allows us to find ourselves anew. And the greatest wonder of all, we learn that it is quite possible to experience both grief and joy. With joyfulness resting comfortably on the far side of despair, we find assurances that courage and tears bear one another's company well.

> Like other great realities, a realistic glimpse of recovery is best found in a story:

> The young athlete was a skier. But he had only one leg, and as he began his routine I could hardly believe what I was seeing. For the entire run, this remarkable young man showed amazing skill on the slopes, doing almost everything the other skiers were doing but using a single ski. It was breathtaking, inspiring and quite simply wonderful.

> Amid the welcoming crowd at the bottom of the slope, his smiling face stood out. But one thought lingered in my mind. "In spite of this young man's remarkable performance, he still has only one leg." (Holtkamp, 1991)

This may be a near-perfect metaphor for those who recover from great trauma. Survivors may do well, they may process all that needs to be processed and accommodate all that needs to be accommodated. They may go on to live full, productive, and loving lives. But no matter how well these survivors make it down the slope, they remain individuals who have suffered great loss. What they accomplish doesn't make them other than what they are.

☐ Closing Thoughts

Since its beginnings in the 1950s, organ transplantation has been surrounded by hard questions about taking organs from living and dead bodies and reusing them for others. The frustrating shortage in the supply of transplantable organs and tissues for those who desperately need them has "prodded society to search for new sources of organs, new methods of procurement, new ways of managing the dying, and innovative strategies for fairly distributing this scarce life-saving resource" (Caplan & Coelho, 1998, p. 10). In keeping with medicine's proclivity for creating new problems every time they solve an old one, every new attempt to address the shortage of organs has increased potential harm to those who mourn the loss of the donor.

A Two-Eyed Vision of Transplantation and Trauma

The old-fashioned stereoscopic viewing machine allowed a viewer to look at two pictures of the same thing, yet see only one image. That image was clearer, more cleanly defined, and was perceived as three-dimensional when viewed with both eyes. When viewed with only one eye, the image appeared blurry and distorted.

The scientific world views organ donation through only one eye—the eye of the mind. The eye of the mind, or in Freudian terms, secondary-process thinking, is rational, logical, and receptive to education and persuasion. While the other level of thought, or primary-process thinking belongs to "the messier and less-than-well-articulated world of emotion, superstition, and magic that is resistant to logic and rational persuasion. Neither perspective is right or wrong. They simply exist and function together, an important and unavoidable quality of the human condition" (Youngner, 1996, p. 34).

A two-eyed vision of trauma and transplantation will reveal a clearer reflection of a triumphant, life-prolonging miracle that exists only because of the mysterious wonder that some families are able to reach beyond their anguish and consent to donation. With that vision in place, we will be willing to acknowledge scientifically shaped magic and to remember that myths and mystery are essential to keeping souls alive and to creating new meaning in a difficult and often meaningless world.

Through all the media hubris and medical jubilation about newfound ways to "slash and suture our way to eternal life" (Ramsey, 1970, p. 238), there has remained one perdurable reality: the trauma-driven grief of the organ donor family. To be congruent in our reverence for life, we must turn our attention to the adventure of learning from these individuals. Those who wish to provide effective care for donor families must learn to gaze upon what can be glimpsed without being seen, to give up a narrow-gauged vision of research, to accept the myths that give some individuals a sense of inner security, and to accept mystical, magical thinking without premature and inappropriate labeling.

It will require courage, this adventure of learning about the donor family. The organ procurement organization must have the courage to consider the welfare of the donor family without one eye constantly focused on promoting organ donation. They must set policy and procedure based on what is known and what is being learned about being a traumatized donor family member. Researchers and caregivers must have the courage to listen to the stories as a means of obtaining data and be willing to ask the hard questions without regard to political correctness or vested interest.

We must be committed to learning more about the organ donor family experience while remembering that human beings have a peculiar habit of refusing to be cast into formfitting molds to be analyzed. It will take courage to admit that some notions we previously held could be wrong. But it is there, in the tension created between conviction and doubt, that we may find answers to what we so earnestly seek, the answer to the original question: "What about the donor family?"

REFERENCES

Aberbach, D. (1989). *Surviving trauma: Loss, literature and psychoanalysis*. New Haven, CT: Yale University Press.

Aguilera, D. C. (1990). Crisis intervention: Theory and methodology. St. Louis, MO: Mosby.

American Psychiatric Association. (1987). *Diagnostic and statistical manual of mental disorders* (3rd ed. rev.). Washington, DC: Author.

Annas, G. (1988). The paradoxes of organ transplantation. *American Journal of Public Health, 78*, 621–622.

Anonymous Parent. (1995, Fall). Perspectives. *For Those Who Give and Grieve, 4*(2).

Arts & Entertainment TV (1999). The organ trade: Life and death for sale. *Investigative reports*. (August 14).

Australians Donate. (February 1999). *National survey series on donor intention*. Black Forest, South Australia.

Back, K. (1991). Sudden, unexpected pediatric death: Caring for the parents. *Pediatric Nursing, 17*, 30–41.

Bartucci, M. (1987). The meaning of organ donation to donor families. *Anna Journal, 14*, 369–371, 410.

Basu, P., Hazariwala, K., & Chipman, M. (1989). Public attitudes toward donation of body parts, particularly the eye. *Canadian Journal of Ophthalmology, 24*, 216–220.

Batten, H., & Prottas, J. (1987). Kind strangers: The families of organ donors. *Health Affairs*, summer, 35–46.

Bernat, J. L. (1992). How much of the brain must die in brain death. *Journal of Clinical Ethics, 3*, 21–26.

Bohr, N. (1989). As quoted by Avery Dulles, *The reshaping of Catholicism*. San Francisco: Harper & Row. Cited in P. Palmer. (1990). *The active life*. New York: Harper Collins.

Bouvard, M. (1988). *The path through grief: A practical guide*. Portland, OR: Breitenbush Books.

Bowlby, J. (1989). Forward. In D. Aberbach, *Surviving trauma, loss, literature and psychoanalysis*. New Haven, CT: Yale University Press.

Brody, H. (1987). *Stories of sickness*. New Haven, CT: Yale University Press.

Bronowski, J. (1995). Quoted in *Roget's super thesaurus*. Marc McCutcheon (ed.). Cincinnati, OH: Writer's Digest Books.

Bruner, J. (1990). *Acts of meaning*. Cambridge, MA: Harvard University Press.

Cain, A. (Ed.). (1972). *Survivors of suicide*. Springfield, IL: Charles C. Thomas.

Cain, L. (1974). *Widow*. New York: Morrow.

Caine, N., & O'Brien, V. (1989). Quality of life and psychological aspects of heart transplantation. In J. Wallwork (ed.), *Heart and heart-lung transplantation* (pp. 389–422). Philadelphia: W. B. Saunders.

197

Callender, C. O. (1987). Organ donation in the Black population: Where do we go from here? *Transplantation Proceedings, 14,* 36–40.

Callender, C. O., Bayton, J. A., Yeager, C. L., & Clark, J. C. (1982). Attitudes among Blacks toward donating kidneys for transplantation: A pilot project. *Journal of the National Medical Association, 74,* 807–809.

Callender, C. O., Hall, L. E., Yeager, C. L., Barber, J. B., Dunston, G. M., & Pinn-Wiggins, V. W. (1991). Organ donation and blacks. *The New England Journal of Medicine, 325,* 442–444.

Cameron, J. (1992). *The artist's way.* New York: Putnam.

Caplan, A. L., & Coelho, D. H. (1998). *The ethics of organ transplants: The current debate.* Amherst, NY: Prometheus.

Cassell, E. (1991). *The nature of suffering: And goals of medicine.* New York: Oxford University Press.

Cerney, M. (1993). Solving the organ donor shortage by meeting the bereaved families' needs. *Critical Care Nurse,* February, 32–36.

Coolican, M. (1990). *Caring for donor families: A unique perspective. Making the critical difference.* New York: National Kidney Foundation.

Corr, C., et al. (1994). Bill of rights for donor families. *United Network for Organ Sharing Update. 10,* 11, 21.

Coupe, D. (1990). Donation dilemmas. *Nursing Times, 86,* 34–36.

Creecy, R., & Wright, R. (1990). Correlates of willingness to consider organ donation among Blacks. *Social Science & Medicine, 31,* 1229–1232.

Davidson, M. N., & Devney, P. (1991). Attitudinal barriers to organ donation among Black Americans. *Transplant Proceedings, 23,* 2531–2532.

Davis, F. D. (1989). Organ procurement and transplantation. *Nursing Clinic of North America, 24* (4), 823–836.

DeChesser, A. D. (1986). Organ donation: The supply/demand discrepancy. *Heart & Lung: Journal of Critical Care, 15,* 547–551.

DeFrain, J. (1991). Learning about grief from normal families: SIDS, stillbirth, and miscarriage. *Journal of Marital and Family Therapy, 17,* 215–232.

DeJong, W., Franz, H., Wolfe, S. M., Nathan, A., Payne, D., Reitsma, W., & Beasley, C. (1998). Requesting organ donation: An interview study of donor and non-donor families. *American Journal of Critical Care, 7:* 13–23.

DeVries, P. (1961). *The blood of the lamb.* Boston, MA: Little Brown.

Editorial: Presumed consent laws. (1997, September–October). *Saturday Evening Post,* p. 10.

Elick, B. (1997). Transplant coordinators. In J. Chapman, M. Deierhoi, & C. Wight (Eds.), *Organ and tissue donation for transplantation* (pp. 325–343). London: Arnold.

Elliott, L. (2001). Benny's heart. *Reader's Digest,* April, 115–120.

Engel, G. (1961). Is grief a disease? A challenge for medical research. *Psychosomatic Medicine, 23,* 18–22.

Fenichel, O. (1972). *Psychoanalytic theory of neurosis.* New York: Norton.

Fiedler, L. A. (1996). Why organ transplant programs do not succeed. In S.Youngner, R. Fox & L. O'Connell (eds.), *Organ transplantation: Meanings and realities* (pp. 56–65). Madison, WI: University of Wisconsin Press.

Figley, C. (1983). Catastrophes: An overview of family reactions. In C. R. Figley & H. I. McCubbin (eds.), *Stress and the family: Coping with catastrophe* (Vol. 2, pp. 3–20). New York: Brunner/Mazel.

Figley, C. (1986). *Trauma and its wake* (Vol. 2). Levittown, PA: Brunner/Mazel.

Figley, C. (1989). *Helping traumatized families.* San Francisco: Jossey-Bass.

Fox, R. C. (1988). *Essays in medical sociology.* New Brunswick, NJ: Transaction Books.

Fox, R. C. (1996). Afterthoughts: Continuing reflections on organ transplantation. In S. Youngner, R. C. Fox, & L. O'Connell (eds.), *Organ transplantation: Meanings and realities* (pp. 252–272). Madison, WI: University of Wisconsin Press.

Fox, R. C., & Swazey, J. (1992). *Spare parts: Organ replacement in American society.* New York: Oxford University Press.

Fowlkes, M. R. (1991). The morality of loss: The social construction of mourning and melancholia. *Contemporary Psychoanalysis, 27,* 529–551.

Fulton, R., & Fulton, J. A. (1971). A psychosocial aspect of terminal care: Anticipating grief. *Omega, 2,* 91–100.

Gallup Organization for the Partnership for Organ Donation. (1993). *The American public's attitude toward organ donation and transplantation.* Boston: Author.

Gilbert, K. (1997). Couple coping with the death of a child. In C. R. Figley, B. E. Bride, & N. Mazza (eds.), *Death and trauma: The traumatology of grieving* (pp. 101–121). Washington, DC: Taylor & Francis.

Gilbert, K., & Smart, L. (1992). *Coping with infant or fetal loss: The couple's healing process.* New York: Brunner/Mazel.

Good Morning America. (2000). Double transplant of forearms and hands. (January 17): ABC.

Gutkind, L. (1988). *Many sleepless nights.* New York: Norton.

Gyulay, J.N. (1989). Sudden death—no farewells. *Issues in Comprehensive Pediatric Nursing, 12,* 71–102.

Hart, D. (1986). Focus on critical care. *American Association of Critical Care Nurses, 18,* 335–339.

Hauerwas, S. (1990). *Naming the silences: God, medicine, and the problem of suffering.* Grand Rapids, MI: Eerdmans.

Helmberger, P. S. (1992). *Transplants: Unwrapping the second gift of life.* Minneapolis, MN: Chronimed.

Hickey, M. (1985). What are the needs of families of critically ill patients? *Focus on Critical Care, 1,* 41–43.

Hill, D. J., Munglani, R., & Sapsford, D. (1994). Haemodynamic responses to surgery in brain-dead organ donors. *Anaesthesia, 49,* 835–836.

Holtkamp, S. (1991). *Catherine: Searching for something more.* Unpublished manuscript.

Holtkamp, S. (1997). The donor family experience: Sudden loss, brain death, organ donation, grief and recovery. In J. Chapman, M. Deierhoi, & C. Wight (eds.), *Organ and tissue donation for transplantation* (pp. 304–322). London: Arnold Publishing.

Holtkamp, S. (2000). Anticipatory mourning and organ donation. In T. A. Rando (ed.), *Clinical dimensions of anticipatory mourning* (pp. 511–535). Champaign, IL: Research Press.

Holtkamp, S., & Nuckolls, E. (1993). Completing the gift exchange: A study of bereavement service for donor families. *Journal of Transplant Coordination, 3,* 80–84.

Horowitz, M. J. (1997). *Stress response syndromes—PTSD, grief, and adjustment disorders.* Northvale, NJ: Jason Aronson.

Hyer, L., & Brandsma, J. M. (1999). The treatment of PTSD through grief work and forgiveness. In C. R. Figley (ed.), *Traumatology of grieving: Conceptual, theoretical, and treatment foundations* (pp. 131–151). Philadelphia, PA: Brunner/Mazel.

Janoff-Bulman, R. (1992). *Shattered assumptions: Towards a new psychology of trauma.* New York: Free Press.

Jasper, J., Harris, D., Jackson, R., Lee, B., & Miller, K. (1991). Organ donation terminology: Are we communicating life or death? *Health Psychology, 1*(10), 34–41.

Jaspers, K. (1951). *Man in the modern world.* London: Routledge & Kegan Paul.

Johnson, C. (1992). The nurse's role in organ donation from brain dead patients: Management of the family. *Intensive and Critical Care Nursing, 8,* 140–148.

Johnson, H. (1992, April 13). The darker side of organ donation. *Sun-Sentinel*. Ft. Lauderdale, FL.

Joralemon, D. (1995). Organ wars : The battle for body parts. *Medical Anthropology Quarterly, 9*, 335–356.

Kachoyeanos, E., & Selder, F. (1993). Life transitions of parents at the unexpected death of a school-age and older child. *Journal of Pediatric Nursing, 8*, 41–49.

Kirste, G., Muthny, F., & Wilms, H. (1988). Psychological aspects of the approach to donor relatives. *Clinical Transplantation, 2*, 67–79.

Klassen, A. C., & Klassen, D. K. (1996). Who are the donors in organ donation? The family's perspective in mandated choice. *Annals of Internal Medicine, 125*(1), 70–73.

Kliman, A. S. (1977). Comments in section on "The Parents." In N. Linzer (ed.), *Understanding bereavement and grief* (p. 171). New York: Yeshiva University Press.

La Foret, E. G. (1976). The fiction of informed consent. *Journal of the American Medical Association, 235*, 1579–1585.

Lange, S. (1992). Psychosocial, legal, ethical and cultural aspects of organ donation and transplantation. *Critical Care Nursing Clinics of North America, 4*(1), 25–42.

Lazarus, R., & Folkman, S. (1984). *Stress, appraisal, and coping*. New York: Springer.

Lebow, G. (1976). Facilitating adaptation in anticipatory mourning. *Social Casework, 57*, 458–465.

Leske, J. S. (1986). Needs of relatives of critically ill patients: A follow-up. *Heart Lung, 15*, 189–193.

Lifton, R. (1979). *The broken connection*. New York: Simon & Schuster.

Lindy, J. (1985). The trauma membrane and other clinical concepts derived from psychotherapeutic work with survivors of natural disasters. *Psychiatric Annals, 15*, 153–160.

Lindy, J. (1986). An outline for the psychoanalytic psychotherapy of post-traumatic stress disorder. In C. Figley (ed.), *Trauma and its wake: Traumatic stress theory, research, and intervention* (Vol. 2, pp. 195–212). New York: Brunner/Mazel.

Lock, M. (1996). Deadly disputes: Ideologies and brain death in Japan. In S. J. Youngner, R. C. Fox, & L. J. O'Connell (eds.), *Organ transplantation: Meanings and realities* (pp. 142–167). Madison, WI: University of Wisconsin Press.

Marris, P. (1982). Attachment and society. In C. M. Parkes & J. Stevenson-Hinde (eds.), *The place of attachment in human behavior* (pp. 185–204). New York: Basic Books.

May, R., & Yalom, I. (1989). Existential psychotherapy. In R. J. Corsini & D. Wedding (eds.), Current psychotherapy (pp. 363–403). Itasca, IL: Peacock.

McCullagh, P. (1993). *Brain dead, brain absent, brain donors: Human subjects or human objects?* West Sussex: Wiley.

McIvor, D., & Thompson, F. J. (1988). Self-perceived needs of family members with a relative in the ICU. *Intensive Care Nurse, 4*, 139–145.

McKissock, M. (2000). *Donor family and recipient communication*. Paper presented at the NSW Human Tissue Act Review Forum. Australian Red Cross Blood Service. Sydney, Australia.

McPhee, A. (1987). Let the family in. *Journal of Emergency Nursing, 13*, 120–121.

Meilander, G. (1996). *Bioethics: A primer for Christians*. Grand Rapids, MI: Eerdmans.

Miles, M. S., & Demi, A. S. (1986). Guilt in bereaved parents. In T. A. Rando (ed.), *Parental loss of a child* (pp. 97–118). Champaign, IL: Research Press.

Moore, B., & Fine, B. (Eds.). (1990). *Psychoanalytic terms and concepts*. New Haven, CT: American Psychoanalytic Association and Yale University Press.

Moore, F. D. (1964). New problems for surgery. *Science, 144*, 388.

Moores, B., Clark, G., Lewis, B., & Mallick, N. (1976). Public attitudes towards kidney transplantation. *British Medical Journal, 1*: 629–631.

Morrow, L. (1991, June 17). When one body can save another. *Time*, 54–58.

Murray, T. (1996). Organ vendors, families and the gift of life. In S. J. Youngner, R. C. Fox, & L. J. O'Connell (eds.), *Organ transplantation: Meanings and realities* (pp. 101–125). Madison, WI: University of Wisconsin Press.

NFO Research, Inc. (1999). *When a child dies.* A survey of bereaved parents conducted on behalf of The Compassionate Friends. (Available from The Compassionate Friends, P.O. Box 3696, Oak Brook, IL 60522.)

National Kidney Foundation. (1997, July 27). *Guidelines for communication between donor families and transplant recipients unveiled.* New York: Author.

National Safety Council. (1998). *Accident facts.* Chicago: Author.

Norris, L. D., & Grove, S. K. (1986). Investigation of selected psychosocial needs of family members of critically ill adult patients. *Heart Lung, 2,* 194–199.

Ochberg, F. (Ed.). (1988). *Post traumatic therapy and victims of violence.* New York: Brunner/ Mazell.

Omar, C. (1936). *Henrietta Maria.* London: Hodder & Stoughton.

O'Neill, R. (2000, February). *The vexed issue of communication between transplant recipients and families of organ donors: A sociological perspective.* Paper presented at NSW Human Tissue Act Review Forum. Australian Red Cross Blood Service. Sydney, Australia.

Ott, B. (1998). Defining and redefining death. In A. Caplan & D. Coelho (eds.), *The ethics of organ transplants, the current debate* (pp. 16–23). Amherst, NY: Prometheus Books.

Owen, G., Fulton, R., & Markusen, E. (1983). Death at a distance: A study of family survivors. *Omega, 13,* 191–225.

Palmer, P. (1990). *The active life.* San Francisco: Harper.

Parkes, C. M. (1972). *Bereavement: Studies of grief in adult life.* New York: International University Press.

Parkes, C. M., & Weiss, R. S. (1983). *Recovery from bereavement.* New York: Basic Books.

Pelletier, M. (1992). The organ donor family members' perception of stressful situations during organ donation experience. *Journal of Advanced Nursing, 17,* 90–97.

Pelletier, M. (1993). Emotions experienced and coping strategies used by family members of organ donors. *Canadian Journal of Nursing Research, 25,* 63–73.

Pennefather, S. H., Dark, J. H., & Bullock, R. E. (1993). Haemodynamic responses to surgery in brain-dead organ donors. *Anaesthesia, 48,* 1034–1038.

Pennington, J. C. (1988). Public information and transplantation from a recipient's point of view: The case for donor confidentiality. *Transplantation Proceedings, 20,* 1036–1037.

Peppers, L. G., & Knapp, R. J. (1980). *Motherhood and mourning: Perinatal death.* New York: Praeger.

Perez, L., Schulman, B., Davis, F., Olson, L., Tellis, V. A., & Matas, A. J. (1988). Organ donation in three major American cities with large Latino and Black populations. *Transplantation, 46,* 553–557.

Peters, T. (1998). Life or death: The issue of payment in cadaveric organ donation. In A. Caplan & D. Coelho (eds.), *The ethics of organ transplants, the current debate* (pp. 196–204). Amherst, NY: Promethus.

Pine, V., & Brauer, C. (1986). Parental grief: A synthesis of theory, research, and intervention. In T. Rando (ed.), *Parental loss of a child* (pp. 59–96). Champaign, IL: Research Press.

Prottas, J. M. (1983). The marketing of organ donation. *Millbank Quarterly, 61,* 292–295.

Radecki, C., & Jaccard, J. (1997). Psychological aspects of organ donation: A critical review and synthesis of individual and next-of-kin donation decisions. *Health Psychology, 16,* 183–195.

Ramsey, P. (1970). *The patient as a person: Exploration in medical ethics.* New Haven, CT: Yale University Press.

Rando, T. (1984). *Grief, dying and death: Clinical interventions for caregivers.* Champaign, IL: Research Press.

Rando, T. (1986). *Parental loss of a child.* Champaign, IL: Research Press.

Rando, T. (1993). *Treatment of complicated mourning*. Champaign, IL: Research Press.

Rando, T. (2000). On the experience of traumatic stress in anticipatory and postdeath mourning. In T. A. Rando (Ed.), *Clinical dimensions of anticipatory mourning: Theory and practice in working with the dying, their loved ones, and their caregivers*. Champaign, IL: Research Press.

Raphael, B. (1986). *When disaster strikes: How individuals and communities cope with catastrophe*. New York: Basic Books.

Raphael, B., & Middleton, W. (1987). Current state of research in the field of bereavement. *The Israel Journal of Psychiatry and Related Sciences, 24,* 5–32.

Redmond, L. (1989). *Surviving: When someone you love was murdered*. Clearwater, FL: Psychological Consultation and Education Services.

Reitz, N., & Callender, C. (1993). Organ donation in the African-American population: A fresh perspective with a simple solution. *Journal of the National Medical Association, 85:* 353–358.

Rene, N., Viera, E., Daniels, D., & Santos, Y. (1994). Organ donation in the Hispanic population: Dondi estan ello? *Journal of the National Medical Association, 86,* 13–16.

Richardson, R. (1996). Fearful symmetry: Corpses for anatomy, organs for transplantation? In S. J. Youngner, R. C. Fox, & L. J. O'Connell (eds.), *Organ transplantation: Meanings and realities* (pp. 66–100). Madison, WI: University of Wisconsin Press.

Riethier, A., & Mahler, E. (1995). Organ donation: Psychiatric, social, and ethical considerations. *Psychosomatics, 36,* 336–343.

Rinear, E. (1988). Psychosocial aspects of parental response patterns in the death of a child by homicide. *Journal of Traumatic Stress, 1,* 305–322.

Rodgers, S. B. (1989). Legal framework for organ donation and transplantation. *Nursing Clinics of North America, 24*(4).

Rosenblatt, P. C., & Burns, L. H. (1986). Long-terms effects of perinatal loss. *Journal of Family Issues, 7,* 237–253.

Rynearson, E. (1987). Psychological adjustment to unnatural dying. In S. Misook (ed.), *Biopsychosocial aspects of bereavement*. Washington, DC: American Psychiatric Press.

Rynearson, E. (1988). The homicide of a child. In F. Ochberg (ed.), *Post traumatic therapy and victims of violence* (pp. 213–224). New York: Brunner/Mazel.

Rynearson, E., & Goeffrey, R. (1999). Bereavement after homicide: Its assessment and treatment. In C. R. Figley (ed.), *Traumatology of grieving: Conceptual, theoretical, and treatment foundations* (pp. 109–128). Philadelphia: Brunner/Mazel.

Sanders, C. (1980). A comparison of adult bereavement in the death of a spouse, child, and parent. *Omega, 10,* 303–322.

Sanders, C. (1986). Accidental death of a child. In T. A. Rando (ed.), *Parental loss of a child* (pp. 181–189). Champaign, IL: Research Press.

Savaria, D., Rovelli, M., & Schweizer, R. (1990). Donor family surveys provide useful information for organ procurement. *Transplant Proceedings, 22,* 316–317.

Schlump-Urguhart, S. R. (1990). Families experiencing a traumatic accident: Implications and nursing management. *AACN Clinical Issues, 1,* 522–534.

Schroeter, K., & Taylor, G. (1999). Ethical considerations in organ donation for critical care nurses. *Critical Care Nurse, 19*(2), 60–69.

Selzer, R. (1990). Wither thou goest. In *Imagine a woman and other tales* (pp. 1–21). E. Lansing, MI: Michigan State University Press.

Shewman, D., Capron, A., Peacock, W., & Schulman, B. (1998). The use of anencephalic infants as organ sources: A critique. In A. Caplan & D. Coelho (eds.), *The ethics of organ transplants, the current debate* (pp. 92–115). Amherst, NY: Prometheus.

Shneidman, E. S. (1972). Forward. In A. Cain (ed.), *Survivors of suicide* (pp. ix–xi). Springfield, IL: Charles C. Thomas.

Signet/Mosby Medical Encyclopedia. (1985). New York: Signet Books.

Silverman, P., Klass, D., & Nickman, S. (1996). *Continuing bonds: New understandings of grief.* Philadelphia, PA: Taylor & Francis.

Simmons, R. G., Klein, S., & Simmons, R. L. (1987). *Gift of life: The social and psychological impact of organ transplantation.* New York: Wiley.

Simos, B. (1979). *A time to grieve: Loss as a universal human experience.* New York: Family Service Association of America.

Soukup, M. (1991). Organ donation from the family of a totally brain dead donor: Professional responsiveness. *Critical Care Nursing Quarterly, 13*(4), 8–18.

Spital, A. (1995). Mandated choice: A plan to increase public commitment. *JAMA, 273,* 504–506.

Spital, A. (1997). Ethical and policy issues in altruistic living and cadaveric organ donation. *Clinical Transplantation, 11,* 77–87.

Spurgeon, D. (1984). *And I don't want to live this life.* New York: Ballantine.

Stamm, B. H. (1999). Empirical perspectives on contextualizing death and trauma. In C. Figley (ed.), *Traumatology of grieving* (pp. 3–19). Levittown, PA: Brunner/Mazel.

Strobe, W., & Strobe, M. S. (1987). *Bereavement and health: The psychology and physical consequences of partner loss.* Cambridge: Cambridge University Press.

Stocks, L., Cutler, J. A., Kress, T., & Lewho, D. (1992). Dispelling myths regarding organ donation: The donor family experience. *Journal of Transplant Coordination, 2,* 147–152.

Swazey, J. (1986). Transplants . . . the gift of life. *Wellesley, 70,* 13–15.

Taylor, S. E., Lichtman, R. R., & Wood, J. (1984). Attribution, beliefs about control and adjustment to breast cancer. *Journal of Personality and Social Psychology, 46,* 489–502.

Toledo-Pereyra, L. (1992). The problem of organ donation in minorities: Some facts and incomplete answers. *Transplant Proceedings, 24,* 2162–2490.

Truog, R. (1998). Is it time to abandon brain death? In A. Caplan & D. Coelho (eds.), *The ethics of organ transplants, the current debate* (pp. 24–40). Amherst, NY: Promethus.

United Network for Organ Sharing (UNOS). (1997). *UNOS annual report.* Richmond, VA: Author.

United Network for Organ Sharing (UNOS). (1999). Cadaveric organ donation increases 5.6 percent in 1998. *UNOS update*(1) Richmond, VA: Author.

van der Kolk, B. (1987). *Psychological trauma.* Washington, DC: American Psychiatric Press.

Van Norman, G. (1991). A matter of life and death: What every anesthesiologist should know about the medical, legal and ethical aspects of declaring brain death. *Anesthesiology, 91*(1), 275–287.

Veatch, R., & Pitt, J. (1998). The myth of presumed consent: Ethical problems in new organ procurement strategies. In A. Caplan & D. Coelho (eds.), *The ethics of organ transplants, the current debate* (pp. 173–182). Amherst, NY: Prometheus.

Verble, M., & Worth, J. (1996). The case against more public education to promote organ donation. *Journal of Transplant Coordination, 6*(4).

Vernale, C. (1991). Critical care nurses' interventions with families of potential organ donors. *Focus on Critical Care, 18,* 335–339.

Vernale, C., & Packard, S. (1990). Organ donation as a gift exchange. *Image: Journal of Nursing Scholarship, 22,* 239–242.

Volkan, V. (1972). The linking objects of pathological mourners. *Archives of General Psychiatry, 27,* 215–221.

Volkan, V. (1981). *Linking objects and linking phenomenon.* New York: International Universities Press.

Volkan, V., & Zintl, E. (1993). *Life after loss.* New York: Charles Scribner.

von Pohle, W. R. (1996). Obtaining organ donation: Who should ask? *Heart Lung, 25,* 304–309.

Wetzel, R. C., Setzer, J. L., & Roger, M. C. (1985). Hemodynamic responses in brain dead organ donor patients. *Anesthesia and Analgesia 64*, 125–128.

Wikler, D., & Weisbard, A. J. (1989, April 21). Appropriate confusion over 'brain death'. *American Medical Association, 261*, 2246.

Willis, R., & Skelley, L. (1992). Serving the needs of donor families: The role of the critical care nurse. *Critical Care Nursing Clinics of North America, 4*, 63–77.

Wilson, J. (1989). *Trauma, transformation and healing.* New York: Brunner/Mazel.

Wittgenstein, L. (1961). *Tractatus logio-philosophicies.* D. F. Pears & B. F. McGuiness, Trans. London: Routledge & Kegan Paul.

Wolf, Z. (1991). Nurses' experience giving postmortem care to patients who have donated organs: A phenomenological study. *Scholarly Inquiry for Nursing Practice, 5*, 73–87.

Wolfelt, A. (1993). Identification of "grief avoidance response patterns": A growing phenomenon. *The Forum Newsletter, 1*, XVIII, 1, 16–18.

Worden, J. (1991). *Grief counseling and grief therapy.* New York: Springer.

Wright, J. (1978). Toward a common goal. *Heart Lung, 7*, 978–979.

Yalom, I. (1980). *Existential psychology.* New York: Basic Books.

Yalom, I. (1989). *Love's executioner and other tales of psychotherapy.* New York: Perennial.

Yalom, I. (1999). *Momma and the meaning of life.* New York: Basic Books.

Youngner, S. J. (1990). Organ retrieval: Can we ignore the dark side. *Transplant Proceedings, 22*, 1014–1015.

Youngner, S. J. (1992). Organ donation and procurement. In J. Craven and G. Rodin (eds.), *Psychiatric aspects of organ transplantation* (pp. 121–130). Oxford, England: Oxford University Press.

Youngner, S. J. (1996). Some must die. In S. Youngner, R. Fox, & L. O'Connell (eds.), *Organ transplantation: Meanings and realities* (pp. 32–55). Madison, WI: University of Wisconsin Press.

Youngner, S. J., Allen, M., Bartlett, E. T., et al. (1985). Psychosocial and ethical implications of organ retrieval. *New England Journal of Medicine, 313*, 321–324.

Youngner, S. J., Landerfield, S., Coulton, C., Juknialis, B. W., & Learly, M. (1989). "Brain death" and organ retrieval: A cross-sectional survey of knowledge and concepts among health professionals. *Journal of the American Medical Association, 261*, 2205–2210.

Youngner, S. J., & Arnold, R. M. (1993). Ethical, psychosocial and public policy implications of procuring organs from non–heart beating cadaver donors. *Journal of the American Medical Association, 269*, 2769–2774.

INDEX